# SHAPING
# INVENTION

D1710352

# SHAPING INVENTION

THOMAS BLANCHARD'S
MACHINERY AND
PATENT MANAGEMENT IN
NINETEENTH-CENTURY
AMERICA

*Carolyn C. Cooper*

COLUMBIA UNIVERSITY PRESS
*New York*

Columbia University Press
New York   Oxford

Copyright © 1991 Columbia University Press

*Library of Congress Cataloging-in-Publication Data*

Cooper, Carolyn.
Shaping invention : Thomas Blanchard's machinery and
patent management in nineteenth-century America,
Carolyn C. Cooper.
p.   cm.
Includes bibliographical references.
ISBN 0-231-06868-9
1. Woodworking machinery—United States—Patents—History
—19th century.   2. Inventors—United States—Biography.
3. Blanchard, Thomas, 1788–1864.   I. Title.
TS850.C476   1991
346.7304′86—dc20
[347.306486]            90-20626
                                    CIP

Printed in the United States of America

c  10  9  8  7  6  5  4  3  2  1

*With*
*love*
*to*
*Ellen and Don Cahalan,*
*who did*
*the first*
*shaping*
*of the*
*author.*

# CONTENTS

# 9
# SUMMARY AND CONCLUSIONS    *237*

# LIST OF ILLUSTRATIONS

# ACKNOWLEDGMENTS

**B**RAINCHILDREN have many godparents. In bringing this book to fruition, Robert Gordon has at all times provided a strong helping hand at tasks large and small. I am immensely grateful to him for unflagging conversations, critical readings, technical advice, and his photographic and drawing talent. Asger Aaboe has supplied moral and institutional support, quotable aphorisms, and excellent scholarly advice for longer than either of us wants to admit. Eda Kranakis and William Parker have both demonstrated a rare ability to find more in what I wrote than I knew was there, and to explain it to me. Earlier, Nathan Rosenberg and Walter Vincenti kindly fostered my first efforts at technological history and encouraged me to go on. I am also much indebted to Derek de Solla Price, who guided my beginning graduate study in the field; he has grievously departed beyond sublunary thanks.

Kendall Dood, Steven Lubar, Judith McGaw, Richard Nelson, Glenn Porter, and Stephen Victor read all or parts of various drafts and gave helpful suggestions. In maps and drawings Lyn Malone has skillfully provided visual renditions of technological processes and comparisons. Daniel Klubock of Cambridge, Massachusetts, Lettie Blanchard of Mc-Farland, California and my father, Don Cahalan, helped me trace the vicissitudes of Thomas Blanchard's family history.

My topic has required me to examine artifacts—old woodworking machines and their products—as well as documents, so I have called on museum keepers as well as archivists. At the National Museum of American History in Washington D.C., Robert Post, Robert Vogel, and Deborah Warner have given encouragement, technical expertise, and sensible advice before, during, and since my postdoctoral fellowship there, while David Shayt and Peter Liebhold have generously supplied exhibit souvenirs, pictures, and information from their files. At the Science Museum in London, Michael Wright helped me look at James Watt's sculpture copying machines, and A. K. Corry showed me the Blanchard lathe from Enfield Armory. At the Springfield Armory Museum, Larry Lowenthal, Richard Harkins, William Meuse, and Stuart Vogt provided guidance to the documents and artifacts of that "model establishment." Judith Parker and the Mudd Library staff at Yale University have been unfailingly cheerful in helping me to their remarkable collection of "less used" old books. William Sacco has applied special care and talent in photographing pictures from them.

At the National Archives Sharon Gibbs and Marjorie Ciarlante put me in touch with unfamiliar patent documents in Washington; in the branches at Waltham and Philadelphia, James Owen, Robert Plowman and their staffs exhumed and copied old patent litigation records for me, while Messrs. Butler and Cotton at the Cartographic Section in Alexandria located old patent drawings on short notice. Nadia Smith at the University of Vermont library fruitfully pursued the otherwise unsung fate of the Winooski patent block manufacturers. Private holders of artifacts were also generous: Merritt Roe Smith and Warren G. Ogden Jr. respectively helped me look at ax handles in process and ornamental turning lathes; Harold Smith of Haverhill, Mass. sent me shoe lasts and lasting memoirs. Ann Leskowitz at Yale University has quietly provided a pleasant and supportive work place in which to write and rewrite this book, while Leslie Bialler at Columbia University Press has kept me of good cheer during its publication.

All these kind people are of course free to disagree with what they have enabled me to produce, and should not be blamed for its defects. They nevertheless have my heartfelt gratitude.

# SHAPING INVENTION

# CONTEXTS

$\text{\normalsize ❧❧❧❧}$

**P**ARLIAMENTARY COMMISSIONERS from England who visited American manufactories in the summers of 1853 and 1854 perceived the manufacturing technology of the United States as different, and in certain respects even superior to that of England, the pioneer in industrialization. They particularly praised "the wonderful energy that characterizes the wood manufacture of the United States."[1] Foremost among the American woodworking machinery they admired was the production line for making gunstocks at the U.S. national armory at Springfield, Massachusetts, which was based on the machinery Thomas Blanchard had developed there thirty years earlier. The Commissioners who came in 1854 ordered a set of gunstocking machines for the new arms factory near London that was to operate according to the "American system of manufactures," as it was later termed.[2]

At the time of the English Commissioners' visits, Thomas Blanchard himself was still showing "wonderful energy" in developing applications for another major woodworking invention, a machine for bending wood. This book discusses Thomas Blanchard's machines and production lines for woodworking, and their application to manufacturing in the United States during several decades in the nineteenth century as "the American system" spread beyond small arms production. It traces the origins of Blanchard's machines, particularly those for irregular turning, patented 1819–20, for blockmaking, patented 1836, and for bending wood, patented 1849, 1856, and 1858. It describes how they operated, and discusses the manufacturing tasks to which they were applied, in relation to Blanchard's management of his intellectual property in the form of patents.

This book, then, is about particular technological inventions that took place in the United States of America in the nineteenth century. It asks, and partly answers, where those particular inventions came from and what happened to them after they came into being. However, it is also about invention in general. It asks how we recognize what is and isn't an invention, and points out that such recognition is a continuing social process that defines invention itself, even as it defines particular inventions. Thus invention itself is a social construct, and particular inventions are socially constructed.[3] To explain what this means, this book presents as case histories the particular woodworking inventions of Thomas Blanchard, and shows how people behaved in relation to them in the course of their social construction. It also describes the gradual process by which the decision rules for invention itself underwent social construction.

The American patent system of Blanchard's day organized the efforts of inventors and brought them into interaction with entrepreneurs in a variety of ways, not only through production of the devices they had invented, but also through assignment and licensing to others of the rights to make, use, and sell those devices. It thus harnessed psychological processes (inventive activity) with economic processes. The system also organized the inventors and entrepreneurs, together with patent officials and other increasingly knowledgeable technological "experts," with lawyers and judges, and with members of the public at large, in the social construction of technical knowledge.[4] This was accomplished through the initial obtaining of patent rights, their trial in courts of law, and sometimes their extension for longer periods or reissue with different wording. Thus it harnessed economic processes with legal, governmental, and ultimately intellectual processes in defining not only who temporarily "owned" which inventions, but also what features of technique were new and important. It provided the arena in which decision rules were gradually established as to the criteria for such technical judgments.

# A BRIEF SURVEY

Chapter 2 narrates a biographical sketch (1788–1864) of the inventor, to establish a personal context for viewing his woodworking inventions. Chapter 3 outlines the most central social system—patent management —through which the inventions of Thomas Blanchard and other American inventors of his day were socially constructed, describes the actions of Blanchard as manager of his patents, and shows what effect the system had on his irregular turning lathe after it was invented. It also describes the gradual process of change in decision rules for invention. Chapter 4 traces the history of the technology to which Blanchard added his invention of the irregular turning lathe, and shows in what respects it was different from the preceding technology, that is, in what respects it *was* an invention. Chapter 5 shows Blanchard's actions as user of his own intellectual property in applying his lathe to the production of gunstocks and integrating it with other special-purpose machines of his design into a prototypical production line. It also reassesses the effect of these machines on productivity at the Springfield Armory, and the extent to which they saved money for the government. Chapter 6 explains Blanchard's design and sale to entrepreneurs of another early production line, of special-purpose machines for making ships' tackle-blocks and deadeyes. It shows in what ways they were different from preceding blockmaking machinery and gives the brief history of their initial application. Chapter 7 describes as "application divergence" the modifications Blanchard and others made to his irregular turning lathe in adapting it to manufacture of equipment for agriculture, transportation, footwear, and decorative art (as well as the art of persuasion). Chapter 8 presents the history of Blanchard's woodbending invention as a case of application divergence and of social construction whose outcomes contrasted with those of the irregular turning lathe. Chapter 9 summarizes and draws conclusions from these stories.

## PATENT MANAGEMENT AS SOCIAL SYSTEM

As chapter 3 explains, the patent management system, in which much invention took place in the early nineteenth-century United States, should be understood to include not only the granting of patents but also, more broadly, their maintenance through assignments, licensing, litigation, reissue, and extension of term. Even as it also underwent changes, the system functioned in several ways within the society of which it was part. It manifestly encouraged inventions in the first place by promising reward for them. By turning an invention into intellectual property, it multiplied the ways by which its inventor could, with further effort, earn pecuniary reward from it. Patenting also promoted the development of practical industrial applications of the inventions, by providing a mechanism by which the inventor could marshall advance funds for research and development. Further, patent management helped disseminate technical information and stimulated interaction and communication among inventors, manufacturers, and other interested participants in the system. Part of this interaction and communication was doubtless unpleasant to them, since it involved conflict at law, but it was useful nevertheless in identifying significant features of the emerging new technologies. This helped build up the widening and deepening structure of technical knowledge and skills in the system's participants.

From the point of view of the society as a whole, of which the patent management system was a subsystem, some of its features had negative as well as positive effects. Beyond a certain point (whose location was a subject of debate), the legal defense of the limited monopoly granted to any one inventor on his intellectual property would have the effect of discouraging improvements of the patented device by other would-be inventors, instead of encouraging them. Sometimes, too, as patents were sold or "assigned" to several persons, they functioned as nodes around which special-interest groups formed to engage in restraint of trade, price fixing, or lobbying for special legislation in their own favor. These features of patent management behavior aroused uneasiness or even outrage, especially among those who felt injured economically by them.

Beyond these positive and negative functions of the patent management system in the nineteenth century, it also functioned, through record-keeping, to determine our history of inventions by continually defining the significant characteristics of particular inventions. It has shaped our very perceptions of what constitutes "newness" in technologies.

Patent management was certainly not the only subsystem of American society within which social construction took place regarding the particular technologies that were rapidly coming into existence during Thomas Blanchard's lifetime. The government itself was a subsystem of society through parts of which—notably the military arm—people made choices among particular technologies.[5] Another important subsystem in which people had a direct or indirect influence on technology was made up of the scattered commercial interactions collectively termed "the marketplace" or "the economy." Other subsystems were also providing for interaction on questions of technology among inventors, mechanics and engineers, entrepreneurs, writers, educators, and the public at large. Some arenas of such interaction were organizations dedicated to the promotion of technological development, like the Franklin Institute in Philadelphia or the American Institute in New York City.[6] Some, such as mechanics' organizations, were occupational interest groups.[7] Some were the workshops, manufactories, and mills themselves where mechanics worked and exchanged "little kinks and devices" of production technique.[8] Some were broader forums, such as schools and colleges where mathematics and sciences were taught, or newspapers and magazines that reported technological developments. Some were much more ephemeral gatherings such as the 1853 Crystal Palace Exhibition in New York (which English Parliamentary Commissioners also visited).[9]

Communications, transactions, and decisionmaking concerning technology took place among people in all such overlapping locations within society.[10] These technology-related interactions in nineteenth-century American society were not value-free; they took part in the growth and maintenance of a cultural value favoring technological "progress." They helped foster the motivation in some individuals to attempt invention. They also helped spread a sufficiently growing stock of technological information and equipment to such motivated individuals to enable them to make a widening variety of inventions.

But the patent management system in which Thomas Blanchard and his contemporaries operated was a very central one of these subsystems that mediated between the individual inventor and the whole society. Overlapping with and drawing upon the society's legal system, its economic system, and its political system, it had a relatively direct influence on the invention of particular technologies, and a special role in the very development of technological cognition.[11]

Explanations for the rise of the American system of manufactures have been advanced in terms of "Yankee ingenuity," of labor scarcity, of resource abundance, or of social attitudes toward work. Historians do not agree on which explanations outweighed others in shaping that era of American technological history. From the example of Thomas Blanchard's career, in which management of patents was a powerful feature, I suggest that we will understand the changing technology of his era better when we consider the effects of the patent management system on inventions and on their application and diffusion.[12]

## BLANCHARD'S INVENTIONS

Inventions do not spring full-blown into an empty mind; instead, in solving technical problems inventors draw upon the cumulative cultural tradition of previous inventions. The cultural tradition of Blanchard's time and place was European-American. Study of the origins of Blanchard's machines therefore inevitably involves questions of technology transfer: were there—as was persistently asserted in Blanchard's numerous patent lawsuits—earlier or contemporaneous European machines for doing "the same" operations as Blanchard's irregular turning lathe of 1819–20? Was Blanchard's truly an "American" invention? To arrive at an answer to this question I have examined how Blanchard's machine for copying irregular shapes and those of his predecessors and contemporaries on both sides of the Atlantic actually worked, and what the relevant differences were. Both in Blanchard's irregular turning lathe and in European copying machines that preceded it, a tracer following a model controlled the actions of a tool to cut out a copy. However, the crucial distinction between Blanchard's lathe and the other machines is not in their components, but in their kinematics. The elements of which the Blanchard lathe is composed may be similar to those of other machines of its day, but the ways in which they *move* produce a totally different effect. Chapter 4 shows how Blanchard's novel kinematics overcame the inherent limitation in other lathes on the amount of material that could be removed during one rotation of the workpiece, which prevented them from cutting highly irregular shapes. The vertical-spindle sculpture-copying and carving machines of Blanchard's day mentioned in chapter 7 were kinematically limited in a different way from the lathes. They could copy irregularities even finer than the Blanchard lathe could do, but they could not reproduce three-dimensional objects all the way around in one operation.

Thus the European copying machines that were invented previously and contemporaneously to Blanchard's lathe were for one or the other of these two reasons incapable of duplicating highly irregular objects such as gunstocks or shoe lasts in one continuous operation, as Blanchard's lathe did. The machine that came closest to Blanchard's in this capability was that of another American, Azariah Woolworth (b. 1779), whose machine was not originally self-acting, as Blanchard's was. Woolworth's machine, patented in June 1820, has been lost to history, but patent litigation records reveal its kinematics. It was also capable of shaping shoe lasts and gunstocks, but worked more slowly than Blanchard's lathe. The reason Woolworth's machine is so obscure and Blanchard's so famous, however, has less to do with their respective capabilities, I believe, than with the social construction of technical knowledge (and therefore of history) through the workings of the patent management system at the time. The effect of those workings, as chapter 3 explains, was that Woolworth's different mechanical solution to the problem of turning irregular shapes was gradually subsumed by the socially expanded definition of the Blanchard lathe.

Next to his invention of the Blanchard lathe, Thomas Blanchard is best known for his design of the earliest American production system comprised of special-purpose machines organized for manufacturing uniform objects. This was his production line for gunstocks at Springfield

Armory. How did this production system actually work? Did he design other such systems? How did his design compare with European precedent in this respect? To investigate how such a production system actually worked we must closely examine the operation of its component machines, in order to see which tasks were apportioned to each machine, and in what sequence. Chapter 5 shows that besides special-purpose saws and drills, Blanchard's set of machinery for gunstocking consisted of variants on three types of machine for copying the exterior of solids and interiors of spaces. It also shows, contrary to contemporary and later commentary, that Blanchard's machines did not supplant hand work among the gunstockers at Springfield.

Blanchard also designed a production system for the manufacture of marine tackle-blocks and deadeyes. He patented ten blockmaking machines that went into operation in an industrial-scale block mill, near Burlington, Vermont in 1836. Like the gunstocking machinery, they included machines for shaping the exteriors of solid bodies and for inletting spaces into them. Chapter 6 shows that Blanchard's design of the individual blockmaking machines and of the production sequence was original, and not a replication of the famous block mill at Portsmouth, England, which had begun operation thirty years earlier. I attribute the differences in design to the differences in circumstances of the American commercial market for pulley blocks, for which Blanchard designed these machines, from those facing the designers of machinery for the Royal Navy.

## APPLICATION DIVERGENCE AND DIFFUSION OF BLANCHARD'S INVENTIONS

Once invented and patented, Blanchard's lathe and his woodbending machine spread by way of assignments and licenses during their patent periods, which ended in 1862 and in 1870, respectively. As discussed in chapters 7 and 8, both of these inventions found widespread application in the manufacturing of agricultural implements and of carriages and wagons. As these industries expanded westward from their beginnings on the east coast they took Blanchard's machines with them. By contrast, lastmaking, like the shoe industry into which it fed, remained primarily in the eastern states. Chapter 7 shows that Blanchard's lathe mechanized lastmaking decades before shoe making was mechanized, and explains Blanchard's licensing relationship to lastmakers in New England.

The way in which one invention leads an inventor to another is rarely logical. Blanchard's total roster of over two dozen inventions certainly shows diversity of interest, from shearing the nap of cloth (1813) to shallow-draft steamboats (1831), from cigarettes (1858) to scoop shovels (1862). His patented machines for woodworking, however, have an internal coherence, even when they are not related to one another in a production line. Such coherence is supplied by an economic motive: to increase the opportunities for applying the machines he had already invented.

Thus, as chapter 8 explains, Blanchard turned his attention to a woodbending machine when he was told that a reliable bending method was needed before his lathe could be used for turning plow handles. Once he had the plow-handle bending machine in 1849, he made it more attractive by inventing a handle smoothing machine, patented in 1854, to sell along with it, which was applicable to other kinds of wooden handles as well. He also proceeded to invent further versions of his woodbending machine in order to expand its possible applications to ship timbers, furniture, and other tool handles. With respect to the economy, Nathan Rosenberg has called this process "technological convergence."[13] I suggest that from the inventor's point of view it should be called "application divergence," and that it was promoted by the patent management system.

In his report of 1854, one of the English Parliamentary Commissioners wrote of "the American working boy"

> The facts constantly before him of ingenious men who have solved economic and mechanical problems to their own profit and elevation, are all stimulative and encouraging; and it may be said that there is not a working boy of average ability in the New England States, at least, who has not an idea of some mechanical invention or improvement in manufactures, by which in good time, he hopes to better his position, or rise to fortune and social distinction.[14]

For Thomas Blanchard, as for other American working boys of his era, the patent management system not only kept such facts constantly before him, it also provided the sometimes arduous means for realizing his hopes to rise to fortune and social distinction. By successful management of his patented intellectual property, Blanchard did become an inventor who won material reward in his lifetime as well as lasting recognition thereafter.

**2**

# FROM
# "WHITTLING BOY"
# TO "MAN OF
# PROGRESS"

# WHITTLING—A YANKEE PORTRAIT[*]
## By Rev. J. Pierpont

The Yankee boy, before he's sent to school,
Well knows the mystery of that magic tool,
The pocket-knife. To that his wistful eye
Turns, when he hears his mother's lullaby;
His hoarded cents he gladly gives to get it,
Then leaves no stone unturned till he can whet it;
And in the education of the lad,
No little part that implement hath had;
His pocket-knife to the young whittler brings
A growing knowledge of material things.

Projectiles, music, and the sculptor's art,
His chestnut whistle and his shingle dart,
His elder pop-gun with its hickory rod,
Its sharp explosion and rebounding wad,
His corn-stalk fiddle, and the deeper tone
That murmurs from his pumpkin-leaf trombone
Conspire to teach the boy. To these succeed
His bow, his arrow of a feathered reed,
His windmill, raised the passing breeze to win,
His water-wheel that turns upon a pin;
Or if his father lives upon the shore,
You'll see his ship "beam-ends upon the floor,"
Full-rigged, with raking masts and timbers staunch,
And waiting near the wash-tub for a launch.

Thus, by his genius and his jack-knife driven,
Ere long he'll solve you any problem given;
Make any gimcrack, musical or mute,
A plow, a coach, an organ or a flute;
Make you a locomotive or a clock;
Cut a canal or build a floating dock;

[*] *The United States Magazine* 4 (March 1857): 217.

Make anything, in short, for sea or shore,
From a child's rattle to a seventy-four;
Make it, said I? Ay, when he undertakes it,
He'll make the thing and the machine that makes it.

And when the thing is made—whether it be
To move on earth, in air or on the sea,
Whether on water, o'er the waves to glide,
Or on the land to roll, revolve or slide,
Whether to whirl, or jar, to strike or ring,
Whether it be a pistol or a spring,
Wheel, pulley, tube sonorous, wood or brass,
The thing designed shall surely come to pass;
For when his hand's upon it, you may know
That there's go in it, and he'll make it go.

T H E English Commissioner quoted earlier gave one reason an "American working boy" in the mid-nineteenth century would be motivated to become an inventor: the boy's desire for social and economic betterment. An American contemporary, Rev. J. Pierpont, offered quite a different reason: the boy's pocketknife.

Rev. Pierpont's nostalgic verse, shown on the opposite page, well evokes the image of the ingenious Yankee "Whittling Boy" that became part of the nineteenth-century myth of the heroic inventor. It is the same image that Thomas Blanchard's and Eli Whitney's early biographers presented.[1] Its idea that the inventor was from childhood "by his genius and his jack-knife driven" will make any present-day historian of technology shrug and grimace, for it is woefully inadequate as historical explanation for inventive activity. Yet the Commissioner's explanation that the American working boy set out to be an inventor simply *in order to* "better his position" is also incomplete.

Neither does the present volume purport to explain completely the phenomenal flowering of the behavior labeled "Yankee ingenuity" in the nineteenth century. It does offer, however, a look at the behavior of people within a subsystem of American society that was particularly important for inventors in the nineteenth century: the system of patent management. Ingenious Yankees, including Thomas Blanchard, were active in that system; it shaped their interactions, which in turn helped shaped the system.

Any inventor, however, also participated in multiple other social subsystems in addition to that of patent management. Like most people, over his lifetime he was born into a family and later formed others; he lived in specific communities; he went to school; he won friends and provoked opponents; he bought from and sold things to other persons; he had employers and employees and colleagues. These social relationships presumably provided opportunities and constraints and affected his motivations as an inventor. This chapter shows Thomas Blanchard in these other contexts so as to provide perspective on his inventive and patent management activities, which receive more detailed attention in later chapters.

*15*

No full-dress biography of Thomas Blanchard has appeared, but several biographical sketches were published in the nineteenth and early twentieth centuries. Almost all derive from sketches by Henry Howe and by Asa Holman Waters.[2] Howe's sketch, based upon "materials obtained . . . from the subject of the memoir," was written before 1840, and necessarily ignores Blanchard's later career. The several sketches by Waters were written after Blanchard's death, but also emphasize Blanchard's early career, when Waters knew him best in person. Both Howe and Waters are uninformative about Blanchard's family life as an adult; both are strong on colorful anecdotes and weak on dates. This chapter draws on information from other sources, including patent and legal records, local histories, directories and vital records, newspapers, and Blanchard's will, to establish a chronology of the main events in Blanchard's "rise to fortune and social distinction" through successful patent management.

Born June 24, 1788 into a large farm family[3] in the township of Sutton, not far from Worcester, Massachusetts,[4] Thomas Blanchard was said to show as a child the usual signs of inventiveness that were *de rigueur* in biographies of nineteenth-century ingenious Yankees. He was described as uninterested in farm work but fond of making mechanical toys with his jackknife. According to Henry Howe, Blanchard's earliest biographer, young Tom witnessed blacksmithing for the first time at age nine and thereupon surreptitiously built himself a "forge" at which he made an abortive attempt in his parents' absence to weld together two pieces of iron. Howe also credits him with making an apple-paring machine at age 13.[5] Asa Holman Waters, Blanchard's most assiduous biographer, emphasizes that Blanchard was a stutterer, which apparently led his early acquaintances to regard him as an uncouth dullard and to call him "stammering Tom." He did not shine at school, attended as little as possible, and was a poor speller as an adult.[6] A neighbor later recalled that

> When Thomas was about 12 years of age his father came to my father and asked him to take the boy into his employ as he could do nothing with him. He would not work, but was constantly at some project in the line of machinery. Thomas . . . soon became a source of trial and vexation and did not remain long. If father sent him into the field to pick and pile up stones Tom would stammer out "T-t-there might b-b-be a ma-machine m-m-made to do th-th-this!" . . . Having been sent to the house from the field one day for a plow he induced the servant girl to shoulder and lug it for him by promising to make her a paring-machine, which he did.[7]

Apparently what people remembered about Blanchard's boyhood was that he was already alert to potential labor-saving devices and that this was not appropriate for a farm boy.

Alternative occupations, however, were available not far from home for a farm boy in Worcester County. Thomas's brother Stephen, who was thirteen years older than Thomas, had already moved to that part of Sutton called Millbury, where he had a horse-powered mill in which he employed "a number of persons, mostly boys . . . in . . . manufacturing tacks."[8]

Another older brother, John Brewer Blanchard, became a scythe maker in Dudley (now Webster), which was somewhat farther away. After his unsuccessful sojourn on the neighbor's farm, Thomas was sent to Millbury to work for his brother Stephen.[9] In response to the job of heading tacks one at a time, Blanchard soon devised an automatic counter to signal when he had accomplished his daily stint at this tedious task, and then at age eighteen set about inventing a machine to make the tacks. With interruptions, he worked on it for six years, during which he also invented and in 1813 patented a "Horizontal or Circular Vibrating machine, for shearing woolen cloth."[10] On October 3, 1817 he obtained a patent for his tackmaking machine, which cut and headed 500 tacks per minute. He sold the rights for $5,000, and set up his own shop in West Millbury.[11]

Meanwhile, he was appointed one of three "field-drivers" by the Millbury town meeting in March, 1815,[12] having married Sarah Segress, from Leicester, Massachusetts, that January. The newlyweds quickly started raising a family. Their daughter Laura was born February 24, 1815, and their son George Washington arrived nineteen months later.[13]

Blanchard's shop was located on a waterpower privilege, of which Millbury had many (hence its name). Already in 1793 there were more than forty waterpowered industrial enterprises in Sutton township; by 1827 fourteen manufacturing establishments were concentrated within 1 1/4 miles on one of Millbury's streams, powered by a total fall of 212 feet in that distance.[14] Among the diverse metal- and woodworking industries at Millbury when Thomas Blanchard set up his shop were the first brass foundry in central Massachusetts, run by one Asa Kenney, opposite Blanchard's shop,[15] and, on a different stream some miles away, the Waters' gun manufactory.[16] The proprietor of this manufactory, Asa Waters, Jr. (1769–1841) was one of the private contractors making U.S. muskets for the Springfield Armory. In 1818 Waters received a patent for a lathe he had invented to turn gun barrels.[17] Although his lathe eliminated the need for grinding to make the barrels a slightly tapered cylinder along their length, it did not eliminate the need for hand-filing to change the circular cross section into the "ovals and flats" of the breech end. After vain attempts to build this capability into his lathe, Waters called on Thomas Blanchard in early 1818 for help. Blanchard reportedly "began a low monotonous whistle, as was his wont through life when in deep study, and ere long suggested an additional, very simple, but wholly original cam motion, which . . . proved a perfect success."[18] Blanchard's solution may not have been quite as instantaneous as this anecdote suggests, for his page in the Waters account book shows he was charged $2.00 on February 19, 1818, for "Sundry refuse gunbarrels which you took for turning but did not return." He also bought a gunstock from Waters for 25 cents.[19]

According to Asa Holman Waters (1808–1887), who was the barrel-lathe inventor's son, Blanchard's success with the cam motion for the barrel lathe prompted him to think about the problem of shaping a gunstock by lathe, and to solve it by an extension of the cam-motion principle.[20] In Henry Howe's anecdote about the invention, the inspiration of the gunstock lathe by the barrel lathe is less direct: after installing his improvement on the gunbarrel lathe at Springfield Armory and hearing a stocker remark that *his* job could not be spoiled by Blanchard's machine, Blanchard began mulling over the problem and on his way home to Millbury "the whole principle of turning irregular forms from a pattern at once burst upon his mind." According to Howe, "the idea was so pleasing and forcible, that, like Archimedes of old, he exclaimed aloud, 'I have got it! I have got it!' " and a farmer who heard him remarked to another farmer, "I guess that man's crazy."[21]

The Blanchard lathe coordinated the motions of a tracer pressing against a revolving model with those of a cutting wheel acting on a revolving workpiece, so that the machine cut a three-dimensional copy of the model. As chapter 4 shows, the gunstocking lathe was a basically different kind of machine from the gunbarrel lathe, and both its effectiveness and its originality were due less to the cam motion principle than to the actions of its independently powered cutter.

Through the Waters armory connection, Blanchard came to the notice of the Springfield Armory and the Ordnance Department, which employed him in spring and summer 1818 to make improvements to barrel-turning lathes at the national armories at Springfield and Harpers Ferry.

Blanchard returned to Millbury and demonstrated a small-scale gun-stocking lathe at Springfield the following spring. The Ordnance Department sent him again to Harpers Ferry to construct a full-size one that summer.[22] When Blanchard applied for a patent for this irregular turning lathe, his neighbor in Millbury, Asa Kenney, claimed it was *his* invention and brought a patent interference suit against Blanchard. After winning the suit in late July 1819, Blanchard received a patent for his irregular turning lathe on September 6, 1819, and on September 14 was exhibiting a model of it in Boston.[23] Following accusations in Boston that he had claimed more in his patent than he had invented, Thomas Blanchard and his brother Stephen made a quick trip to Waterbury, Connecticut. There they paid a visit to the workshop of James Harrison, a clockmaker, to look at a crude lastmaking machine that Harrison's erstwhile partner, Azariah Woolworth, had invented and put into operation. As they came away, Stephen remarked to his brother that he had nothing to fear from *that* machine.[24] Nevertheless, Thomas Blanchard withdrew the patent of September, revised his patent specification, and received a reissued patent for the same machine on January 20, 1820.

For a period Blanchard apparently made trips back and forth between Worcester and Hampden Counties while building machines in Millbury for the Springfield Armory. The Blanchards' son Samuel, born in Millbury in May 1820, died there only fourteen months later.[25] In mid-1823 Blanchard began working as an inside contractor at the Armory, manufacturing gunstocks at 37 cents per stock, while using Armory facilities and materials but hiring his own helpers. In the next few years Blanchard devised and used, but did not patent, a series of thirteen additional special-purpose machines to use with the irregular turning lathe in performing the various operations of "half-stocking" muskets. His brother John Brewer Blanchard moved his scythe factory in 1824 from Dudley to a larger millsite in Palmer, Hampden County, after Thomas informed him it was for sale.[26] A generation later, John B.'s sons equipped the scythe factory with woodworking machines invented by their uncle Thomas, and were major assignees of Blanchard's patents.

By the end of 1825 Thomas and Sarah had produced two more children, both born in Millbury, and then acquired a house in Springfield.[27] When Blanchard's "inside" contract ended on December 31, 1827, his machines remained at the Springfield Armory and he began to collect royalties of 9 cents on each musket produced at the two national armories.[28]

In addition to setting up and running his production line of gunstocking machines at the Armory in Springfield, Blanchard engaged in other engineering activities in the 1820s. He spent several summer months in 1826 setting up waterpowered machines for pulley-block manufacture near Hudson, New York, an episode discussed in chapter 6. He also turned his attention to steam-powered transportation. He built a steam carriage in 1826, presumably making use of the device he patented on December 28, 1825, a "Traction Wheel for Regulating the Speed of Carriages."[29] He attempted unsuccessfully to get a steam railroad established in Massachusetts at that time, and met a similar lack of interest from the state of New York for this proposal.[30] (The first U.S. railroads, e.g., the Camden and Amboy in New Jersey, went into operation around 1831.)

He had more success in getting backers for steam transportation by water, which had already been proved feasible. In late 1826 the Connecticut River Company sponsored a test run by a steamboat named *Barnet* from Hartford, Connecticut, to Bellows Falls, Vermont.[31] Remaining in Springfield several years beyond his "inside" contract with the Armory, Thomas Blanchard designed, built, and operated shallow-draft steamboats to navigate the rapids of the Connecticut River between Hartford and Springfield before the completion of the Enfield Canal.

His steamboat *Blanchard,* propelled by side paddlewheels, was available for excursions in 1828 and was carrying passengers and freight on daily runs between Springfield and Hartford in 1830. It was subsequently renamed *Springfield.* In May 1829 Blanchard launched his stern-paddler *Vermont*—eighty feet long, fourteen feet wide—causing great local excitement in Springfield. It was "intended to ply in the river between Hartford and Bellows Falls and elsewhere."[32] The *Vermont's* paddlewheel "was set extremely far aft between two outboard supports . . . [to avoid] the turbulence close to the hull."[33] According to one account, Blanchard took the *Vermont* upstream to Bellows Falls for the first time in September 1829. At Brattleboro he encountered "a particularly vicious rapids" that halted the boat's progress even though "the fire was so great that the blaze poured out of the smokestack and Captain Blanchard, with the energy of despair, was punching against the bed of the river with a spiked pole."[34] In his efforts Blanchard fell overboard, but was pulled out without injury. Then the *Vermont* was winched over the rapids by a stationary windlass and the next day it proceeded upstream with its passengers to Bellows Falls.[35]

His steamboating enterprise took Blanchard westward in Pennsylvania and eastward to Maine: "Within the year he was commissioned to construct *Alleghany,* an excursion steamer out of Pittsburgh, and *Ticonic,* the first steamboat on the Kennebec to go from Gardiner to Waterville."[36] An observer commented "This kind of steamboat draws about one foot, all on board. So far as we have experience, her performance is extraordinary."[37] While in Pittsburgh, Blanchard submitted plans to the Allegheny Arsenal there for a series of eight machines to use in making gun carriages.[38] In Springfield again in spring 1831, Blanchard obtained a patent for his shallow-draft steamboat design[39] and launched the *Massachusetts,* which is thought to be the boat that later carried Charles Dickens from Springfield to Hartford in 1842.[40] In his *American Notes* Dickens described it disparagingly as "a warm sandwich about three feet thick," but at its launching the ninety-six-foot long *Massachusetts* was termed "much the largest and most complete boat ever seen at Springfield."[41]

At about that time Blanchard arranged the withdrawal of the Springfield and Hartford stagecoach company from competition with the steamboats for a few months. After the steamboats proved themselves faster as well as smoother than the land transport between Springfield and Hartford, in July 1831 "the stage people bought out Blanchard's interest in the vessels and he bowed out of the boating business for good."[42]

Blanchard's son George left high school in Springfield in the spring of 1832.[43] About then, I infer, Thomas Blanchard moved to New York City and shifted his inventive efforts somewhat from steamboating to woodworking for nautical purposes. He was a resident of New York City when he petitioned Congress for an extension of his patent for the irregular turning lathe in December 1833. While in New York City he obtained a patent on March 20, 1834 for "Planking Vessels." Three months later, on June 30, Congress passed an act granting him an extension of his irregular turning lathe patent. Then he received a patent for a "Shifting Circular Saw Mill" on August 8. He is listed in the city directory for New York only in 1833–34 and 1834–35, with two different addresses, both near the East River.[44] His wife Sarah died on July 20, 1834, at age forty-one.[45]

In the next two years Blanchard developed a set of machines for manufacturing ships' tackle-blocks and deadeyes, for which he obtained ten patents in the month of August 1836.[46] These machines were valued at $30,000 when they went into operation in a large block mill near Burlington, Vermont, whose production line is discussed in chapter 6.

Blanchard lived in or near New York City through the 1830s, expanding his sphere of activity to include Newark, New Jersey and its environs. He apparently grew interested in hat manufacture, conceivably through acquaintance with hatmakers' use of hatblocks made by his irregular turning lathe, for in 1837 he obtained a patent for "Making a Batting or Web for Hat Bodies."[47] It may have been in this period that he acquired property in Newark, New Jersey that was later listed in his estate appraisal.[48] In June 1838 he was residing in Springfield, New Jersey, a small town near Newark.[49] He was living in New York City in June 1839, when he won a patent infringement suit in Boston against shoe-last maker Chandler Sprague of North Bridgewater, Massachusetts, who had to pay him $521.27.

By now Blanchard had apparently achieved a higher economic status: according to records of this trial, he was valuing his time at $8.00 per working day, compared to $2.00 a day for a machinist of his age from Springfield, New Jersey, who was another witness in the trial.[50] By now he had also gained sufficient eminence to be the subject of a biographical sketch in Henry Howe's book, *Memoirs of the Most Eminent American Mechanics,* which appeared in 1840. It included the likeness shown in figure 2.1.

Soon afterward Blanchard moved to Boston, where the city directories

THOMAS BLANCHARD

FIGURE 2.1. Thomas Blanchard, c. 1839. At the age of fifty years, Blanchard impressed his earliest biographer as "an unassuming, yet talented individual." (From Henry Howe, *Memoirs of the Most Eminent American Mechanics,* 1840, p. 196.)

list him at four different addresses from 1840 to 1845, and on Dover Street for a decade thereafter.[51] He probably married his second wife, Marcia Pierce of Grafton, Massachusetts, about the time he moved to Boston, for their daughter, Delia P. Blanchard, was born about 1841.[52] In March 1843, Blanchard patented an improvement in his irregular turning lathe, which eliminated the overhanging framework of the 1820 version. This new "rocking" version of the lathe was more effective for turning long items like ax handles and wheel spokes well as gunstocks, as is discussed in chapters 5 and 7.

Blanchard lived in Boston for the rest of his life, but traveled to New York, Newark, and Washington, D.C. in the course of patent management activities. He continued making inventions and managing their patents; his most lucrative was the woodbending machine for which he obtained a patent in 1849 (see chapter 8). His wife Marcia and his son George participated to some extent in his business, for their names appear occasionally in various legal papers, as do those of his English son-in-law, Alfred Maddock, and his informally adopted son, Thomas Blanchard, Jr., who was Maddock's younger brother, Samuel. Blanchard maintained relations with his nieces and nephews, including the children of his older brothers John B. in Palmer, and Simon, who had long lived in Boston.[53] By 1855 Blanchard had acquired sufficient means to move his family from quarters near his workshop on Dover Street to a Charles Bulfinch-designed house overlooking the Boston Commons,[54] and to afford such luxuries as a trip to the Paris Exposition that summer. His estate was valued at nearly $100,000 when he died in 1864.[55]

To attain this degree of affluence, however, he had to engage in "protracted and expensive litigation" on many occasions to claim recognition and royalties as patentee of the irregular turning lathe. Associate Supreme Court Justice Joseph Story, rendering a decision in favor of Blanchard in 1839, said "with much pleasure" that "after much trouble, care, and anxiety he will be able to enjoy the fruits, unmolested, of his inventive genius."[56] Nevertheless, Blanchard's fruits continued to be molested: he had to bring suit against many more infringers in the late 1840s and in the 1850s in protection of his intellectual property, as we will see in chapter 3. A beneficial side effect of so much litigation was that he overcame his stutter. According to A. H. Waters, "By means of books, social intercourse in courts and elsewhere . . . his speech impediment was conquered, and he finally attained a good degree of culture and expansion of mind."[57]

In addition to such utilitarian objects as gunstocks, ax handles, wheel spokes, scythe snaths, shoe lasts and hat blocks, Blanchard's biographers also credit his lathe with the ability to carve busts. When Blanchard was lobbying Congress for the second extension of his 1820 patent in 1848, he testified, as he had already done in 1834, that piracy of his invention had been so great that he so far had netted little reward from it. This time he also took a machine with him to Washington and used it to sculpt marble copies of plaster busts of influential members of Congress, including Senator Daniel Webster of Massachusetts. He also performed this feat at the Paris Exposition in 1855, where he replicated the head of Empress Eugenie in marble.[58] As discussed in chapter 7, however, the machine that Blanchard used was not really a Blanchard lathe, which was not capable of undercutting cavities (such as nostrils) that were smaller than could be entered by its cutting wheel.

Besides irregular turning, Blanchard's other major woodworking invention was machinery for bending wood. "The Boston manufacturers of Agricultural Implements" drew his attention to the need for improvement in the usual methods of bending plow handles, by which the breakage rate was high. Blanchard invented a method of compressing the wood endwise just before bending, making it much stronger in the process. At the end of 1849 he obtained a patent for a machine to bend the handles for plows, harrows, scythes, and other agricultural implements. With further experiments, he succeeded by 1854 or 1855 in bending timber fourteen inches square, large enough for "ship knees of the heaviest class."[59] At the Paris Exposition in 1855, Blanchard won first-class medals for his sculpture-copying and timber-bending machines.[60] He obtained three more woodbending patents in the years 1856–58.[61] As chapter 8 shows, the application of Blanchard's woodbending machines spread westward in the 1850s and 1860s along with the carriage and agricultural implement industries.

Blanchard had a variety of relationships to the enterprises using his inventions. Sometimes he accepted a lump-sum fee for the use of one of his patented inventions for a particular application or in a particular locality, and sometimes a periodic fee varying with the output of the user. Other times he accepted a percentage of the returns from a firm's use of a patent, or took shares in the capital stock of the company. In 1851 and 1852 Blanchard made major sales of rights to his bending machine and turning lathe to J. M. Quinby, a carriage maker in Newark, New Jersey, and to A. V. Blanchard and Co., his brother's sons in Palmer, Massachu-

FIGURE 2.2. American "Men of Progress," 1862. In his seventies Thomas Blanchard appeared, second from right, among these scientists, inventors, and entrepreneurs fictitiously assembled beneath Benjamin Franklin's presiding image. He is turned toward Elias Howe. The others are, left to right, William Morton, James Bogardus, Samuel Colt, Cyrus McCormick, Joseph Saxton, Charles Goodyear, Peter Cooper, Jordan Mott, Joseph Henry, Eliphalet Nott, John Ericsson, Frederick Sickels, Samuel Morse, Henry Burden, Richard Hoe, Erastus Bigelow, and Isaiah Jennings. (John Sartain engraving after a painting by Christian Schussele, 1862, National Portrait Gallery, Smithsonian Institution, Washington, D.C.)

setts, who made scythes. For these assignments he received fixed fees totaling $68,000 in installments over six years. A little later he also accepted $600,000 worth of shares in the capital stock of the Ship Timber Bending Company in New York City. From this venture, however, he later calculated that he realized only $12,000, for the company failed.[62] He also earned a steady income from license fees for the use of his lathe by shoe-last makers in eastern New England, as chapter 7 shows. Blanchard's flexible patent management, described in chapter 3, made him a "successful" inventor.

Blanchard continued inventing on through his sixties and into his seventies. In addition to his timber-bending machines, he obtained patents for a "Machine for Polishing Handles and Other Articles," February 7, 1854 (#10,497); a "Mill for Reducing Substances," March 9, 1858 (#19,541); an "Improvement in Cigars," March 30, 1858 (#19,746); and an "Improved Scoop-Shovel," January 21, 1862 (#34,193). His lifetime total of patents was more than the two dozen for which he is usually given credit.[63] In 1862 he was depicted, along with Samuel Morse, Charles Goodyear, Elias Howe and other famous inventors and scientists, in Christian Schussele's well-known collective portrait, "Men of Progress"[64] (see figure 2.2).

Along the way to public fame Thomas Blanchard suffered a number of personal shocks and losses, in addition to the early deaths of his baby son in 1821 and of his first wife in 1834. None of Blanchard's first five children outlived him. His oldest son, George Washington Blanchard, survived the longest, but went west to California in the gold rush and died there in 1850, thirty-three years old.[65] Delia, the daughter of his second marriage, married Alfred Maddock, who committed suicide in 1862, whereupon she went insane and was still *non compos mentis* in 1864. Blanchard's second wife, Marcia, presumably died before Blanchard, for in his seventy-fifth year he was married for a third time, to thirty-one-year-old Laura A. Shaw.[66] Ten months later he died of apoplexy on April 16, 1864. Thomas Blanchard was buried in Mount Auburn Cemetery in Cambridge, Massachusetts, where his monument depicts two of his inventions—his lathe and his woodbending machine—in bas-relief marble panels. The epitaph calls him "An eminent American Inventor whose great mind conceived ideas and brought into operation works of art that will live for ages." The bust of Blanchard himself that used to surmount the monument[67] has disappeared.

In his will, Blanchard devoted much attention to arranging continued care for his deranged daughter, and to forseeing all possible contingencies of surviving heirs in future generations. He didn't mention his pocket-knife, but he singled out for particular disposition his volumes of the annual Patent Office Report and the models he had used in patent applications and trials. These symbolized his career's strong involvement with patent management.

# 3

## SOCIAL
## CONSTRUCTION
## OF INVENTION
## THROUGH PATENT
## MANAGEMENT

WHAT did a nineteenth-century American inventor have to do to earn recognition and reward for his invention? Thomas Blanchard's career as inventor demonstrates patent management as the course to pursue toward those goals.[1] It also demonstrates the social construction of invention: the workings of a social subsystem that powerfully affected not only what got invented, but also what got recognized and recorded in history. The interactions of "interested" people in the course of managing patents determined features of particular patented devices, *and* over time they defined and redefined implicit rules for judging whether a proposed invention was really new. Since originality is the defining characteristic of any invention, the gradual social formation of decision rules for originality was tantamount to defining invention itself. Of course, we recognize that not all inventions received patents. Still, all patents were, by definition, for inventions. Publicly acknowledged patented inventions provided powerful standards for recognition of nonpatented inventions also. Patent management was the social subsystem to which our society allocated the continuing task of constructing "invention" as well as particular inventions.

## THE RATIONALE AND EVOLUTION OF A PATENT SYSTEM

Thomas Blanchard was able to make a career of inventing because the society in which he lived gave him material reward as well as fame. Not all societies have so rewarded their inventors, but modern Western societies have tended to do so.[2] From this we can infer that these societies have generally approved of invention and intended to encourage it. From the point of view of a society intending to encourage invention by rewarding inventors, it is important that the reward be sufficient for such encouragement, but not excessive. It is also important that particular inventions not disappear, but become part of the society's available stock of technology. Thus, the optimal social system to satisfy these criteria is one that holds out the maximum credible prospect of reward to a potential inventor, in order to induce that person to make an invention and to share it with society, but one that then gives the inventor the minimum actual reward consistent with continued credibility.

Sometimes, as in pre-Revolutionary France, modern Western societies have chosen to award prizes out of public funds directly to the inventors who have persuaded designated judges (such as the *Académie des Sciences* in Paris) that their inventions deserve approval.[3] Since the early seventeenth century, however, the usual English and American way of rewarding invention has been less direct: these societies have given inventors an opportunity to earn reward through the private economy, by granting them patents for their inventions, in return for making them public knowledge.[4] A patent for invention is a temporary monopoly on the making, use, and sale of a new device, in return for describing it so fully that anyone "skilled in the art" can understand it. The patent thus has two functions: one is to define and publicize what was original about an invention, and the other is to turn the invention for a limited duration of time—usually fourteen to seventeen years—into a piece of private property, to which the owner has rights that are enforceable in court. Because of this duality, the patent system operated in possibly unforeseen ways and had effects other than simply rewarding invention.

Through the interplay of these two functions—the promotion of technological knowledge and the protection of intellectual property, particular inventions continued to be socially defined and redefined (i.e., socially "constructed") even after their patents were granted. The material devices themselves, the embodiment of the inventions, changed as their features were modified during different uses, and unintended opportunities arose for official redefinition of the invention, when patents were re-issued or extended or litigated. Then, since the patent office and the courts kept records of these actions, subsequent inventors who wanted patents were able to get information about previous inventions and to build on them, being of course careful not to imitate them too closely. How close was "too close" became a matter of social construction through patent management.

An inventor in possession of a patent found it required management if it was to yield a return. He had entered the patent management system, in which patentees could *use* their own patents to produce something, or they could *sell* or *license* them to other people. They also had to *defend* their patents in lawsuits against infringers. Before 1861 they might also restate the specification and get it *reissued* for the same patent term, or ask to *extend* their patent term. And they might attempt to appeal directly to Congress for special extension of their own patents or for changes in laws pertaining to patents in general. These were all patent management activities.

In order to fulfill its functions of knowledge promotion and property protection, the patent system has kept various records. By keeping records that necessarily emphasize success in patent management rather than some unattainably pure, objective account of invention, the patent system has encouraged historians to create an oversimplified history of technological change as large discontinuous leaps forward instead of continual small evolutionary modifications. Some inventors, like Thomas Blanchard, or Thomas Edison in a later generation, were relatively successful in managing their patents and became famous; some inventors, like Azariah Woolworth and many others of whom we've never heard, were poor at patent management and therefore dropped out of history.

Like any other social system, the American patent system was subject to change. Thomas Blanchard's career spanned a period of several such changes.[5] In 1790 the founders of the new republic had already decided that the nation would encourage inventors by allowing them temporary monopolies on their inventions, rather than awarding them an outright prize from public funds. Thus inventions were defined as private property, albeit property that was intellectual and therefore intangible. By issuing patents the federal government undertook to protect and regulate the property rights of the individual inventors with respect to other inventors and to the public at large.

After a brief period 1790–93 in which the Secretary of State (then Thomas Jefferson) decided whether or not a proposed "invention" was original as well as useful, the United States adopted a simple registration system for patents, such as the English had. This system, which was in effect during Thomas Blanchard's early career until 1836, required no examination of patent applications, but relied entirely on the courts to decide questions of originality. The nation granted anyone a patent for fourteen years' exclusive rights to make, use, and sell the object or process patented, once he had followed this procedure: described his invention in writing and drawing, swore that it was original, survived a period of public notification or "caveat" during which anyone who disagreed could file an "interference" suit, and paid a $30 registration fee. After receiving a patent, a patentee then had the right to sue anyone who used his intellectual property without his permission. Such "infringement" suits took place in the federal circuit courts. Before 1836 Thomas Blanchard and other inventors paid their fees and submitted their specifications for nearly 10,000 inventions, and then duly obtained their patents and began conducting infringement suits.

After forty-odd years experience with this register-and-sue system, which became increasingly unwieldy as the annual number of patents swelled, Congress took action to relieve the courts and put the Patent Office on a more professional footing. In 1836 it reorganized the Patent Office to include salaried patent examiners, who would advise the Patent Commissioner to issue a patent only if they judged the application to indicate a truly original invention. Senator Ruggles of Maine, promoter of the patent office reform in 1836, acknowledged that a man meeting all the criteria for patent examiner was rare. He should have:

> a general knowledge of the arts, manufactures, and the mechanisms used in every branch of business in which improvements are sought to be patented, and of the principles embraced in the ten thousand inventions patented in the United States, and of the thirty thousand patented in Europe. He must moreover possess a familiar knowledge of the statute and common law on the subject, and the judicial decisions both in England and our own country, in patent cases.[6]

Nevertheless, from one patent examiner in 1836 and two in 1837, the number grew by 1861 to twelve examiner positions and by 1870 to twenty-two principal examiners plus forty-four assistant examiners.[7]

Informal practices grew up that were incorporated into the formal procedures of the patent office, or became expected, though not obligatory. Thus the patent office came to require inventors to reveal the necessary information about their inventions through three-dimensional patent models, in addition to written patent specifications and drawings.[8] Outside the patent office, the occupational specialties emerged of patent agent and patent attorney, to help inventors obtain and manage patents. For a fee, they would advise inventors as to the patentability of their inventions, help them write patent specifications, and represent them in dealing with the Patent Office and in lawsuits. Patent agents and agencies such as Munn & Co., associated with the publication *Scientific American,* were located in New York, Washington, D.C., and other large and small towns.[9] As figure 3.1 shows, at least one midwestern patent agent late in the century also went on the road to drum up business in rural areas.

**OUR EXHIBITION WAGON,**

WM A. BELL & CO. PATENT BROKERS & SOLICITORS

OF WHICH THE ABOVE IS AN ACCURATE REPRESENTATION.

**ATTENTION! READ WITH CARE!**

Have Your Patent Placed for Sale in Our Agency at Once.

**MAKE MONEY OUT OF YOUR PATENT WHILE YOU HAVE AN OPPORTUNITY.**

FIGURE 3.1. Patent diffusion by wagon. In 1891 William A. Bell & Co., patent brokers and solicitors of Sigourney, Iowa, outfitted this wagon for mobilized display of up to 150 patent models and copies of patent specifications. It toured midwestern states in the summer and fall, southern states the following winter. Bell & Co. told inventors that besides attending state fairs and other large expositions, "our agents having the wagon in charge . . . call on Manufacturers, Speculators and Buyers . . . Do not miss this good opportunity of having your patent brought before those most likely to buy territory. . . ." (National Museum of American History, Washington, D.C.)

## APPLICATION FOR A PATENT

Since the claims of originality in a patent specification constituted the legal equivalent of the boundaries stated in a real estate deed, it was important to claim no more and no less than what was original about the purported invention. If an inventor claimed too much, his whole patent could be declared invalid in a lawsuit; if he claimed too little, someone else could appropriate the unclaimed intellectual property. The patent examiners communicated with the inventors, or with their agents, about *which* features of a proposed invention were new and which had already been invented. Then the inventors and patent agents could rewrite the specification to disclaim the originality of some features and claim others. Or they could argue with the examiner. They could resubmit the application for decision again and again. Eventually, either the patent was granted or the applicant gave up.[10]

The patent examiners' decisions were ostensibly objective, but inevitably the examiners differed among themselves in the degree of originality they thought sufficient to warrant a patent.[11] No one had spelled out their decision rules in any formal way; they were left to construct them in practice. Robert C. Post's study of the rejection rate for antebellum patent applications demonstrates that as a group, the examiners varied over time in the stringency with which they applied their implicit decision rules.[12] We may suppose they formed these implicit rules in communication with one another as well as with inventors, patent agents, and other people in the growing community of persons interested in inventions. Sometimes patent examiners became patent agents themselves, and vice versa.

## REISSUE AND EXTENSION

Even after a patent was granted, if the inventor decided—perhaps in the course of a lawsuit—that the wording of his specification had been inaccurate or unclear, he could withdraw his patent, reword the specification, and apply to get the patent *reissued* for the remainder of the original patent term. The Patent Act of 1836 also allowed for a seven-year *extension* of the term of a patent if the patentee showed that he had failed to reap "a reasonable remuneration for the time, ingenuity and expense bestowed upon [his invention], and the introduction thereof into use."[13] A patented invention was supposed to remain the same in an extension or a reissue; in fact, however, these provided unintended occasions for making changes—hence for social construction—in the scope of a patent after experience with it. Reissues and extensions were much diminished by changes in Patent Office rules in 1861 and 1870.[14] In 1861 the patent term was lengthened from fourteen to seventeen years, and extensions were no longer allowed by Patent Office procedures.

## USE, ASSIGNMENT, AND LICENSE

As with tangible property, an inventor's intellectual property required management if he were to earn money from it during the term of his patent. There were many possibilities open to the inventor once he became a patentee. Even as a landowner can farm his own land, the inventor could of course use his invention himself to produce an object for sale. (This he could have done without a patent, but with risk of competition.) Or he could sell his patent outright for a lump sum or for installment payments. Or he could lease or rent it for a fixed or variable royalty fee. Sales were called assignments; leases or rentals were licenses. The difference between licenses and assignments was not always as clear as this analogy to real estate suggests. The legal distinction hinges on the right to sue an infringer: an assignee may do so on his own, but a licensee may not.[15] These possibilities were in turn multiplied by as many geographical territories as the inventor designated, so he could simultaneously assign his patent in some territories, license it in other places, and use it himself in still others. For an invention, like Blanchard's, with more than one industrial application, these possibilities were multiplied yet again by the number of different applications. Such an inventor could use, assign, or license his patent for the same purpose in different territories or for different purposes in the same territory.

As a landowner decides among his choices of occupying, selling, and renting his real estate, so the inventor had to decide about the long- and short-term advantages of using his own invention or assigning or licensing his patent. Eli Whitney, for instance, made what proved to be the wrong decision in attempting to produce cotton gins himself instead of licensing others to make and use them.[16] Ithiel Town, in contrast, was happy to let other bridge builders use his 1820 patented lattice truss design and to collect from them royalties of $1 per foot. (He sued them for $2 per foot if they tried to cheat.)[17]

Such a decision required an assessment of the market demand for the use of his invention for a given purpose in a given territory, not only at the time, but for the future duration of the patent. Presumably the market price for an assignment tended to decline, other things being equal, as the remaining term of the patent shortened. A license for the same territory could be expected to yield a constant income stream, but more opportunities for default, hence greater risk and need for sustained attention by the inventor. Assignment usually shifted to the assignee the right and onus of defending the patent against infringement; a license left this responsibility to the patentee. In either case, the patentee also had to remember the uses and territories for which he had already assigned and licensed his rights, in order not to infringe upon them.

In decisions about assignments and licenses, an inventor could conceivably develop a long-range strategy based on a sense of what size territory would be optimal for a given application of his invention, and then sell his rights for standard territories the size of cities, counties, or states. He might prefer to be paid outright for assigning his invention, or to receive "an interest" or ownership rights in the assignees company, or to be paid a variable amount based on the company's sales. These different modes of payment imply different degrees of continuing involvement by the inventor in the enterprise making use of his invention. As we will see, Thomas Blanchard was flexible both as to size of territory and mode of payment in his assignments and licenses.

Conversely, potential assignees and licensees had to weigh the short- and long-term costs of pirating, buying, or leasing patent rights in a desired territory. They had to decide whether they wanted an assignment, with the right to issue licenses and to sue infringers on their own, or wanted instead to leave those tasks to the patentee, and take a license. And they had to decide from what size territory they wished to exclude competitors from operating. Other things being equal, the larger territories cost more.

The assignment of patent rights also carried with it the right to sell them again or to license others within the territory specified, so an assignee need not himself be a user of the patented device; he could be simply a speculative purchaser of the right, intending to license it and collect royalties, or intending to sell it again for a higher price, perhaps by subdividing the territory. The network of assignees and licensees that grew up around a patent formed a nascent interest group that could be mobilized on occasion, such as testifying in lawsuits against infringers and lobbying in Congress for legislation beneficial to their interests. They also frequently made, in the subdivision of separate territories, agreements to fix the prices of what they produced under the patent.

Once the invention was embodied in an actual material object—such as a machine—in the hands of an assignee or licensee, he was free to modify it informally for his own use if he wished. In fact, he may have built his own in the first place, more or less following the design of the patentee. Useful modifications tended to spread by communication among the other assignees and licensees. Any such "improvement" that was sufficiently different from the original equipment might prompt the originator to go the trouble of taking out a separate patent (thereby risking litigation over it), but many such improvements were individually too small to inspire such effort. Over time, such small informal modifications tended to accrete, by tacit consent, to the original invention, and came to be regarded as covered by the patent. Such an expansion of the patent right could then be confirmed (or rejected) in lawsuits.

## PATENT LITIGATION

Thus, besides patent application, reissue, and extension, litigation provided additional occasions for social construction of a patented invention. The Patent Act of 1836 did not eliminate recourse to the legal system. It just meant that there were now two locations in society in which the originality of inventions was scrutinized and socially determined: one location in the patent office, and one in the courts. The judgment of the courts could, implicitly, overrule the judgment of the patent examiners in individual cases. Conducting lawsuits remained a task of patent management, for the more useful an invention was, the more likely there was to be infringement, and therefore litigation. Although deplored, lawsuits were a normal feature of the system, not a symptom of its malfunctioning or of cranky personal temperaments.

The patentee had the right to sue anyone who made, used or sold "his" device without his permission, in order to make the infringer stop doing so and to pay damages. At stake in the lawsuits was not just the inventor's claim to fame, but the economic wherewithal of a network of persons who may have bought or licensed his intellectual property for a given purpose in different geographic territories or for different purposes in the same territory. If no one sued infringers, who had avoided paying royalties for the patented device, the inventor's assignees and licensees would be at a disadvantage in competing. Without infringement suits against unlicensed users of his invention or against other patentees who had incorporated crucial features of his invention into theirs, an inventor's intellectual property would be eroded and gradually rendered worthless.

Infringement suits were held in federal district courts, presided over by circuit-riding Supreme Court justices. Sometimes the judges decided the case; sometimes a jury decided it. The usual defense against a complaint of infringement was either that the plaintiff's patented device was not in fact original, but the same as a previous device, or that the defendant's device was substantially different from the patented one. Or both of these arguments might be used at once. For either argument, it was necessary to make comparisons of two objects at a time: the plaintiff's device was compared with some device in the past, or it was compared with the defendant's device. More or less expert witnesses on both sides would identify various features of the devices as materially different from each other or the same as each other.

In the law courts, as with the examiners in the Patent Office, there were no objective and explicit decision rules for these more or less expert witnesses to follow in comparing one device with another; they simply had to use their own perceptions. After hearing their testimony, it was up to the judges or jury to decide whether an infringement had taken place. They took decisions—how else?—by vote. Witnesses and judges continued to dispute and to dissent, frequently on up to the Supreme Court, for their own eyes saw clear differences or similarities in the designs of disputed inventions. Such lawsuits were occasions for social delineation of the boundaries on intellectual property. No characteristics made the disputed inventions unambiguously "different from" or "the same as" one another, except as perceived by the eye of their beholders. The lawyers marshaling evidence on both sides of these cases encouraged witnesses to make comparisons on grounds that had been convincing to judges and juries in previous trials, so there tended to be a rough convergence over time as to what were the relevant grounds for comparing one device to another.

Thus, both in the granting and maintaining of patents, the nub of the process was to get people—examiners in the patent office or witnesses in lawsuits—to compare two things and say yes, gizmo $x$ and $y$ are the same in relevant respects, or no, gizmo $x$ and gizmo $y$ are significantly different. In both contexts we may observe these comparisons that were made in the past and try to discern what the criteria were for the decisions.[18] In making these decisions the examiners and witnesses were of course interacting directly or indirectly with judges, juries, lawyers, patent agents, and inventors, for the decisions of the courts were known and responded to by the patent examiners; the decisions of patent examiners had weight in the decisions of the courts. Patent agents and attorneys advised the inventors, and so on. All of these people were actors in the social system that was continuously creating and shaping an inventor's intellectual property, both before and after the initial granting of the patent. We shall now turn to the case of Thomas Blanchard's irregular turning lathe to see how it was socially constructed by this process.

## THE BLANCHARD LATHE

The gunstocking lathe for which Blanchard obtained a patent in 1819 copied a model all around, as distinct from a key-copying machine, which copies a key only along its edge. As is explained in chapter 4, it was also different from an ordinary lathe, which could only shape objects that were circular in cross section. But in Blanchard's machine a rapidly rotating cutting wheel removed material from around a slowly rotating workpiece, down to the shape of any model, including a gunstock or other irregular object that was *not* circular in cross section. It took just a few minutes to accomplish this in one continuous operation. It was a versatile machine, for with relatively little effort it could be "retooled" to make a different object by use of a different model. Besides gunstocks, Blanchard and his assignees and licensees adapted the machine to make shoe lasts, hat blocks, ax helves and other tool handles, and wheel spokes and other carriage parts, all of which had formerly had to be made by hand tools. The patent drawing (figure 3.2) shows the lathe adapted to turning shoe lasts.

Although he invented many other machines as well, Blanchard's experience with this machine for the rest of his life provides an excellent example of all the actions an inventor of his day could possibly take in relation to the patent management system. In attempting to gain reward for his invention, Blanchard not only used his own patent to make and sell machines, but also managed to overcome problems posed by interference, reissue, infringement, extension, assignment, and license. In addition, his management activities included congressional lobbying in Washington. Blanchard's experience as patent manager was not that of the average inventor, for it was longer and more successful than most. But he demonstrated the full range of the behavior of an inventor as patent manager, and thus can be regarded as a model for that role.

## INTERFERENCE AND REISSUE OF BLANCHARD'S PATENT

Blanchard received a patent for his lathe in 1819, but only after winning an interference action brought by his neighbor in West Millbury, brassfounder Asa Kenney. An appointed panel of experts held a trial in Millbury in July 1819, and decided, despite the superior appearance of

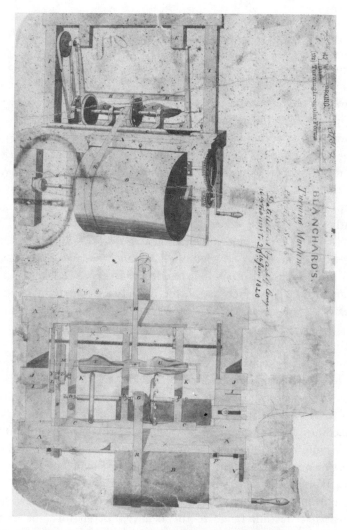

FIGURE 3.2. Oldest patent drawing of the Blanchard lathe. Thomas Blanchard's first patent drawing for his irregular turning lathe presumably perished in the Patent Office fire of 1836, but this copy was restored to the record soon afterward. It shows a working model of the machine copying a model last (left), to turn a rough workpiece (right), into a shoe last. (National Archives Cartographic Section, Alexandria, Virginia.)

Kenney's brass model, that Blanchard's had precedence.[19] After obtaining his patent on September 6, 1819, Blanchard demonstrated a model of his machine in Boston. Some people who viewed the machine considered buying the right to use it, but some others, among them one William Hovey of Worcester, questioned its originality, scaring off the potential customers.[20] Blanchard withdrew his patent, revised his claims of originality in the specification, and obtained a reissue on January 20, 1820. The differences in the two versions of Blanchard's patent specification suggest that he informed himself in the interim about four other machines —for making pulley blocks, wool-card handles, ornamental turnings, and shoe lasts. His reissued patent specification ends by stating that "the principle of his machine or invention is different" from each of these other machines.[21]

The lastmaking machine had been put into operation in Waterbury, Connecticut by a man named Azariah Woolworth, who at various times in his career worked as house carpenter, ship carpenter, and clock-maker.[22] In November 1819 Blanchard and his brother Stephen traveled to Waterbury to see the machine in operation at the waterpowered clock shop of James Harrison, Woolworth's partner in lastmaking. Operated partly by hand and partly by water, it was much cruder than Blanchard's machine, and worked about six times more slowly, but it was an improvement over Woolworth's earlier "machine #1," which was totally hand powered.[23] Figure 3.3 shows four points of comparison between Woolworth's "machine #2" and Blanchard's irregular turning lathe. Each comparison reveals both a similarity between the machines and a difference. First, like Blanchard's machine, Woolworth's machine #2 copied a model by means of a tracing mechanism, but instead of one model, it used two. Second, both machines differed from ordinary lathes in having separately powered cutters, but Blanchard's was a rotary cutter and Woolworth's was a reciprocating cutter. Third, in both machines, the workpiece and model(s) were keyed together to rotate simultaneously, but in Blanchard's they rotated continuously, while in Woolworth's they rotated intermittently, at the end of each lengthwise cut along the workpiece. Finally, as a result of their respective actions, both machines were capable of turning out irregular objects like shoe lasts, but where Blanchard's lathe cut a single continuous spiral path around the workpiece, Woolworth's lastmaking machine cut a series of parallel paths lengthwise along the object.

His brother Stephen told him he had "nothing to fear from *that* machine,"[24] but Thomas Blanchard took the precaution of withdrawing his patent, revising his specification explicitly to deny his lathe resembled the Waterbury lastmaking machine in "principle," and getting a reissue in January 1820. He and his financial backers were incorporated in February as the Blanchard Gunstock Turning Factory. Woolworth sold his unpatented invention to William Hovey, who with Woolworth's occasional assistance in Worcester and Boston built an improved version of his lastmaking machine. It was much more like Blanchard's, having a powered continuous rotation of the workpiece and a single model, and an additional rotary saw-tooth "burr" cutter for smoothing off the edges left by the first cutter.[25]

In early 1820 the financial backers of this Woolworth machine #3 were threatening to sue Blanchard and his backers, and vice versa. They reached a "compromise" out of court: the Blanchard group bought from the Woolworth group an assignment of all rights to the Woolworth machine, which duly received a patent in Woolworth's name in June 1820.[26] In 1834, when both patents expired, Blanchard got his extended, but Woolworth did nothing about his, so his machine #3 should have been in the public domain. A fire in the Patent Office destroyed all records in 1836, however, and no one restored Woolworth's patent specification to the record afterward. Blanchard had his own patent restored.

# BLANCHARD'S ASSIGNMENTS AND LICENSES

Meanwhile, once he obtained his reissued patent in January 1820, Blanchard was able to divide up his intellectual property in two ways: by use —for making shoe lasts, tool handles, wheel spokes, etc.—and by geographical territory. He sold and licensed his machine for the same use in different territories and for different uses in the same territory.[27] Blanchard and potential buyers or renters of his intellectual property had to decide about the long- and short-term advantages of assignments or licenses, and agree on the size and price of territories. The assignment

FIGURE 3.3. *(opposite)* Blanchard and Woolworth lathes compared. Thomas Blanchard's irregular turning lathe and the contemporaneous "Waterbury last-making machine" show both similarities and differences in their modes of copying a three-dimensional model by machine. What do *you* think? Are the two machines "different" or the "same" overall? By what rules have you made your decision? (Drawing by Lyn Malone.)

# COMPARISON OF FEATURES

BLANCHARD'S IRREGULAR TURNING LATHE
(PATENTED SEPT. 6, 1819)

WOOLWORTH'S IRREGULAR TURNING LATHE "#2"
(OBSERVED IN AUTUMN 1819)

MODELS

ONE MODEL, ONE WORKPIECE

TWO MODELS, ONE WORKPIECE

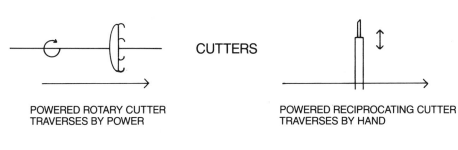

CUTTERS

POWERED ROTARY CUTTER
TRAVERSES BY POWER

POWERED RECIPROCATING CUTTER
TRAVERSES BY HAND

MOTIONS

MODEL AND WORKPIECE ROTATE
CONTINUOUSLY BY POWER

MODELS AND WORKPIECE ROTATE
INTERMITTENTLY BY HAND

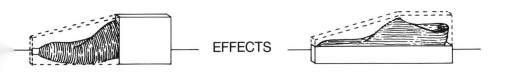

EFFECTS

UTS SPIRAL PATH AROUND WORKPIECE

CUTS LINEAR PATH ALONG WORKPIECE

and litigation records indicate that the result of these decisions was a mixed strategy of his own use, plus assignments and licenses in territories of no standard size, but ranging from the whole country down to one "shop right" in one town. Blanchard seems, then, to have adapted to the offers he received in this respect, and therefore maintained several management roles—user, seller, and licenser—in relation to his own intellectual property and to the other persons who used it.

Thus, for instance, as inside contractor for making gunstocks at Springfield Armory in the 1820s, he *used* his lathe himself and sold the gunstocks to the Ordnance Department. When he left the Armory he *licensed* the Ordnance Department to use his stocking machines, at 9 cents per gunstock. For a lump-sum settlement he finally *assigned* rights in 1839 to the U.S. for gunstocking in national armories, but retained the right to make gunstock lathes for private or foreign arms factories. For making shoe lasts and boot trees, Blanchard assigned several territories, including the right for New England east of the Connecticut River, which he sold to one James Hendley in 1834. He bought this territory back in 1847, and began collecting license fees of 3 cents a pair from Hendley's former licensees.[28] In the 1840s Blanchard received either lump-sum payments or royalties per spoke from users of his lathe to make wheels or other carriage parts in specified territories; for making tool handles he assigned his rights to different assignees in the same or overlapping territories as for wheel and carriage applications. Over the decades the assignments of Blanchard's lathe for various purposes changed hands, spreading westward across the expanding nation (see map in chapter 7).

Some features were added to Blanchard's lathes in actual operation over the years, such as the arrangement of levers for making well-proportioned lasts or hatblocks of several sizes without changing the model (see figure 3.4). One of his licensees, Collins Stevens, started using this feature around 1835, and it came to be regarded as an integral part of the Blanchard lathe, despite a difference of opinion at first as to whether the wording of Blanchard's specifications actually covered that device.[29] Its integration was gradually confirmed during repeated lawsuits. This gradual repeated process is an example of the social construction of a particular invention. Some assignees were machine manufacturers who presumably bought the rights in order to make and sell Blanchard lathes; others were manufacturers of what the Blanchard lathe could make, and presumably bought the rights to use the machine and sell what the assignments specified, such as spokes, plow handles, whiffle-trees, ax handles, and so

FIGURE 3.4. Lastmaking lathe advertisement, 1875. This machine could be adjusted to cut proportionally correct right and left shoe lasts of several different sizes of the right, following the same model on the left. Sliding rods and gears to make the adjustments were built into Blanchard lathes by assignees and licensees in the 1830s, and gradually became accepted as a feature covered by Blanchard's patent. (From *New England Business Directory, 1875,* p. 1380. Warshaw Collection, National Museum of American History.)

forth. Some assignees, such as wheelwright Samuel Reed of North Brookfield, Massachusetts, became both user and maker of Blanchard's machines. Two of Blanchard's assignees, Amos K. Carter and James M. Quinby, were carriage makers in Newark, New Jersey, but seem to have bought Blanchard's rights largely for the secondary purposes of collecting royalties or reselling subdivided territories.[30]

Because of the extension twice of his irregular turning lathe patent,

Thomas Blanchard's relationship to some of his more durable licensees lasted twenty to thirty years. The relationship went beyond just paying and receiving fees; some of them—even lastmaker Chandler Sprague, who had become a licensee only after losing a two-year court battle with Blanchard in 1838–39—testified on Blanchard's behalf in later patent suits, and joined him in an attempt in 1850 to lobby Congress to prohibit the importation of lasts from the British provinces in the north that were made with unlicensed Blanchard lathes.[31]

Through a shadowy chain of responsibility via James M. Quinby, Amos K. Carter, and Lewis M. Linsley, yet another "agent" from Newark, Blanchard and his seven Boston-area lastmakers sent payment to a lobbyist in Washington. These lastmakers, plus six others in New England, had each agreed with Blanchard to a royalty fee of 3 cents per pair and to a standard list of prices for sale of lasts; they were now acting as an interest group in lobbying Congress on behalf of the lastmaking industry.[32] They made it known to the House of Representatives that

> at twenty different places along the frontier, just on the British side of the line, persons have set [Blanchard's] machine, and are largely engaged in operations which are greatly destructive to those who have fairly purchased of him the right of manufacturing shoe-lasts.[33]

Presumably as a result of their lobbying campaign, petitions to Congress arrived not only from Blanchard and from his licensees, but also from lastmakers "and other citizens" of many states, protesting the "gross fraud" and "piracy" of the "depredators" who avoided patent fees by operating in the British Provinces, and urging passage of a bill to prevent the importation of their products into the United States. This apparently provoked a countercampaign of petitions from manufacturers and dealers in shoes and boots, who claimed that the price of lasts had risen 20 percent since renewal of Blanchard's patent, and protested against the proposed bill.[34]

## EXTENSION OF BLANCHARD'S PATENT

Blanchard also lobbied Congress in person in the course of patent management. He managed to extend the duration of his patent twice by act of Congress instead of normal Patent Office procedures, from its initial fourteen-year term to a total of forty-two years, from 1820 to 1862. To obtain the first extension, Blanchard argued that his employment in the

1820s as inside contractor to make gunstocks at Springfield Armory had prevented him for several years from exploiting his patent for commercial purposes and from "maintaining the patent privilege against conflicting pretensions." He estimated that the fair value of his machine was at least $215,440, while he had netted only $3,665.84 in the fourteen years of his patent.[35]

Unfortunately for Blanchard, there was a lapse of several months between the expiration of his patent in January 1834 and its renewal in June. The congressional act of renewal (6 Stat. 589) explicitly exempted from infringement suit (and from royalty payments) anyone who had not previously been using Blanchard's lathe, but who had in good faith started doing so during those few months in which it was unknown that it would be renewed. This "free" period caused Blanchard trouble later: whenever an accused infringer claimed he had built his Blanchard lathe during those few months, Blanchard would have to seek evidence to disprove it. The renewal act also mistakenly dated Blanchard's 1820 patent as January 12 instead of January 20. In a later lawsuit, a defendant seized on this error, claiming that the renewal wasn't legally binding, since it referred to a nonexistent patent![36] Blanchard had to go to the additional trouble of getting another act through Congress in 1839 (6 Stat. 748) to put the act of 1834 into effect.

When the second term of his patent expired in 1848, Blanchard managed better. He obtained renewal for an unprecedented third fourteen-year term, by an act of Congress that left no dating gaps or defects (9 Stat. 683). To do so, he added showmanship to his patent management behavior: he obtained plaster busts of influential congressmen and used a sculpture-copying machine to make marble copies, which he exhibited in the Capitol. As the flattered congressmen admired these marble sculptures, Blanchard told them this was a new use of his irregular turning lathe, for which he needed a patent extension. This episode added sculpture-copying to the popular list of uses for the Blanchard lathe, even though the machine he used could not have been the patented Blanchard lathe, whose cutter would be unable to cut such fine detail as the features of a face.[37] The counsel for opposition to Blanchard's extension bill, Rufus Choate, who was a former representative and senator from Massachusetts, quipped afterward that Blanchard had "'turned the heads' of Congress and gained his point."[38]

Not everyone was amused at Blanchard's 1848 extension. An outraged correspondent, James Johnston, wrote to the *Scientific American* predicting darkly that the extension would result in an intolerably "antirepubli-can" regime imposed on all manufacturers of shoe lasts and ax helves, in which they would have to let Blanchard's agents inspect their books and repossess machinery in case of default, and would not "be allowed to dispose of any last by barter, nor receive any payment except money, nor give longer credit than six months." Johnston hoped that

> the renewal of Blanchard's patent will thump so hard upon the heads of our Last Manufacturers that some of them no doubt will invent a machine shortly, that will successfully evade Blanchard's patent.[39]

Soon afterward, another correspondent announced that such a machine had indeed been invented in Gardiner, Maine, by Mr. Elbridge Webber, and would appear in a few weeks, so that

> notwithstanding the broad ground which Mr. Blanchard has been allowed to enclose by a special act of Congress giving him a second renewal, it is hoped that he will not be allowed to make a turnpike of it and hold the office of tax-gatherer.[40]

Outrage at Blanchard's patent management presumably grew when it was reported he had got the U.S. Marshal in Boston to board the train in Boston and seize Webber's patent model from Webber and his partner Charles Hartshorn as they were traveling to Washington to apply for a patent.[41]

Webber's machine used as a model a "reverse pattern," whose contours a tracer followed, while another part of the machine reversed these into positive motions for cutting the workpiece. This blatant attempt at eva-sion was rejected by the patent examiner as a claim to invention. A patent was issued in 1849, however, on the basis of two other claims, after Webber and Hartshorn wrote defiantly:

> We shall construct and use the whole machine and invite Mr. Blanchard and all other persons to commence suit for infringement . . . and if we obtain a judgement we shall . . . demand a patent for whatever is allowed us by the court, that is now refused us by the Patent Office.[42]

## LITIGATION OVER BLANCHARD'S PATENT

Like other petitioners for patent extension, Blanchard claimed that he had been unable to earn a reasonable return on his irregular turning lathe during its original patent term because people had used it without paying him and he had to spend so much on lawyers' fees defending his patent in court. Reportedly "more than fifty violators had pirated his invention" during his years at Springfield Armory.[43] From the 1820s through the 1850s, Blanchard and his assignees sued dozens and dozens of users of machines for making spokes, lasts, and tool-handles.

Despite Webber and other new "evaders" of his patent, Blanchard not only continued to win most of his court cases against them, but also won the right to collect royalties after the extension in 1848 from those who had first built their machines in those "free" months in 1834, and had therefore never paid royalties before.[44] He failed, however, in the attempt to collect additional royalties from Eli Whitney, Jr., who had bought a stocking lathe in 1843 from Blanchard himself, for a price that included royalties for the then-remaining term to 1848. In the case of *Thomas Blanchard vs. Eli Whitney,* Justice Nelson reasoned that in "a case where the patentee has manufactured and sold the machine himself . . . such a transaction . . . implies and carries with the purchase of the article the right to use it, at least till it is worn out."[45]

Frequently the "infringing" users were licensed by other patentees of other irregular turning lathes, many of which were some improved version of Azariah Woolworth's Waterbury lastmaking machine. For despite Stephen Blanchard's reassurance in 1819 that Woolworth's machine was nothing to worry about, its descendants kept cropping up, especially in Connecticut, with various modifications that made them more like Blanchard's lathe and more of a competitive threat to Blanchard's machine in performance. Some of these were granted patents, in spite of Blanchard's vociferous protests to the Patent Office that they were merely "useless or *non*improved modes of endeavoring to evade his patent."[46] Figure 3.5 shows one descendant that appeared in France, beyond Blanchard's range of litigation.

Witnesses in Blanchard's lawsuits were called on to testify whether the two machines—Blanchard's and the defendant's—were substantially "the same" or "different" from each other. The witnesses identified themselves as mechanics, machinists, engineers, millwrights, inventors, lastmakers, ax-handle makers, wheel-spoke makers, shoemakers, gunmakers, carriage makers, patent agents, and former patent examiners. Different features of the machines struck different witnesses as decisive. Some thought it was enough to say that both made the same product, so they were the same machine. Some said both machines copied models, so they were the same; others said one machine required two models and the other, one model,

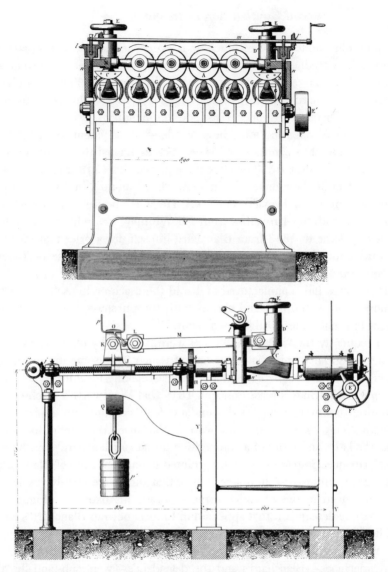

FIGURE 3.5. French lastmaking machine c. 1855. This machine was descended from Azariah Woolworth's lastmaking machine patented 1820, in using two model lasts (G, far right and left in the end elevation) and two feelers (C) to control the rising and falling of rotary saw-tooth cutting wheels (A) over the four workpieces in the middle. It is shown making two pairs of right and left lasts. It could also make gunstocks. In the United States, patent management including litigation had defined such machines as Blanchard lathes. (From Armengaud Aine, *Publication Industrielle des Machines, Outils et Appareils,* vol. 7, plate 9, Paris, 1856.)

so they were different. Some said reciprocating cutters were of a different form from circular cutters, so they were different machines. Others said difference in the cutter form was immaterial; the machines were mechanically equivalent. Some said the cutters followed different paths on the workpiece, so they were different. Others said the one machine could or couldn't do smoother work than the other, or make more copies at once, or make larger or smaller sizes than the models, so the machines were substantially different or the same.

Over time, some arguments emerged as more persuasive than others. Over time, the more-or-less expert witnesses tended to emphasize process more than product, and the kinematics of the machines more than their components. Evidence for sameness that sounds naive to us today, such as the fact that both machines made lasts, gradually dropped out. Distinctions that now sound more sophisticated stayed in use. This gradual process was taking place over the very period in which there was a great proliferation of mechanical experience and increase in mechanical skills by people making and using new machines of many sorts for many purposes in this country. The process is an example of social construction, at a deeper level, of the decision rules for invention itself in the realm of machinery.

These implicit rules for invention, or originality, were gradually put into practice by the increasing mechanically informed community, including patent agents and patent examiners, as well as makers and users of machines, when called upon in lawsuits or when communicating in other contexts, such as patent applications. The implicit rules for originality also gradually underwent change and became more refined in subcategories where there were more machines to be compared to one another. Patent Office reclassification was one manifestation of this social construction. Where the Patent Office recognized 22 classes for patents for most of the nineteenth century, in 1870 it recognized 145 classes, because of subdivision of former classes as well as creation of new ones. Today the Patent Office employs a whole division for continual reclassification.

At a more particular level, over time a body of belief or understanding or knowledge concerning the specific machines at question was also built up within the social subsystem for patent management, defining what Blanchard's particular "invention" had actually been and therefore what his intellectual property currently was, for which he deserved to enjoy a temporary monopoly. In this process of social construction, the boundaries of Blanchard's intellectual property—his lathe—expanded to subsume many similar machines, including, strangely enough, a machine that Blanchard originally said his lathe did *not* resemble: the Waterbury lastmaking machine.

# ISAAC ELDRIDGE'S MACHINES

A dramatic demonstration of this expansion took place when Blanchard sued several lastmakers in Philadelphia in the late 1840s. The court enjoined defendant Isaac Eldridge to stop using his lathe. But during the trial Eldridge heard testimony from several witnesses, including the elderly Woolworth himself, describing Woolworth's machines #1, #2, and #3.[47] He "experimented upon the vibrating cutter, as in a certain machine called at the trial of this case No. 2,"[48] and built himself a version of the Waterbury lastmaking machine. With it he resumed making lasts, reasoning that although it was slower and less efficient it was surely safe from an accusation of infringement, since Blanchard's specification *said* it was different.

The court commissioned Philadelphia patent solicitor W. W. Hubbell to report on the features of Eldridge's new machine. During Eldridge's demonstration for Hubbell, the building shook, the power transmission belt broke three times, and a bearing caught fire, but Hubbell saw enough to decide that Eldridge's machine differed from a Blanchard lathe only in having a double-edged reciprocating cutter instead of a rotary one, and a "friction column" as a tracer instead of a friction wheel.[49] This was insufficient difference to satisfy Judge Kane, although he did compliment Eldridge for his "considerable mechanical ingenuity." Remarking that "there appears to be but a single point of difference"—the cutter—and that the two types of cutter were in principle the same, he issued a second injunction to make Eldridge stop using his new machine, too. Judge Kane said, "The patent law would give but an illusory protection to the meritorious inventor, if it respected devices like this." He scolded Eldridge for spending his "inverted energies, not to improve or advance, but to devise something less useful and more costly than that which was known before."[50] Clearly, the judge was not about to tolerate this inelegant machine at its face value, but was taking Eldridge's evasive motivation into account.

Perhaps rashly, Judge Kane went on to express "the essential principle that resides within" Blanchard's invention:

A tracer so arranged as to pass in a spiral or helix line over the surface of a model while the rough material revolves in a similar line under a cutter, guided by the tracer, but acting with independent, rapid motion—the combination of these for a declared purpose, this is the principle of the Blanchard patent. All the rest is detail . . . [51]

Picking up on this, the invertedly ingenious Eldridge rebuilt his machine so that the circular and lateral motions causing the spiral path of the cutter on the workpiece were no longer simultaneous, but sequential. Now his machine cut lengthwise paths on the lasts. Encountering Blanchard and his assignee A. K. Carter in Boston, Eldridge taunted that "they could not stop me," for "Judge Kane had very properly decided what was Mr. Blanchard's principle and that was more than any other judge had done, which was the cutting in a spiral line." [52]

The court next sent a blue-ribbon commission of three eminent members of the Franklin Institute to inspect Eldridge's third machine. They reported that it had a cutter wheel and a tracer that passed "rapidly from one end of the model to the other and backward . . . and at each end of the motion the model and rough material receive a small and equal motion around their longer axes." [53] So Eldridge's machine now resembled Woolworth's machine #2 not in the cutter, but in the intermittent rotation of the workpiece. The commissioners pointed out that these were different kinematics from those set forth in Blanchard's specification: "the only method proposed by Mr. Blanchard is that in which the friction wheel or tracer describes a spiral over the whole surface of the model and causes the cutters to act in a similar direction." All three concluded Eldridge's method "is not a mere colourable and unimportant change from the method described in Mr. Blanchard's patent, but that it is essentially different"; so that "the machine of Mr. Eldridge is different in its principle and mode of operation from that described in Mr. Blanchard's patent." [54] After this report, the court refused Blanchard's motion for attachment of Eldridge's property. [55]

Taking Eldridge to trial yet again, to seek an injunction against his third machine, Blanchard not only marshaled additional expert witnesses to contradict the commissioners' report and testify to the mechanical equivalence of the continuous and intermittent motions. He also brought into court a model lastmaking lathe that was capable, by the shifting in or out of a simple mechanical linkage, of either motion. It could perform either in the Blanchard-specified continuous, spiral-forming fashion *or* in the Woolworth mode, with intermittent rotation of the workpiece between lateral lengthwise passes of the cutter.

Justice Grier, the judge in this case, complained of the hot weather and said:

> I should have had much less difficulty in arriving at a conclusion satisfactory to my own mind in the present case but for the opposite opinions expressed by gentlemen of the highest reputation for learning, judgment, and practical skill in mechanics.[56]

Although tempted to leave the question to a jury in yet another trial, the judge granted the injunction. He based his opinion on an analysis of the spiral motion into the separate lateral and circular motions of the cutter and workpiece, respectively, as Blanchard's courtroom model had demonstrated. He said "such a change . . . affecting the motions of the model and guide only in the figure of their path or the relative lines of their movements in no case changes the principle . . . of the machine," adding "We cannot shut our eyes to the fact that the defendants have pirated the invention . . . in all its essential parts."[57] Like Judge Kane, Justice Grier was taking Eldridge's evasive motivation into account, in seeing one Woolworth-like feature after another as "the same" as those in a Blanchard lathe.

## LONG-TERM EFFECTS OF PATENT MANAGEMENT

Thus, under treatment as a piece of intellectual property, Blanchard's invention had expanded in concept to include by 1850 all the features of a machine that Blanchard had explicitly disclaimed at the beginning in 1820. If such a social redefinition was taking place in this case, I consider it likely that it was taking place, perhaps less dramatically and completely, in many other cases also, and that our retrospective view of the history of technology has been distorted, when two initially separate inventions can be regarded as one invention a few decades later.

This episode clearly demonstrates that the definition of any particular invention and its delineation as intellectual property was the result of a social process that was in continuous operation, not just during the drawing up and approval of patent specifications, but also throughout the duration of the patent. It also suggests this process had a built-in bias against cheap (royalty-free) operation of obsolete, less efficient machinery like Woolworth's machine #2. This bias may be seen as reinforcing market forces against technological inefficiency and against the small operators who might otherwise find economically viable niches using old-fashioned equipment. Thus, from the point of view of the society as a whole, for whose ostensible benefit the patent system existed, this bias probably had a "progressive" or ratchet effect on its developing technology.

On the history of technology, this bias had the effect of suppressing later recognition of how diverse the devices had been that had evolved in the past to achieve given ends, for example, lastmaking. It therefore reinforced a misleading "great man" theory of invention. Should we conclude from this story that Blanchard deserved fame and fortune for inventing exceedingly useful and versatile machines? Or that he simply claimed and managed his intellectual property more adroitly than less "successful" inventors like Woolworth?

The case of Blanchard's bending machine, as explained in chapter 8, shows quite a different outcome of the social construction that took place; one invention did not always subsume another to become the eponymous winner in the contest. But it also shows that social construction did take place. Regardless of how we assess Blanchard's personal achievement, we should recognize that his story reveals patent management as the social system in which people continuously constructed and intertwined definitions of particular inventions with considerations of property rights.

Furthermore, in the deeper, definitional sense of "invention," the patent management system had an additional special relationship to American society's store of technological knowledge, for it was the arena in which the implicit rules were determined for deciding what was new. As Thomas Blanchard's experience illustrates, the interactions of persons during patent management brought about social decisions that identified not only whom to reward for particular inventions, but also what to remember as important differences or dismiss as unimportant samenesses between items of technology. These decision rules, constructed during interactions among economically as well as intellectually interested persons, not only guided prospective inventors' technical choices, but also shaped for everybody our very categories of thinking about technological change. Our society had allocated to its patent management subsystem this task of constructing "invention" itself.

Where does this leave *us* as observers after the fact? How can we, who are part of the society and receivers of its socially constructed perceptions of reality, including its history of technology, hope to achieve an independent view of it? This is perhaps impossible to do completely, but one exercise in gaining perspective is to compare technologies in different societies; another is to "get behind" a specific technology by tracing its historical origins in some detail, to see when "new" features were incorporated or old ones dropped out. This is risky too, since we are dependant on socially constructed historical information, but at least the process can reveal anomalies and persistent silences in the record across time, during which the situations of social construction have themselves varied. This exercise, when applied to lathes, as reported in the next chapter, reveals the Blanchard lathe as indeed something new under the sun, but only when *in motion*.

# 4

## LATHES

## BEFORE BLANCHARD

## AND HOW HIS WAS

## DIFFERENT

**A** "down-east" Maine joke tells how to make a decoy for a duck: "First, you take a piece of wood. Next, you take a knife. Then, you cut away everything that doesn't look like a duck." Before Thomas Blanchard invented his irregular turning lathe, you could make duck decoys, or other such highly irregular shapes as gunstocks or shoe lasts, only by using hand-held tools. Instead of just a knife, you would use a saw or axe to rough out the workpiece, and chisels, gouges, and drawknives to shape it. Blanchard's machine held and moved a workpiece and cutting wheel and a three-dimensional model in such ways that the cutters cut away everything from all around the workpiece down to an object shaped like the model. We may therefore say that he mechanized the making of gunstocks, shoe lasts, ax-handles, and other highly irregular shapes.

Machines existed before Blanchard's, however, that were able to cut certain *less* highly irregular shapes. The previous technique for making these more nearly regular shapes was to use the lathe, which had itself already undergone a long history of mechanization. To appreciate just what it was that Thomas Blanchard invented, we need to consider not only the mechanization of gunstocking and lastmaking, but more broadly, the mechanization of lathe turning, with respect to the lathe's ability to copy irregularities in shape.[1]

In many of the patent lawsuits mentioned in chapter 3, Blanchard's opponents claimed that his invention was not original, by citing the copying mechanisms of previous lathes as precedents to Blanchard's lathe. Close consideration of how those earlier lathes operated, however, confirms that Blanchard's lathe was indeed unprecedented.

In the following descriptions of machines' operations, I refer to linear motions in the three dimensions relative to an operator facing the front of the machine, as: (1) vertical (up-and-down), (2) transverse (forward-and-back or in-and-out), and (3) lateral (sideways or side-to-side or right and left) The machines discussed in this chapter have horizontal axes of rotation, usually extending laterally rather than transversely.[2]

## SIMPLE LATHES

The origin of the turning lathe is "lost in the shades of antiquity,"[3] but is thought to have occurred after development of the drill.[4] Even in its very early and simple form the lathe mechanized two distinguishable hand-tool tasks: the shaping of basically cylindrical objects (such as chair rungs) was mechanized by "turning between centers,"[5] and the shaping of basically circular disks or dished objects (such as plates, bowls, or cups) was mechanized by "flat" or "hollow" turning.[6] Cylinders and disks are both solids of revolution, i.e., any section of the object at a right angle across its axis of revolution will be a circle. The ordinary "hand" lathe, in which the workpiece rotates and the turner holds a chisel or gouge to it, persists today in underdeveloped countries and among hobbyists (see figure 4.1.).

For "turning between centers," such a lathe holds a workpiece at both ends between its headstock and tailstock; as the workpiece rotates rapidly on the lengthwise axis the turner cuts it by moving a gouge or chisel sideways parallel to the axis and in-and-out at right angles to the axis, to remove more or less material from the workpiece. But while moving the tool sideways and in-and-out, the turner keeps it as steadily as possible at an angle to the workpiece such that its action on the workpiece is a paring or shaving action (see figure 4.2). To remove more material at a given location along the axis of the workpiece, the turner does not change the cutting angle of the tool, but advances it forward toward the axis while more rotations of the workpiece take place and more material is shaved off. The shape that results must be a solid of revolution: it may be quite varied and nonsymmetrical in profile along its length, but it cannot vary in profile around its circumference. Any right-angle cross-section of an object turned in this manner is inevitably circular if the object has been cut over its whole surface,[7] for the rotary speed of the workpiece is much faster than the cutter's movements.

For cutting a disk or bowl, the workpiece is "chucked" or fastened to the face-plate at the *end* of the lathe's rotating shaft, and no tailstock is used. The turner reorients his actions by 90 degrees; he advances and withdraws the cutter in lines parallel to the axis of rotation, while sweeping sideways to and from the circumference of the workpiece, to shave away material until the desired flat or dished surface is achieved. Again, since the rotation of the object on its axis is very rapid relative to any motion of the tool, the object made is a solid of revolution and all right-angle sections across its rotational axis are circular.

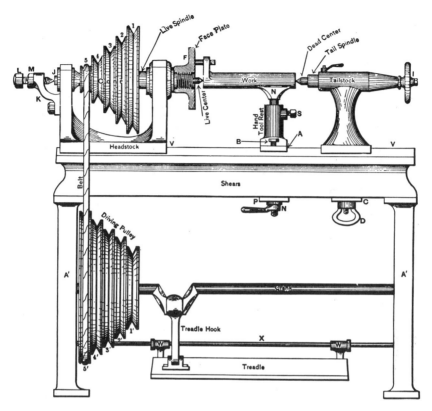

FIGURE 4.1. Foot-powered "hand" lathe. The turner either shapes a cylinder (as shown) from a rapidly rotating workpiece held between "live" and "dead" centers in the headstock and tailstock, or he shapes a disk from a workpiece fastened only to the face plate at the end of the headstock. He steadies a gouge or chisel on the tool rest, which he can move to different positions along the shears and adjust to various angles relative to the work, e.g. to change from work between centers to disk work. By foot treadle he turns the driving pulley at left; by belt it turns the "live spindle." (From Joshua Rose, *Modern Machine-Shop Practice* [New York: Scribner, 1888], vol. 1, p. 130.)

The very earliest type of lathe was driven by a cord wrapped around the workpiece itself, if it was cylinder work, or around the shaft to which the workpiece was fastened, if it was flat or dished work. After each pull in one direction, the cord was pulled back to its beginning position by any of various means: by hand, the stroke of a bow, the springing of a pole, or the action of a weight. The direction of rotation therefore alternated with the pulls of the cord, and the cutting, which took place only with one direction of rotation, was intermittent.[8]

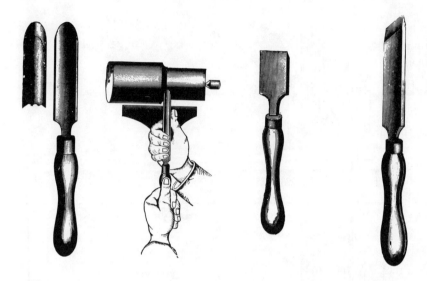

FIGURE 4.2. Cutting tools for lathe work: gouge and chisels. The turner's hands steady a gouge against the rest and hold it at an angle to shave away material as the workpiece rotates toward him, forming a cylinder from right to left. (From Joshua Rose, *Modern Machine-Shop Practice* [New York: Scribner, 1888], vol. 1, p. 339.)

In late medieval or early Renaissance times, the substitution of a crank action and a fly wheel for the alternate pulls of the cord made possible a continuous rotation in one direction, and therefore an uninterrupted cutting action.[9] Now a "live" spindle or mandrel could be used to rotate the workpiece, as figure 4.1 shows. The crank could be turned by treadle or by an assistant with a "great wheel."[10] It was next a fairly easy matter to connect the live spindle through belting and pulleys to a remote power source, for example, horse, water wheel, steam engine, or electric motor, once these became available.

In all of these simple "hand" lathes, no matter how they are powered, the tool is held and moved into cutting positions by hand, while the cutting is actually done by the workpiece rotating against the cutter. A bar or "rest" against which to steady the tool is usually provided; the steady rest can be adjusted and fixed into the appropriate position for the cylinder or disk work at hand. Exceedingly elaborate and accurate work can be accomplished on a simple lathe by a skilled turner in control of hand-held tools. A highly skilled turner can even cut a regular screw thread along a cylinder by moving a notched cutter along the axis at a speed that is coordinated with the speed of rotation. This is called "cutting flying" in Rees's *Cyclopaedia,* and is an excellent example of "workmanship of risk."

## LATHE CONTROL MECHANISMS

In the early Renaissance period, lathe makers began building mechanisms into the lathe for controlling the depth of cut and for moving the cutter sideways at the desired rate relative to the rate of rotation of the workpiece.[12] These mechanisms made it much easier to cut an accurate screw, and reduced the risk of error in other kinds of lathe work. Two such mechanisms appearing in the Renaissance were the slide rest and the lead screw. The slide rest is a holder for moving a cutting tool that becomes part of the machine and no longer hand-held during operation. By means of a rack and pinion or by a lead screw and nut, a tool held in a slide rest can be made to move along ways (tracks) parallel to the axis of rotation of the workpiece, and, in a cross slide, perpendicular to it.[13] A slide rest carrying a "cross" slide on top is called a "compound slide rest.[14]

If the workpiece and lead screw are keyed together so as to rotate at the same speed, the cutter will, with repeated deeper passes of the cutter in the same spiral groove, cut an exact copy of the lead screw into the workpiece. Figure 4.3, a very early representation of an adjustable tool holder together with a master screw, dating from 1480, shows a machine capable of copying a screw by moving the workpiece past the cutter, which remains stationary during operation.[15] But in figure 4.4, Jaques Besson's improbable drawing in 1569 of a screw-cutting lathe, the tool holder has become a slide rest, which the lead screw advances along the workpiece during the cutting operation. In later screw-cutting machines, the slide rest moves parallel to the lead screw instead of at its end. The technology of making and using screws has a compelling history of its own,[16] but the point of interest here is that a screw is not quite regular in shape. That is, cross sections at right angles to its axis of rotation are not quite circular. Although the difference of a screw from a cylinder of the same diameter is crucial to its function as a screw, it is a difference that can be easily specified as pitch and thread form. Nor is it a difference that requires much material to be cut away to make it.

The control of the slide rest by the action of a lead screw was a combination of mechanisms that proved useful for purposes other than copying the screw itself. One use was to produce a tapered shape in the

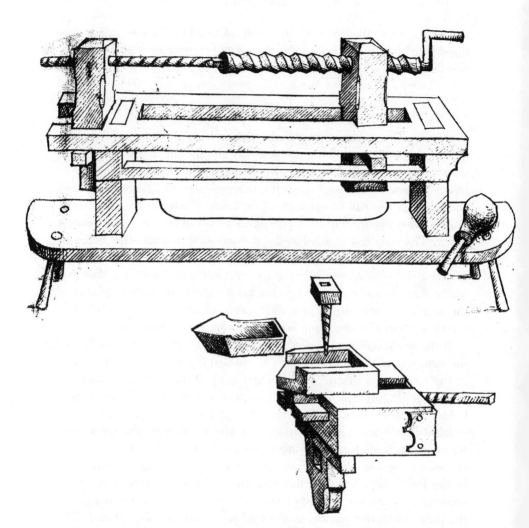

FIGURE 4.3. Screw cutting by master screw, c. 1480. An adjustable tool holder, shown detached and enlarged in the foreground, held a pointed cutter to the cylindrical workpiece, which was fastened endwise to the master screw. The workpiece moved laterally as the master screw, turned by the crank handle, worked through an internal screw in the headstock. The lateral movement per rotation was thus determined by the master screw, and the cutter inscribed the same spiral on the workpiece as the thread of the master screw. The artist has mistakenly reversed the spiral from that of the master screw. (From *Das Mittelalterliche Hausbuch,* 1480, Helmut Bossert and Willi Storck, eds. [Leipzig: E. A. Seeman, 1912], p. 53b.)

workpiece, by setting the lead screw at an angle, so that while traversing along the length of the workpiece the cutting tool gradually moves closer to its axis, removing more material as it goes (see figure 4.5). A taper, or cone, is also a solid of revolution, a regular figure. This feature was later used in gunbarrel lathes, such as that of Asa Waters in 1818, mentioned in chapter 2.

The lead screw and slide rest opened up capabilities for the lathe at both ends of the size range for turning. They were incorporated into lathes that were large and powerful, like Polhem's 1710 waterpowered lathe in Sweden for turning cylindrical rolls for rolling mills, and also lathes that were small and precise, like Ferdinand Berthoud's 1763 "fusee engine" in France, for cutting the exact hyperboloid form of a clock fusee.[17] The power-driven lead screw and slide rest became the *sine qua non* of the industrial lathe when they were incorporated into medium-to-large-scale iron-working lathes in the late eighteenth century by Jacques Vaucanson in France, Henry Maudslay in England, and David Wilkinson in the United States (see figure 4.6). In the early nineteenth century, Thomas Blanchard made use of the lead screw in his lathe as a matter of course; as we shall see, his version of the cutter in the slide rest was unusual.

Another mechanical device that was added to the lathe during the Renaissance was the cam for producing elliptical shapes. It was a circular plate adjustable to any angle across the axis of rotation. When adjusted to a nonperpendicular angle, the rotating plate continuously lengthened and shortened the distance between the tool and the workpiece, producing an elliptical cross section in the workpiece. The elliptical cam is shown in Besson's sixteenth-century work (see figure 4.7) and also appears in the equipment of lathes depicted in the mid-eighteenth century French *Encyclopédie* by Denis Diderot and Jean le Ronde d'Alembert. Large "swash lathes" with this capability for elliptical turning were used to make Baroque balustrades in the seventeenth century. One English maker of such "swash-engines and oval-engines" was Thomas Oldfield, whose workshop was located "near the Savoy in the Strand."[18] An object with an elliptical cross-section is not a solid of revolution, so this *was* irregular turning, but its irregularity was easily specified by the cam, and not much material had to be removed in any one revolution of the workpiece. Blanchard used this cam principle in making a gunbarrel lathe cut "flats and ovals."

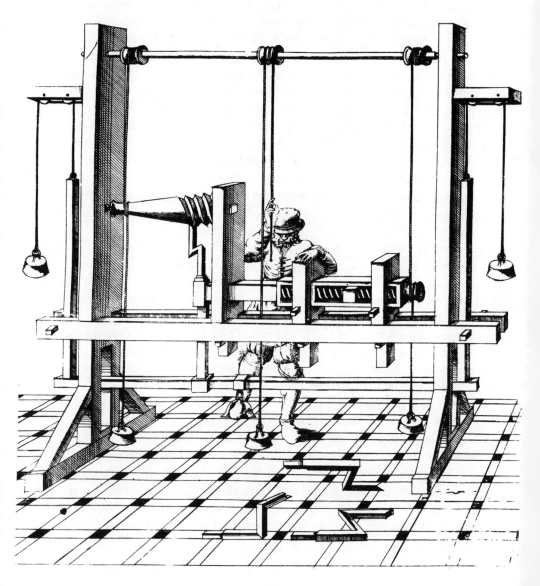

FIGURE 4.4. *(opposite)* Screw-cutting lathe with master screw and slide rest, c. 1570. This lathe lacks a live spindle, so the direction of rotation alternates as the weighted cord wrapped around the end of the workpiece unwinds and rewinds on the overhead pulley when the operator pulls and releases the middle cord. But the cords are long, so that each pull can power many rotations. The cords to the overhead shaft are supposed to coordinate the rotation of the workpiece and the master screw, while the screw advances the z-shaped cutter held in the slide rest. (Three more cutters lie on the floor.) Cutting can occur only in one direction of rotation, so at every rewinding of the cords, the operator has to remove the cutter from the workpiece by treading down the stirrup to lower the whole slide rest apparatus, which is counterweighted at both ends. He also thus controls the height of the tool as it progresses along the taper of the workpiece. L. T. C. Rolt calls this creation of Besson's "weird and wonderful" and says "it cannot be taken seriously as a practical machine tool." The conical workpiece, however, appears to be a realistic depiction of a fusee for a turn-spit, or roasting jack. (From Jaques Besson, *Theatrum Instrumentorum et Machinarum* [Lyon, 1578] plate 9.)

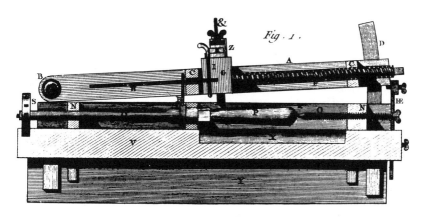

FIGURE 4.5. Cutting a taper, eighteenth century. As workpiece (P) rotates, it is shaped into a taper by the cutter in slide (G) as it traverses along the lead screw (F), at an angle to the axis of (P). (From Denis Diderot and Jean le Rond D'Alembert, *Encyclopédie, Recueil des Planches* [Paris, 1772] vol. 10, plate 53.)

FIGURE 4.6. Lathes with and without a slide rest, nineteenth century. A lathe equipped with a mechanical compound slide rest (right), could be operated relatively effortlessly compared to the strenuous labor required to cut with a hand-held tool and an ordinary steady rest (left). With the top slide, the operator (right) is traversing the cutter along the workpiece, having adjusted the depth of cut with the bottom slide. Both operators are turning a length of iron shafting, rotated by belt from an unseen pulley above. (From James Nasmyth, "Remarks on the Introduction of the Slide Principle," in Robertson Buchanan, *Practical Essays on Mill Work and Other Machinery* [London: John Weale, 1841], p. 396.)

FIGURE 4.7. *(opposite)* Ellipse-producing cams, c. 1570. To produce an elliptical cross section in a workpiece, two circular plates are arranged at the same angle across the axis of rotation in order to move the tool rest (the bar with a wavy slot) up and down the same distance every time, and at a speed coordinated with the rotation, to turn the fancy workpiece shown. The lathe is powered by treadle-and-bow action, so cutting has to be intermittent. The pronged implements hanging on the wall are cutting tools. The turner slides one prong along the wavy slot; the other prong cuts. The turner is shown reaching for a mallet. As in figure 4.4, Besson's drawing is more fanciful than realistic, but illustrates a principle. (From Jaques Besson, *Theatrum Instrumentorum et Machinarum* [Lyon, 1578], plate 7.)

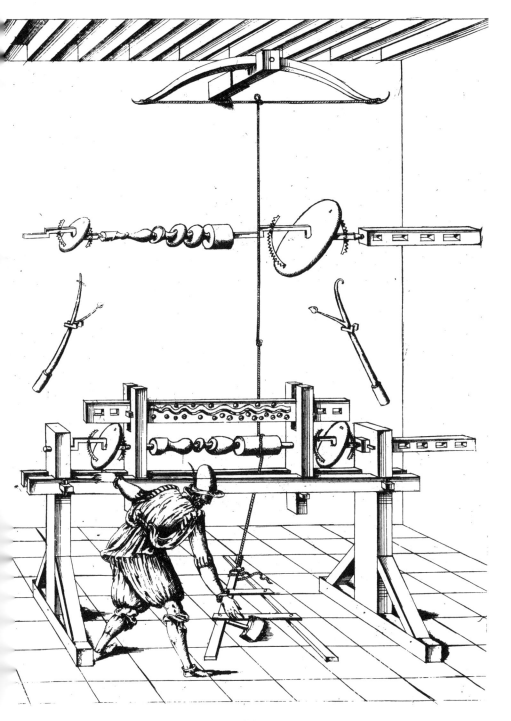

# ORNAMENTAL TURNING

An offshoot of the live-spindle or mandrel lathe during the Renaissance was the ornamental turning lathe,[19] used primarily for making small decorative objects (see figures 4.8 and 4.9). Makers of ornamental turning lathes built mechanisms into them for control in the machine production of objects whose cross-section or whose ornamentation were "to be more or less esteemed as they are the more opposed to the circular figure."[20] In the ornamental turning lathe the live spindle or mandrel was now made capable of two kinds of linear motion in addition to its rotational motion. While rotating, the spindle was made to move along its axis laterally, or to move transversely, at right angles to its axis. For motion along its axis, this so-called "traversing" spindle of an ornamental turning lathe is either pushed by a spring or worked, like a lead screw, through a nut or half-nut within the headstock.[21] The other motion, the whole spindle's transverse movement toward and away from the operator, is achieved by rocking on an axis that is below the bench and parallel to the spindle's axis.[22]

From Emperor Maximilian's lathe in the early 1500s through the "rose engines" of eighteenth-century English gentry, the ornamental turning lathes for use by leisured amateurs or hobbyists usually included both of these motions of the mandrel, which made possible three kinds of copying operations: (1) screw cutting along the axis of rotation of a cylindrical workpiece, (2) inscribing of "rosette" or "guilloching"[23] tracery onto the face of a disc by cutting multiple concentric wavy lines, and (3) reverse reproduction of medallions in relief or *intaglio*. To cut screws by an ornamental turning lathe, the stationary cutter in its slide rest cuts a helical path along the length of a rotating workpiece as the workpiece is moved past the cutter at a rate controlled by the master screw that is being copied. A "key" in the headstock acts as a nut or a half-nut by pressing into the grooves of one of several sections of different screws along the mandrel, and the mandrel then acts as a lead screw, as figure 4.8 shows.[24]

For rosette tracery and medallion cutting, the disk-shaped workpiece is chucked onto the end of the mandrel, and the cutter operates on the rotating face of the workpiece. To make rosette or guilloching decorations, the wavy lines incised on the face of the workpiece are controlled by a pattern disk, usually brass, that is mounted on the mandrel, against

FIGURE 4.8. Ornamental turning lathe with traversing or rocking mandrel, late seventeenth century. By means of its crank and flywheel, this treadle-operated lathe achieved continuous rotation in one direction, transmitted to the workpiece by the mandrel, or "live spindle." To the left of the drive pulley protrudes the hind end of the mandrel, on which are cut sections of various master screw threads. A lever or "key" below can raise a half-nut to engage a screw thread, so as to work the mandrel to the right at a rate coordinated with the rotational speed. Thus the cutter held in the rest midway along the lathe can copy a short section of screw thread onto a cylindrical workpiece (not shown) supported between the live and dead centers. Brass disks with wavy edges, called rosettes, are shown to the right of the drive pulley. When, while rotating, a rosette presses against a stationary "rubber" (positioned this side of the rosettes), the whole mandrel rocks transversely on the pivot below the bench, so that a disk-shaped workpiece (not shown) chucked on the end of the mandrel also oscillates transversely while rotating. Thus the cutter, repositioned to face the disk, copies onto its face the rotating rosette's outline. (Science Museum photograph, London.)

whose wavy periphery a fixed "rubber" presses, causing the mandrel to rock on the pivots located beneath the bench. Repeated tracing with different pattern disks and the cutting tool fixed at different radii will

FIGURE 4.9. Medallion lathe/rose engine, c. 1760. With its traversing or rocking mandrel, this lathe could cut either rosette decorations or a portrait onto a disk. In the rocking mandrel mode, a "rubber" (shown in its elaborate holder this side of the headstock) pressed onto the edge of a rotating rosette would control the mandrel's transverse motions for cutting a wavy line onto the disk. In the traversing mode, a spring holds a tracer against the pattern. As the mandrel, blank, and pattern rotate, the tracer moves slowly across the face of the pattern and the cutter across the face of the blank. The mandrel is forced forward along its axis by the higher areas of the pattern and backward at the lower areas, so the cutter cuts into the blank an inverse copy of the bas-relief or *intaglio* original. The transverse motions of the tracer and cutter across the faces of the rotating pattern and blank were coordinated by the apparatus of wires and pullies shown behind the elaborate headstock. For ordinary turning and cutting of screws or tapers, the operator set up different attachments that included the complex slide rest shown at right. (Science Museum photograph, London.)

incise complicated effects onto the flat surface of the disk-shaped workpiece.[25] The wavy edges of such pattern disks are shown in figures 4.8 4.9, and 4.10.

Another use for these "rosette" pattern disks is to control the cutting of waves or scallops around a cylinder. Since more material is being removed in this operation than in the incising of lines for rosette decorations, "great care must be taken to advance the tool very gradually."[26] Many scallops side by side produce a fluted effect, or with a slight advancement of the pattern at regular calculated intervals, a textured spiral effect. Each scallop requires a separate operation, and the operator stops the lathe between times to rotate the pattern disc to a new position. Alternation of different patterns can achieve basket-weave or latticework textures around the cylinder. A pattern disk with a wavy *ridge* at its periphery can be used to move the mandrel back and forth along its axis. By this means one can inscribe decorations on the surface of a cylindrical workpiece or cut scallops into the face of a disc-shaped workpiece. When rosette disks of both types—with the same number of waves—are used together, according to Rees's *Cyclopaedia,* "the surface of the cylinder may be waved, at the same time that waved lines are drawn upon it."[27]

For "oval turning," the plain or wavy circles that the rose engine traces can be changed into plain or wavy ellipses of varied proportions by the use of the ellipse-producing cam. From the early eighteenth century, oval chucks, whose action is based on the ancient ellipse-generating device of the simple trammel, have also been used for oval turning in ordinary mandrel lathes as well as rose engines.[28]

In these rosette or screw-cutting operations of the ornamental turning lathe, the lathe is stopped between cuts in order to adjust the cutter to a new position in either dimension—sideways or crosswise—relative to the axis of rotation. In medallion cutting, however, as shown in figures 4.9 and 4.10, the cutter moves continuously across the face of the disk-shaped rotating workpiece that is chucked to the front end of the mandrel. On the rear end is mounted a medallion pattern. A spring presses the rapidly rotating mandrel backward against a slowly traversing tracer, which causes the mandrel to move right and left along its axis as the tracer presses against the irregular contours of the medallion's face. By wires winding during operation, the tracer and the cutter are coordinated in their transverse motion across the faces of the pattern and workpiece, respectively. In this way, the high and low points of the rotating pattern surface push the rotating mandrel and blank against a co-ordinated traversing cutter, so that it cuts high where the pattern is low, and low where the pattern is high. A bas relief pattern will yield an *intaglio* copy, and vice versa. Cross sections of a medallion at right angles to its axis of

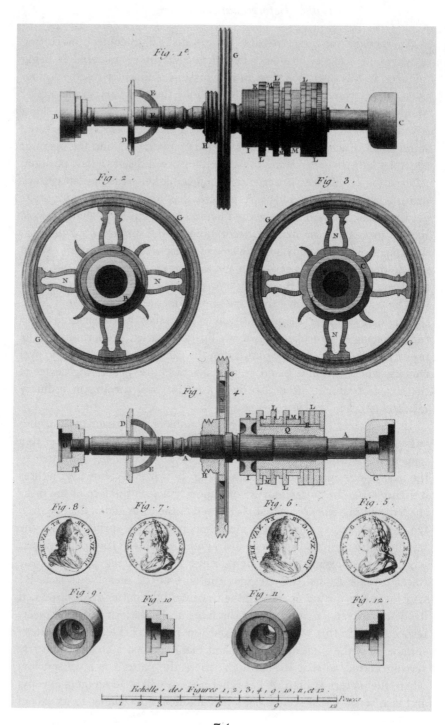

Fig. 1.ᵉ

Fig. 2.

Fig. 3.

Fig. 4.

Fig. 8.

Fig. 7.

Fig. 6.

Fig. 5.

Fig. 9.

Fig. 10.

Fig. 11.

Fig. 12.

Echelle des Figures 1, 2, 3, 4, 9, 10, 11, et 12.

Pouces

rotation are circular, but a section across its face may be highly irregular in profile. Still, the height of the irregularities away from the flat cross section of the disc is not great; the slowly traversing cutter does not need to remove a great deal of material during each rotation of the workpiece.

## POSITIVE COPYING LATHES

Even in its heyday the ornamental lathe was never widely used in commerce, for it required hours of meticulous, repetitive start-stop-adjust operations to achieve its variegated effects on the workpiece. Its greatest use was among rich and royal hobbyists who enjoyed spending leisure hours creating intricate and pretty bibelots of wood, brass, ivory or horn, to be admired not only for their "extreme delicacy, or elegance," but also for "the difficulties of the execution."[29] In Russia, Peter the Great employed the skilled artificer A.K. Nartov (c. 1693–1756) as head of the royal lathe shop to make ornamented objects for the royal household, to design and build new lathes, and to instruct Peter himself in their use. Peter sent Nartov on a study tour during 1718–20 to western, including French, lathe and engineering workshops.[30]

Among the lathes that Nartov designed in the early eighteenth century were several for copying medallions and others that went beyond the capability already described for copying in reverse: they were capable of making positive copies of bas relief pictures on cylinders (see figure 4.11). To do so, they moved a tracer along the length of a model and a cutter along a somewhat smaller workpiece rotating on the same axis. Both model and workpiece rocked on pivots below the bench as the tracer pushed the model against a spring. Nartov may have used the medallion-copying machines to help prepare dies for minting coins, which became his responsibility in 1726. He may have intended the bas-relief cylinder machine to help make models for a monumental column commemorating

FIGURE 4.10. *(opposite)* Inverse medallion cutting (details). Fig. 1 at the top shows the mandrel with its pulley (G), rosette patterns (L), and its chucks for the pattern (C) and blank (B). Figs. 2 and 3 depict the mandrel assemblage end on from the left and right, respectively. Fig. 4 shows it cut away lengthwise. Figs. 5 and 6 show patterns; Figs. 7 and 8 are the medallions copied from them. Figs. 11 and 12 show the chuck for the pattern, whole and in section; Figs. 9 and 10 are the whole and sectioned chuck for the blank that becomes the medallion. (From Denis Diderot and Jean le Rond D'Alembert, *Encyclopédie, Recueil des Planches* [Paris, 1772] vol. 10, plate 67.)

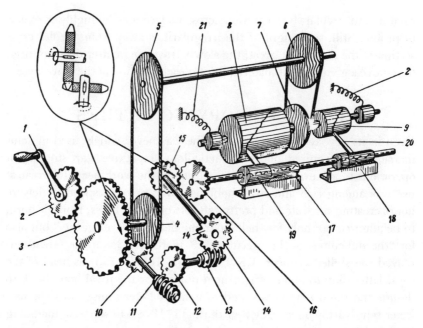

FIGURE 4.11. Kinematic diagram of Nartov's large copying lathe, 1718–1729. Nartov's machine made positive copies of bas-relief or *intaglio* pictures on cylinders. The tracer (19) and cutter (20) traversed laterally while the pattern and workpiece cylinders (8) and (9) rotated on a common axis and, pushed by springs, moved transversely in and out according to the design on the pattern cylinder. Ignore the misleading diagonal lines shown on workpiece and pattern cylinders. For each rotation of the pattern and workpiece, the tracer and cutter traversed laterally .089 mm. The enlarged inset indicates right-angle meshings of gear wheels. (From V. V. Danilevskii, *Nartov and his Theatrum Machinarum,* [Jerusalem, 1966], p. 151.)

events in the life of Peter the Great, a project for which he received a *ukase* in 1725.[31]

Nartov's large copying lathe, model 1718–1729, could copy a bas-relief scene onto a cylindrical workpiece 180–188 mm in diameter and 110 mm in length. It was slow work. "With 60 turns of the handle per minute, 13.1 hours were required for the complete machining of the workpiece." Right-angle cross sections of the completed object were indeed highly irregular in outline, but the irregularities were only superficial relative to the cylinder into which they were cut. Not much material had to be removed in any one of the 2250 rotations for cutting the whole object.[32]

Medallion-copying machines were used in the eighteenth century in

76

France and found their way to England. In 1790 Matthew Boulton bought a "reducing machine" from French engraver and lathe maker J. B. Dupeyrat for use in his Soho manufactory of ornamental objects.[33] Inverse medallion lathes were superseded by the positive medallion-copying machine whose invention is credited to another French lathe maker, P.C. Hulot *fils*.[34] About 1800 Hulot *fils* made one that could make a positive copy on a disc mounted side by side with the pattern medallion. For greater clarity of detail, one could vary the gear ratios of this machine so as to reproduce smaller sizes from a larger original model. This *tour à portrait* was described and illustrated in the 1816 Paris edition of a monumental volume about the art of turning.[35] In England this type of machine was called a "portrait lathe" or a "likeness lathe." The Science Museum in London has an 1824 portrait lathe, which was used in the Royal Mint. (see figure 4.12). The Philadelphia mint obtained one from Paris around 1836.[36] As in the negative medallion lathe, the objects copied in Nartov's and Hulot's positive machines had slightly irregular cross-sections, but not much material had to be removed to create the irregularity.

Having surveyed the art up to Thomas Blanchard's time of reproducing irregularities in an object by lathe, we now turn to the question of what the Blanchard lathe did that was new. Except for Nartov's machine, all of these control devices for cutting screws, ovals, tapers, rosette patterns, and medallions were cited in one lawsuit or another as a reason for thinking that Blanchard's machine was nothing new. For instance, in *Blanchard vs. Eldridge* in 1848, witness John H. Schrader, a machinist in Europe and the United States for forty years, who had experience since 1816 building rosette lathes and portrait lathes, said there was nothing in Blanchard's lathe that was not in a rosette lathe, and that Eldridge's machine was the same as a portrait lathe, and therefore different from Blanchard's. In Boston the next year, the defendants in *Thomas Blanchard vs. John Kimball* argued instead that the portrait lathe, translated as the "image lathe," was the same as Blanchard's lathe, which was therefore not a true invention. In what sense were both wrong?

## BLANCHARD'S INVENTION

It is clear that by the time of Blanchard's invention in 1819, lathe design, especially European design of ornamental lathes, had developed several kinds of mechanisms to replace hand control by machine control to some extent, and several kinds of copying capabilities, some of which were for

FIGURE 4.12. Portrait lathe, early nineteenth century. This French machine of about 1824, used at the Royal Mint in England, is virtually identical to Hulot's machine of c. 1800, illustrated by Bergeron in 1816. It made positive instead of inverse copies of medallions. As the larger pattern medallion on the right and the smaller medallion blank on the left rotate at the same speed on separate parallel axes, they are traced and cut, respectively, by the tracer and cutter mounted on the horizontal bar that is pivoted at the left and slowly lowered by the vertical screw at the right, into which its curved end is keyed. Thus the cutter and tracer touch all parts of the their respective medallion disks. As they do so, the tracer is pushed in and out (transversely) by the raised or sunken design on the pattern medallion, which is thus transferred by the cutter to the blank medallion. (Science Museum photograph, London.)

irregular surfaces on regular forms. Except in the case of screws, these capabilities were only occasionally applied to utilitarian purposes. But in cutting screws, tapers, swash moldings, and scallops along cylinders, and in cutting ovals, waves, and rosette traceries on discs, the potential for machine copying of various sorts of noncircular patterns had gone well beyond the simple turning of chair rungs and dishes. In both the positive and negative medallion or portrait lathe there was an even higher degree of continuous machine control of the cutting process to reproduce a complex and irregular image in bas relief or intaglio on a disk. Nartov's copying lathe could, in many hours, reproduce an irregular bas relief image on the surface of a cylinder.

Except for Nartov's and Hulot's machines, these lathe mechanisms for copying noncircular patterns of various sorts were described in Rees's *Cyclopaedia* before 1820 and had been depicted in the plates of the French *Encyclopédie* nearly fifty years earlier. We may never know if Thomas Blanchard saw such an encyclopedia before or while inventing his irregular turning lathe (nor indeed whether he had ever seen an actual ornamental turning lathe).[37] But these volumes do contain a fairly comprehensive statement of the technology up to that time for turning objects "opposed to the circular figure," and therefore set a benchmark beyond which, by definition of "invention," Blanchard had to go in shaping irregular forms by machine.

Was his further act of mechanization large or small? Was Blanchard's gunstock and last machine only a rose engine by another name? Did he just rearrange its mechanisms, build them bigger, simplify and strengthen them, and add water power to make them run faster and more economically in a serviceable, reliable, factory production machine? Did he, perhaps, unwittingly re-invent a more robust version of Nartov's copying lathe, or of Hulot's positive "likeness lathe"? No, he did not, for it would not have worked. His gunbarrel lathe can be regarded as simply a strengthened taper lathe with an elliptical cam action, but his irregular turning lathe was entirely different in principle.

None of these operations of the ornamental turning lathe, rose engine, oval lathe, screw-cutting lathe, medallion lathe, portrait lathe, swash lathe, nor of Nartov's copying lathe, can produce an object whose cross-sections across its axis of rotation vary as far from a circle as those of a gunstock or shoe last. To produce such an object in a lathe would require the two linear motions of the cutter relative to the rotating object—one small sideways motion along the axis of rotation, and one large transverse motion (the irregular one) at right angles to the axis—not only to be performed simultaneously, but also to be completed during *one* rotation of the object. That is what a Blanchard lathe does, but it can do so only by separating the cutting action from the rotation of the object.

What Blanchard invented was an elegant solution to the problem caused by the basic incompatibility, by previous methods, of the two tasks required of a machine to make a gunstock or a last. In both ordinary and ornamental turning (and in gunbarrel lathes by Blanchard and others) the cutting action results from the rotation of the workpiece itself. But two tasks need to be performed in order to cut a highly irregular object by machine: (1) to cut the material, and (2) to vary the relative position of workpiece and tool so as to cut away *enough* material, *in the right places,* to make the irregular object. The difficulty is that the lowest rotational speed required for cutting by machine is higher than the fastest speed possible for changing the relative positions of workpiece and tool to achieve the desired effect. The rotation of the workpiece in a traditional lathe therefore has to be too rapid to allow the cutter to remove that much wood during each rotation of the workpiece. Expressed another way, a cutter and slide rest rugged enough to cut deeply while the workpiece was rotating rapidly could not be moved fast enough into position to do so in synchronization with the rapidly rotating workpiece. Since the non-Blanchard lathe has to act by paring or shaving a little at each rotation of the workpiece, there is simply no way it can remove enough during a single rotation to produce a highly irregular cross section at that point along the axis.

This incompatibility of tasks for a lathe can be regarded as analogous to the incompatibility facing James Watt with regard to the wastage of fuel by the Newcomen engine: a single cylinder cannot be kept simultaneously hot enough for vaporization of water and cold enough for condensation of steam. Just as Watt's insight was to escape this incompatibility by separating the two tasks of condensation and vaporization into two separate chambers, so Blanchard's insight was to escape the incompatibility facing him in the lathe by separating the two tasks of cutting and positioning into separate motions of the machine. He removed the rotary *cutting* motion from the workpiece and assigned it to the cutter, and left the rotary *positioning* motion to the workpiece. That way the cutting could be fast enough and the positioning slow enough.[38]

With the rapidly rotating cutter, the Blanchard lathe can remove enough material from the appropriate places on the slowly rotating workpiece, during one rotation of the workpiece, to give it a highly irregular right-angle cross-section at that point along its axis. Then, as the cutter traverses along the length of the workpiece, the continuous cutting of all these highly irregular cross-sections along its length renders the whole workpiece highly irregular in shape.

In the Blanchard lathe of 1819–20, the workpiece and model are fastened between centers, either on the same axis (for lasts) or on parallel axes (for gunstocks) that are on a hanging or swinging frame suspended from an overhead cross beam.[39] The spindles holding the workpiece and model are keyed to rotate at the same slow speed. The weight of the frame keeps the workpiece and model pressed respectively against a rapidly rotating cutter wheel and a dummy tracer (or "friction") wheel of the same diameter and thickness.[40] As the model slowly rotates, it pushes to varying extent against the slowly traversing tracer wheel, so that the model and workpiece move out and in according to the contours of the model. Guided thus by the model, the cutter removes more or less material from the workpiece at each point during each rotation of the workpiece. The cutter wheel therefore cuts a spiral path around the workpiece to match the path of the tracer around the model, and the workpiece ends up, at the end of a single passage of the cutter wheel along its length, the same size and shape as the model. By extra gears and levers to vary the direction of rotation, the speed of traversing, and the distance of the cutter wheel from the workpiece, the machine could produce a mirror image of the model (as a right or left shoe last), or an object different from the model in length or thickness or both.

## BLANCHARD'S PATENT CLAIMS

The important difference, then, between a Blanchard lathe and all lathes that preceded it is not that Blanchard merely recombined already-known copying mechanisms into a more robust and economic arrangement for a particular industrial use, but that he created an altogether new capability for the lathe: the ability to make a highly irregular three-dimensional object. Tracing an irregular bas-relief surface on a disk or cylinder was not new, but tracing all around a highly irregular three-dimensional form was new. Strangely enough, neither of Blanchard's own patent statements telling what was original about his invention emphasizes the fact that, unlike all other lathes, in his the cutting was accomplished by the motion of the cutter instead of the motion of the workpiece. His specification for the patent granted September 6, 1819, for "a machine for turning Gunstocks tackle and Shipping Blocks," does at least mention it, however. In this specification Blanchard claims to have invented four "principles," starting with (1) "the use of a . . . guide or model . . . revolving in conformity with the revolution of the . . . article . . . to be made . . . " and (2) "the application of a wheel, with circular or crooked knives or cutters . . . upon the periphery of it to the turning of wood in a lathe."[41]

He seems, however, to have backed off from these two claims, probably in response to the incident in Boston in which he was accused of claiming "more than he had invented."[42] They do not appear in his revised specification for the reissued patent of January 20, 1820, for "an Engine for turning or cutting irregular forms out of wood, iron, brass or other material or substance . . . called Blanchard's self-directing machine." In this version Blanchard no longer explicitly claimed originality for the use of a revolving model nor for the application of a cutting wheel to lathe work, but only for "the mode of operation" as described in the specification itself, whereby "out of the rough material placed in the engine there may be turned or formed at one continued operation . . . an exact resemblance in all respects of a model to be imitated," plus resemblance in reverse (as with right and left shoe lasts) and in different sizes. He even explicitly disavowed any "claim as his invention the cutter wheel or cutters or friction wheel as such nor the use of a model to guide the cutting instrument," remarking that "all these are common property and have been so for years."[43]

One can infer from the differences between the two versions of his patent that in the interim Blanchard decided it would be incorrect, or at least too risky, to claim as original his application of a cutting wheel to the turning of wood in a lathe, as in the September version, and retreated to narrower ground in his revised patent of January 1820. By this time he was apparently thinking about the "cutter wheel" of the Portsmouth scoring engine, for he alludes to the shape of its cutters in this version.[44] No evidence shows whether Blanchard had read or heard about the Portsmouth blockmaking machinery in England before developing his lathe in Millbury and Springfield, although articles on that subject were published in the *Edinburgh Encyclopaedia* and in the Rees *Cyclopaedia* before 1820. In fact, however, neither the scoring engine nor the deadeye machine (the only Portsmouth machines that use a cutting wheel) is a lathe. The blocks and deadeyes do not revolve while being scored, so the kinematics of Blanchard's lathe are completely different from those of the Portsmouth machines (see chapter 6 on blockmaking machinery).

In the revised specification in January, but not in the earlier version, Blanchard also alluded to making a cutter wheel up from a gang of circular saws, as a possible though less desirable form than his wheel with "circular or crooked knives" set around its circumference. As mentioned in chapter 3, this form of "burr" cutter wheel made of saws was a feature that was to be added to Azariah Woolworth's lastmaking machine, which Blanchard had observed in Waterbury, Connecticut between the issuing and reissuing of his patent.[45] He may therefore have had Woolworth's machine in mind in mentioning a saw-like cutter. In Woolworth's machine #2, however, as in the Portsmouth machines, the cutter was not applied to the workpiece while it was rotating. The workpiece was rotated by hand to a new position between cuts. Circular cutters "as such" had indeed become common property by his time,[46] but Blanchard's retreat from claiming originality for the *way he used* the circular cutter on a revolving workpiece in a lathe seems overcautious. Blanchard's visit to Waterbury may also have prompted his disclaimer of originality for "the use of . . . a model revolving in conformity with the article to be made"[47] for Woolworth's machine did use models—two of them—"to guide the cutting instrument"[48] in cutting the workpiece in the right places. Again, however, the "revolving" of models and workpiece in Woolworth's machine #2 was intermittent, between each cutting pass of the cutter, rather than "at one continued operation."

Blanchard's patent revisions between September 1819 and January 1820 are puzzling to us, because they seem to concede too much, but they do sidestep certain communication difficulties he may have been encountering. His lathe's *kinematics* were original, but its *components* were not, and components may have been more salient to observers at the time, as they were later to many of the witnesses testifying in his patent suits. What the revised specification claims as original compresses the kinematic idea into the inelegant phrase that the machine does its work "at one continued operation by the mode of operation in this second article explained."[49] This second article is long and detailed in its description of the machine's mode of operation, and leaves only implicit that no other machine was capable of doing what it could do all "at one continued operation."

At the very end of the 1820 patent specification, however, Blanchard states plainly that he does *not* acknowledge relying on the precedence of certain other machines, past and contemporary, to which his invention may have been likened by others. He says:

> it is apparant [sic] that the principle of his machine or invention is different [from] . . . the last making machine made and used in Waterbury in Connecticut and the card handle machine used for a long time past in Boston and also from the machinery described in the Edinburgh Encyclopedia for making Ships Blocks & Dead-eyes and from the modes of turning irregular surfaces described in the French Encyclopedia.[50]

It remains a question whether Blanchard was aware of any of these machines before patenting his lathe in September 1819. Taken at face value, this statement makes it clear enough that he did not derive inspiration from them for his invention. The evidence presented in this chapter and in chapters 3 and 6 shows that they were indeed significantly different from his machines.

With hindsight, it seems to us that Blanchard threw out the baby with the bath water when he retreated from his patent claims of September 1819 to those of January 1820. The mechanical components of the machine had indeed already been used in various combinations in various other machines, in no one of which, however, did they continuously *move* in relation to one another during the *same* lapse of time. Somehow this fact, whose implications seem remarkable in retrospect, was underemphasized in the claims of the 1820 patent. Although it is accurate, the phrase "at one continued operation" seems inadequate for expressing the unprecedented kinematics of the Blanchard lathe.

Having solved the problem and developed a machine for copying highly irregular forms, and obtained a patent for it, Blanchard might, like many inventors, have left its fate to others. Instead he took an active role in attempting to reap the reward that the patent promised. This led him into designing still other machines and organizing them into manufacturing systems in which his basic invention would have enhanced value. The first and most famous of these was the gunstock production line at Springfield Armory.

# 5

# THE
# GUNSTOCKING
# PRODUCTION LINE
# AT SPRINGFIELD
# ARMORY

A FTER Blanchard had installed barrel-turning machines at the two national armories, Roswell Lee, Superintendent of the Springfield Armory, wrote to him early in 1819, somewhat ambiguously asking about his "machinery."[1] With characteristic self-confidence and poor spelling, Blanchard replied

> I conclude you meen a machine I have recently invented for turning gunstocks and cuting in the locks and mounting. . . . I have got a moddle built. I can cut a lock in by water in one minute and a half as smoth as can be done by hand. The turning stocks is very simple in its oporation and will completely imatate a stock made in proper shape. I shal bring the moddle to Springfield in the course of 3 weeks.[2]

What Blanchard here called "a machine" we would of course recognize as two distinct machines. One, for turning the exterior contours of the gunstock, was the irregular turning lathe for which he subsequently received a patent; the other, for "cuting [sic] in the locks and mounting,"[3] was an inletting machine, for which he received no patent. These two machines formed the basis for the production line to manufacture gunstocks that Blanchard subsequently developed at Springfield Armory.

Blanchard's gunstocking machines and their successors at the Armory received wide acclaim in their own day.[4] Since then, historians of technology have come to regard Blanchard's ingeniously designed machinery, comprising the earliest known production line of sequential special-purpose machines in an American manufacturing industry, as a technological paradigm, "a microcosm of the American system of manufactures." They tend to believe that it "eliminated the use of skilled labor in stockmaking."[5] Blanchard's machines and their "second-generation descendants" developed later at the Armory did eventually replace much of the hand-tool work of gunstockers, although not as quickly or completely as popular opinion and historians have been led to believe. Thus, in order to understand what Blanchard's machines did, we shall first consider the work process of stocking guns by hand tools.

# GUNSTOCKING BEFORE BLANCHARD

Even before mechanization of gunstock manufacture began in 1820, the tasks of a gunstocker at Springfield Armory were different from those of an all-around handicraft gunsmith. Under the division of labor there, a stocker did only woodworking, which followed the metalworking tasks in the production sequence for a musket. The forgers, filers, barrel welders, and machinists had first to make the metal parts and drill screw holes in them and make the screws for fastening them onto the stock. The stocker then had to shape the wooden stock and fit all the metal parts onto it.

Starting with a blank of black walnut sawn roughly to an outline shape of a gunstock, the stocker had to excavate or "let in" sunken places having the proper shapes and depths for receiving the metal parts, and to drill screw holes for fastening them into these sunken "beds." Figure 5.1 shows the stock and the metal parts of a musket. The *barrel* with a *breech plug* screwed into its "breech" end was bedded on top of the fore-end of the stock; the *barrel bands* held the barrel in place, the *band spring*s held the barrel bands in place. Below the barrel, the ramrod (not shown) rode in a partly enclosed groove along the bottom of the stock. On the opposide side of the stock from the *lock,* or firing mechanism, the *side plate* served as washers for threaded side pins to hold the gun together. The *trigger* protruded through the *trigger plate; the trigger guard* protected it. A threaded "tang" pin from the breech-plug tang through the stock to the guard held the gun together top to bottom. The *butt plate* protected the end of the butt. Besides inletting for parts, the stocker also had to shape the exterior of the gunstock so that it would have smoothly rounded contours instead of sharp corners. Then he smoothed and polished and oiled its surface.

The premechanized gunstocker accomplished this job with hand tools: saws, drills, gouges, chisels, and stockshaves. He did so at a bench equipped with a vise to hold the stock steady while he worked on it. His method was literally "cut and try," to see if the metal part would fit yet, and then cut a little more wood away, repeatedly, until it did fit snugly and smoothly, and then when all the parts fitted he fastened them into place with threaded pins, or screws. A good stocker could complete about three guns every two days.

At Springfield Armory in the late 1810s, stockers were paid at a piece

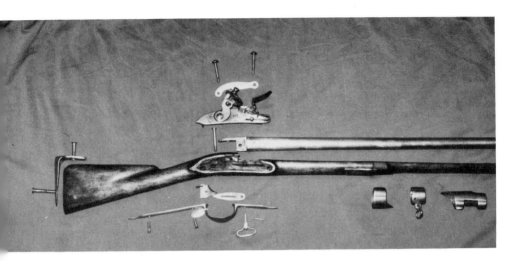

FIGURE 5.1. Parts of a muzzle-loading flintlock musket. Clockwise from top, besides screws and pins: side plate, lock, barrel with breech plug, stock with lower bandspring, upper, middle and lower bands, swivel for strap, trigger guard, trigger plate and trigger, butt plate. (The ramrod is not shown.) In addition to shaping the wooden stock, the stocker had to cut holes and recesses into it for fitting the metal parts. (Model 1795 Springfield musket, Springfield Armory Museum. Photograph by Robert B. Gordon.)

rate of $1.06, $1.12, or $1.16 per gun.[6] There were about thirty-five gunstockers at the Armory within a total production workforce of about 230.[7] On average, they each stocked about thirty guns a month.[8] They worked, along with the lock filers and finishers, in the largest building on Armory Hill.[9]

## DEVELOPMENT OF BLANCHARD'S MACHINERY

Some metalworking tasks at the Armory were already mechanized by 1819, and powered by water in the three "water shops" on the Mill River about a mile away from Armory Hill. Superintendent Lee was looking out for ways to mechanize more operations, and had been quick to adopt Blanchard's improvement to the barrel-turning lathe. When news of Blanchard's stocking lathe reached him, he acted quickly on that, too.

Blanchard demonstrated a model of his gunstocking machine(s) at the Springfield Armory in March 1819, and was commissioned to build a full-scale stocking lathe at Harper's Ferry Armory. By the end of May it was successfully turning a gunstock in nine minutes, and Blanchard returned to Millbury to prepare patterns for erecting one at Springfield.[10] Blanchard's lathe was installed in the Armory's "lower water shop," the farthest downstream on the Mill River at Springfield. Exactly when this took place is not clear, but by June 1820 some "turned stocks" were available for completion by the gunstockers on the Hill, at a piece rate 10 cents lower than they received for starting with "rough stocks."[11] Blanchard having obtained his reissued patent in January, the Armory paid him a royalty of 2 cents per turned stock.[12] During the next months, in which he installed his lathe at Lemuel Pomeroy's contract gun manufactory at Pittsfield, Blanchard also worked to improve the inletting capability of his machines. In early 1821 he wrote to Lee that he had put a machine into "good operation" at Pittsfield and that

> I have made grate improvement in cuting in the work . . . I have discovered a method by which I can vary the jig and set it to every lock [part] side or heel and make a good joint. it is done by a very simple method. I am about to commense building a machine for the above mentioned purpose and wil practice on the same in my shop until I can do as good work as can posably be done by hand.[13]

Blanchard's work had apparently elicited some negative reaction among gunstockers. In the same letter he told Lee "if I cut the inside of the lock the stockers say that is no help to them, and theay stil say that turning the stock is of little or no saving and they are determined if possible to run the machine down, but I am determined they shal not."[14] To overcome the opposition of such stockers, Blanchard proposed an experiment:

> I will get my machine in perfect operation and will hire one first rate stocker and get it up in Springfield and after a fair trial we can asertain how manny muskets two hands (that is I and a stocker) can half-stock in a day or week and by deducting out the rent of machinary and other expenses we can fairly asertain what saving (if eny) their is or can be made by the help of the machine . . . it may be argued that the work will not be done so well as by hand, but who can tell until a fair trial is made.[15]

Two months later, Blanchard wrote to Lee that his machine could "make a closer joint in one minute than a Stocker can in one hour," and that he would "soon be prepared to combat a whole battallion of stockers."[16]

Eventually, after negotiation with the Ordnance Department through Roswell Lee, this proposal for a fair trial of his machines won Blanchard a job as "inside contractor" at the Springfield Armory, to "half-stock" muskets at a price of 37 cents each. This meant he used the work space, materials, and waterpower available at the Armory, but had to hire his own helpers to man his machines.[17] He began working at Springfield on this basis in May 1823 and proceeded to develop a sequence of woodworking machines for shaping the exterior of a gunstock and cutting out cavities in it for the metal parts of the musket. Lee explained to the Chief of Ordnance in 1822:

> What we term half Stocking is to face and turn the Stock, fit on the heel plate, let in the barrel, put on the bands, fit on the Lock & trigger plate and bore the holes for the side & tang pins;—the other half is to let in the side plate & guard, hang the trigger, make the groove & bore the hole for & fit the ramrod, let in the band springs, smooth & oil the Stock.[18]

Lee, who calculated that Blanchard's inside contract would gain for the Armory an immediate "saving of three cents at least on a stock," remarked that it was even more important to encourage development of Blanchard's machines: "the principle object is to bring the machinery to the most perfect state."[19]

At that time Lee expected Blanchard would need a trial of "on[e] years labor, say half-stock 23,000 arms . . . [to] ascertain what can be saved by adopting his improvements,"[20] but in the event it took considerably longer. Lee had no way of foreseeing that "to bring the machinery to the most perfect state" would mean to proliferate it into fourteen machines for subdivided special purposes. But under the incentives and constraints of his inside contract for actual production of gunstocks at a fixed price per piece with his own labor force, one supposes Blanchard attempted to minimize his costs. He did so by creating a greater number of specialized labor-saving machines, to be operated by lower-paid, less experienced workers.[21] He therefore had to "build skill into" his machines. To save time he also had to apportion the separate tasks of gunstocking among the machines so as to promote a smooth flow of gunstocks from machine to machine. Thus, he had to design the machines both individually and all together as a production system.

By midyear 1825, Blanchard had finished this job. He had created machines valued at $1025 for his half-stocking production line, and was planning to leave employment at the Armory. "He had made arrangements to bring his invention into use in turning of other articles and setting up other establishments for operation elsewhere."[22] He had also agreed to a new contract by which the Ordnance Department would pay him a royalty of 9 cents per gunstock produced by his machinery until his patent on the lathe would expire. But fire broke out on July 1, 1825, and destroyed Blanchard's machinery, so instead of receiving the agreed-upon royalty on Springfield musket production, for about five months he was "oblidged [sic] to remain in the service of the United States and reconstruct other machinery in place of it." During this time, he later complained, he was paid "common mechanic's wages."[23]

In Blanchard's petition to Congress in 1833 for extension of his patent, he said that after two or three months' operation in 1826 in unsuitable quarters in a sawmill, the new machinery was dismantled until the beginning of 1827, when a new shop was ready on the site of the sawmill. The Armory's payroll and work returns for this period suggest, however, that the machinery was in successful operation through 1826 and half of 1827, the disruption took place after that, and the machines were back in operation in May 1828. We know Blanchard engaged in other activities in this period, including a sojourn near Hudson, New York in the summer of 1826, when he set up pulley-block machinery at Livingston Mills. Thereafter he reappeared on the Springfield Armory payroll in various capacities for periods until autumn, 1829.[24]

Blanchard ended his inside contracting at Springfield Armory at the end of 1827, and on February 7, 1828 signed the postponed new contract with Ordnance Chief George Bomford for the 9 cents royalty—6 cents per musket "for the use of said turning machine" plus 3 "for the use of the other auxiliary machines."[25] This royalty rate, the Chief of Ordnance explained to the Secretary of War, was "less than one half of the value of the labor saved by using those machines."[26] The machines listed in the contract include Blanchard's two metalworking machines for "turning the barrels" of muskets and for "turning the flats and ovals on the breech of the barrels" and fourteen woodworking machines, "one each for each of the following purposes":

1. for sawing off the stock to its proper length.
2. for facing the stock and sawing it lengthwise.
3. for turning the stock.
4. for boring for the barrel.
5. for milling the bed for the breech of the barrel, and for the breech-pin.
6. for cutting the bed for the tang of the breech-plate.

7. for boring the holes for the breech-plate screws.

8. for gauging [for] the barrel.

9. for cutting for the tang of the breech-pin.

10. for forming the concave for the upper band.

11. for dressing the stock for and between the bands.

12. for forming the bed for the lock-plate.

13. for forming the bed for the interior of the lock.

14. for boring the holes for the side and tang-pins.[27]

We should note that this list omits any mention of forming the bed for the trigger plate, but it is otherwise consistent with Blanchard's job of *half*-stocking as described by Lee five years earlier. That is, it also excludes machinery to prepare the stock for the side plate, guard, trigger, ramrod, or bandsprings. The gunstockers continued to perform these operations by hand. But even though they accomplished only "half" of the total job of stocking the gun, Blanchard's machines did noticeably increase productivity, although not spectacularly.

Thus, Blanchard's "fair trial" for his lathe had resulted in the creation of a production line of coordinated machinery within which the lathe could be most effectively exploited. After the famous blockmaking machines at the Royal Dockyard in Portsmouth, England, Blanchard's machines at Springfield have been recognized as the next earliest example of a set of machinery arranged as a rational production system. It would be instructive to see how these machines worked, individually and together. Unfortunately, only one of the fourteen machines survives today—the wood-framed Blanchard lathe at the Springfield Armory Museum—and no contemporary description tells in detail how they worked. In his "Report on the Manufactures of Interchangeable Mechanism," in 1883 Charles H. Fitch wrote sadly, "Of most of these machines little more than the names remain."[28] Except for the lathe, none were patented, so neither specifications nor patent models exist.

However, a second generation of Blanchard's machines was created at the Springfield Armory in the 1840s and early 1850s, and information about the working of these machines is much more plentiful. Thomas Warner was the master armorer who undertook the retooling of the Armory overall for the 1841 model musket. This retooling, plus use of multiple sets of accurate gauges, brought about the interchangeability of musket parts that the Ordnance Department had been seeking to achieve for at least thirty years.[29] Chief Machinist Cyrus Buckland is credited with most of the design work on the mid-century generation of gunstocking machines.[30]

The fifteen or sixteen gunstocking machines at the Springfield Armory in 1853 and 1854 were greatly admired and described in some detail by the English Parliamentary Commissioners who visited Springfield and other American manufactories in those summers.[31] They ordered gunstocking machinery from the Ames Company in Chicopee, Massachusetts and metal-working machinery from the Robbins and Lawrence Company in Windsor, Vermont.[32] The machines from New England were set up at Enfield Armory outside London and operated under the direction of Virginian James H. Burton, who had been acting master armorer at Harpers Ferry. Several of the Enfield machines survive in museums today. The operation of the machinery at the Enfield Armory was described in detail in 1859 in a series of six illustrated articles in *The Engineer*.[33] By this time there were eighteen gunstocking machines, "as arranged by Mr. Burton."[34] Nearly twenty-five years later, Charles Fitch described Ames Company and Springfield Armory stocking machinery, which with very minor changes was the same as the Springfield and Enfield stocking machinery described in the 1850s.

Charles Fitch characterized this mid-century generation of machines as "modified designs of the Blanchard stocking machinery."[35] The English observers at the U.S. National Armories in 1854 were apparently also informed at the time that "Blanchard's machines or lathes for tracing or copying any pattern . . . form the basis . . . of that machinery."[36] The old Blanchard lathe itself, "which has been in operation nearly 30 years,"[37] was the machine for "rough-turning the stock" at the beginning of the gunstock production sequence they observed at Springfield. Moreover, the *sequence* of operations appears almost exactly the same in Blanchard's Ordnance Department contract of 1828 as in the longer descriptions of the second-generation machines in 1853, 1854, and 1859.

We can therefore infer that the 1828 list was not a random list of the machines, but, like the later accounts, specified the production line sequence. Further, in the absence of eyewitness descriptions of the first-generation machinery, we may regard the second-generation of gunstocking machinery as generally indicative of Blanchard's designs and production sequence, and "read back" from descriptions of their operation to surmise how Blanchard's production line worked.

Some of the second-generation machines that Cyrus Buckland de-

TABLE 5.1

| | *Blanchard's "Half-Stocking" Machines, 1828* | | *Buckland's Stocking Machines, 1853* | | | |
|---|---|---|---|---|---|---|
| Does work of 1853 machine ( ) | | Does work of 1828 machine ( ) | | | Machine times in 1853: min. | sec. |
| | | (2) | [1] | facing and slabbing machine | 3 | 30 |
| | (1) ... sawing off the stock to its proper length | (3) | [2] | Blanchard's rough-turning lathe | 4 | 11 |
| 1] | (2) ... facing the stock and sawing it lengthwise | | [3] | "spotting" machine to cut flat surfaces for bearings in succeeding machines | | 7 |
| 2] | (3) ... turning the stock | (4,5,9) | [4] | barrel-bedding machine (hand finishing of groove)          (hand | 1 1 | 7 42) |
| 4] | (4) ... boring for the barrel | (8) | [5] | machine to cut butt and muzzle to proper angle and length with reference to barrel | | 11 |
| 4] | (5) ... milling the bed for the breech of the barrel and breech-pin | | [6] | bedding for side plate and facing of stock | 1 | 26 |
| 7] | (6) ... cutting the bed for the tang of the breech-plate | (6,7) | [7] | butt-plate machine, recessing bed, and drilling screw holes | | 21 |
| 7] | (7) ... boring the holes for the breech-plate screws | (10,11) | [8] | band-fitting machine to cut for three bands and bevel and upper band | | 23 |
| 5] | (8) ... gauging for the barrel | (11) | [9] | band-finishing machine to plane stock between bands | | 28 |
| ] | (9) ... cutting for the tang of the breech-pin | | [10] | lathe for smooth-turning stock from butt to lock | 8 | 35 |
| 8] | (10) ... forming the concave for the upper band | | [11] | lathe for smooth-turning stock from lock to end of stock | 5 | 28 |
| ] | (11) ... dressing the stock for and between the bands | (12,13) | [12] | lock-bedding machine | | 47 |
| ] | (12) ... forming the bed for the lock-plate | | [13] | guard-bedding machine to cut recess for trigger guard, trigger, ramrod stop | | 51 |
| ] | (13) ... forming the bed for the interior of the lock | | [14] | band spring- and ram-rod-fitting machine | | 55 |
| ] | (14) ... boring side and tang-pin holes | (14) | [15] | machine to bore holes for side screws and tang screws | | 24 |

...n contract between Thomas Blanchard and Chief of ...nance George Bomford, February 7, 1828. (Record ...up 156, National Archives.)

From parliamentary Commissioners' Reports. (Reprinted in Nathan Rosenberg, ed., *The American System of Manufactures,* pp. 137–142, 364–65.)

signed were for operations in the "other half" of gunstocking, which Blanchard's "half-stocking" production line had left to hand work. Such machines performed inletting for the trigger, trigger guard, bandsprings and, in part, for the ramrod. Buckland's second-generation machines also combined the "half-stocking" operations somewhat differently from the ways in which Blanchard's machines had combined them. Table 5.1 lists both sets of machines and indicates which machines in each set performed the tasks of machines in the other set. Machines (#1), (#2), and (#3) in Blanchard's production line reduced the rough blank to the shaped stock. Four more bedded the barrel and breech pin (#4), (#5), (#8), and (#9); two inlet for the butt plate and its screws (#6) and (#7), two prepared the fore-end for the barrel bands (#10) and (#11), two bedded the lock (#12) and (#13), and one drilled for the side- and tang-pins (#14).

Appendix A describes, step by step, how Blanchard's machinery performed the "half-stocking" of muskets at the Springfield Armory in the 1820s and 1830s, as inferred from the the second-generation machines for that purpose in the 1850s. Figures 5.2 through 5.6 show the cuts that machines made in "half-stocking" gunstocks, and the corresponding second generation machines for doing so.

## COMPARING THE FIRST- AND SECOND-GENERATION PRODUCTION LINES

Besides the machines corresponding to Blanchard's original set, the second-generation machinery interpolated additional machines [#3] [#6] [#13] [#14] for making indentations and flat spots to aid in positioning the stock in subsequent machines, for planing various areas, for bedding the trigger guard (see figure 5.7a and b), for bedding bandsprings and ramrod springs, and for making a ramrod groove. Hence the English

FIGURE 5.2. Springfield Armory gunstocking lathe, c. 1825. In this massive machine the gunstock and model hang parallel to each other in a double frame swinging on pivots overhead. The frame presses the gunstock model at rear against the tracer wheel (obscured), and the gunstock blank against the rapidly rotating cutter wheel at front. The tracer and cutter wheels traverse simultaneously, cutting the contours of the slowly rotating stock from the butt to somewhat beyond the lock area, in about four minutes. Compare with figure 3.2 to see how this double-spindle gunstocking lathe differed from the single-spindle lastmaking lathe. In the mid-1850s this machine was still in use for rough turning, and is extant today at the Springfield Armory Museum. (Photograph of original machine by National Museum of American History, which exhibits a full-sized replica.)

Original Blanchard Lathe
—1822—
Turning Butt for Gun Stock.

97

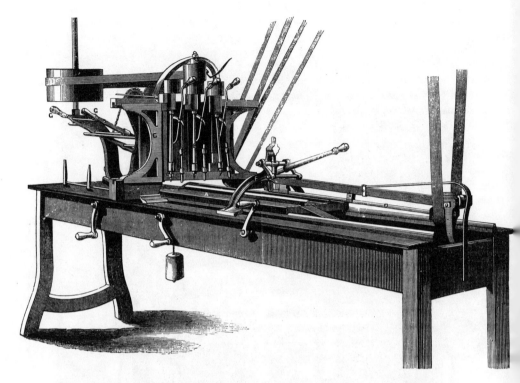

FIGURE 5.3a. Barrel-bedding machine. In the 1850s the stock went to this "second-generation" machine, [#4] in table 5.1, after rough-turning of its thick end by Blanchard lathe. The operator fastened the stock onto the lengthwise-sliding carriage, positioned it under the cross-sliding vertical-spindle cutters by using the cranks at the side of the bench, and manipulated the cutters up and down by the upright levers. Using two controls, he moved each tracing pin around within a steel form (not visible), which was shaped like the barrel groove and the bed for the breech plug and tang. With the lengthwise horizontal rotary cutter suspended from bracket (F) in the middle he cleaned out a ridge remaining in the barrel groove; with the horizontal cutter in the swinging frame at (G) on the left, he squared the shoulder for the bed of the barrel breech. These operations required less than 1¼ minutes total. (From *The Engineer* 7 [April 15, 1859]: 258.

Commissioners observed at Springfield and bought for Enfield machines that performed both "halves" of the gunstocking process more nearly completely than had Blanchard's own machines.

The mid-century production line for gunstocks at Springfield and Enfield also included a larger number of Blanchard lathes [#10] [#11] of the improved 1843 patent "rocking" variety (see figure 5.8 ). These machines were specialized in two ways: (1) to turn the stock either from butt to lock *or* from lock to the first barrel-band; and (2) either to rough-turn, which preceded the rest of the production, or to "second-" or "smooth-turn," which occurred late in the production line (see figure 5.9). This specialization of task among a *greater* number of lathes presumably speeded up the production line. But, as we have seen, some other second-generation machines performed multiple jobs, which *reduced* the number of machines needed. The net result of these changes in the division of tasks among the machines was that Blanchard's fourteen machines for half-stocking were superseded by only fifteen or sixteen for whole-stocking.[38] These terms of "half" and "whole" should not be taken

FIGURE 5.3b. Breech area of barrel and stock, showing the excavation for the breech plug and its tang at the end of the barrel groove. (M1816 Springfield flintlock musket made in 1834, later converted to percussion, Springfield Armory Museum. Photograph by R. B. Gordon.)

FIGURE 5.4a. Butt plate machine. To prepare the butt for its plate with this machine, [#7] in table 5.1, the operator used levers (K) to bring the two vertical-spindle cutters successively to bear on the stock to cut the tang recess and the tang screw hole, their depth and shape controlled by the corresponding tracer pins' motions in pattern shown below the cutter on left. With a horizontal-spindle drill (not easily visible), controlled by a guide pin and hole in the model butt, he cut one or two hole(s) in the end for screw(s), and cut internal thread(s) with a horizontal-spindle tapping tool. At Springfield Armory these operations required less than half a minute to complete. (From *The Engineer* 7 [April 15, 1859]: 258.)

literally; as is discussed below, considerable amounts of work remained to be done by hand in both production systems.

Some questions must arise about the accuracy of inferring Blanchard's 1820s production line from the descriptions of the 1850s production line. Can we distinguish Blanchard's designs from those of Cyrus Buckland at Springfield or of James Burton at Enfield? How much from the second-generation machines can we safely "read back" into the first generation? We must of course grant to common knowledge in Blanchard's day the saws for slabbing and drills for drilling. If we further concede to Blanchard's successors at Springfield and Enfield an improved arrangement and design of the second-generation machines, we can still at a minimum ascribe three main types of machine to Blanchard's original production line. These are (1) the irregular turning lathe, with its traversing horizontal-spindle rotary cutter and dummy "friction" wheel to copy the exterior

FIGURE 5.4b. Butt (or "breech" or "heel") of musket and its plate. Depending on the model of gun, the butt and its butt plate are more or less shaped to fit the shooter's shoulder. Military muskets in Blanchard's era had flat butts. The butt plate's right-angle tang fits into a recess on the top of the stock. In this model, one screw through the tang and another through the butt end hold the butt plate to the stock. (M1816 Springfield musket made in 1834, Springfield Armory Museum. Photograph by Robert B. Gordon.)

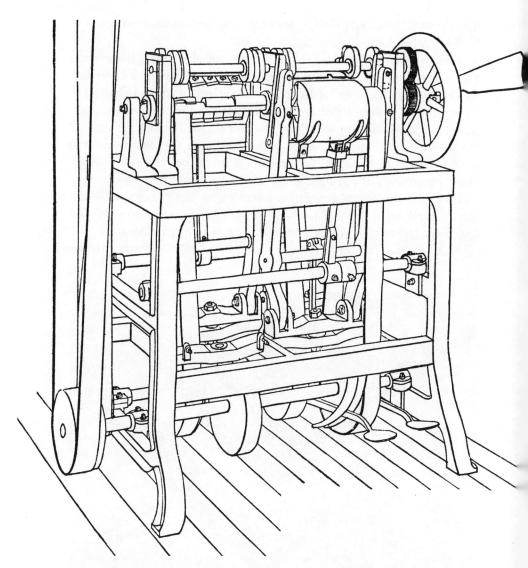

FIGURE 5.5a. Machine for smoothing stock between barrel bands. In this "second generation" machine, [#9] in table 5.1, four large cutting cylinders or heads, each as wide as an area between the barrel bands on the fore-end of the stock, shaped and planed the wood between the bands. (Only two cutting heads are indicated here, facing opposite sides of the machine.) The operator inserted the fore-end, barrel-side down, through the center of a chuck, which he turned by handwheel (at right). By operating the pedals he brought the four powered cutting heads to bear, two at a time, against the wood on either side. Tracers rubbing over pattern cams that rotated in unison with the stock controlled the depth of cutting, as the operator turned the stock part-way around in either direction by the hand

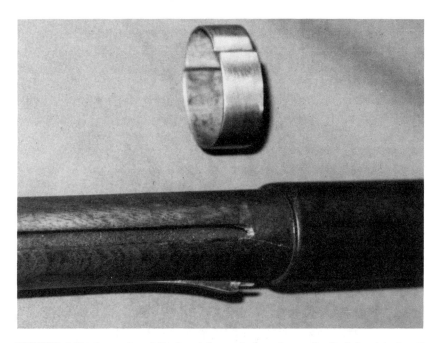

FIGURE 5.5b. Lower barrel band and fore-end of musket stock. Each band had to fit against a shoulder along the tapered fore-end. Also shown are a bandspring and beginning of the ramrod groove, which becomes a closed hole in the thicker part of the stock. (M1855 Springfield rifle-musket, Springfield Armory Museum. Photograph by R. B. Gordon.)

of a solid form; (2) the variant lathes for barrel-band bedding and turning the fore-end between bands, in which the cutter edge is wide enough so that it does not need to traverse; and 3) the recess-inletting machines, in which a rotary cutting tool at the tip of a vertical spindle cuts out a recess whose shape is determined by a connected similar "dummy" spindle tracing the area and depth of a recess in a metal pattern.

Of these three, it is the irregular turning lathe (figures 5.2 and 5.8) that was patented and has received the most recognition. As mentioned above, however, Blanchard already included the recess-inletting machine in his offering to Roswell Lee in 1819, "a machine I have recently invented for turning gunstocks and cuting in the locks and mounting."[39]

wheel. Thus the cams determined the cross section of the fore-end. This operation required less than thirty seconds. (From Charles H. Fitch, "Report on the Manufactures of Interchangeable Mechanism," p. 632.)

FIGURE 5.6a. Lock bedding machine. In this machine, [#12] in table 5.1, five vertical-spindle rotary cutters of varied sizes, carried in a rotating carousel frame, successively cut the various levels and shapes for the lock bed into the side of the stock. The operator used each of five handles to bring each cutter to bear on the lock area, which had been planed flat. Each cutter was connected with a matching guide pin, which could be moved around at a certain level of the steel pattern (D). By using lever (B) to move the gunstock forward and back and each handle to move the cutter and guide pin side to side and up and down, the operator could copy all contours of the pattern with the successively smaller cutter bits. A fan (not visible) forced air through the curved pipes onto the lock area to blow away the chips. The total time for all five operations was less than one minute. (From *The Engineer* 7 [April 29, 1859]: 294.)

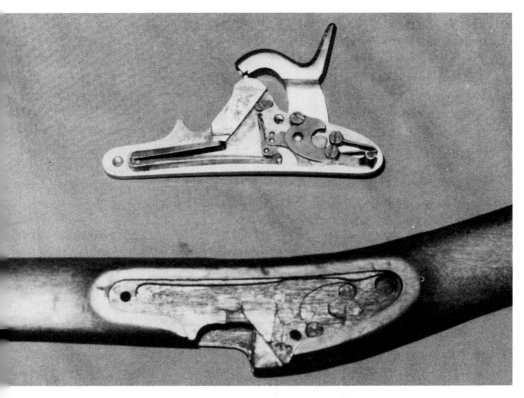

FIGURE 5.6b. Lock and lock bed. The lock mechanism for making the hammer strike a percussion cap in the 1850s (shown here) was virtually the same as that for the cock of a flintlock musket in the 1820s. When assembled, the parts of the lock form an irregular three-dimensional solid that needs a corresponding irregular cavity in the gunstock. To keep from weakening the stock, the lock bed should be just big enough to allow the lock parts to move during firing. The lock plate fits in the shallowest cut; the other parts of the lock fit into the deeper recesses of the lock bed. (M1855 Springfield rifle-musket, Springfield Armory Museum. Photograph by R. B. Gordon.)

FIGURE 5.7a. Guard bedding machine. At Springfield and Enfield Armories in the 1850s, the gunstock went from the lock bedding machine to a similar guard bedding machine, [#13] in table 5.1, which drilled the screw holes and cut out the recesses in the stock for the trigger guard, the trigger, and the ramrod stop at the end of the ramrod hole. Its carousel tool holder carried four vertical-spindle cutters with corresponding guide pins that the operator moved around in a steel form (not visible here). He brought each cutter

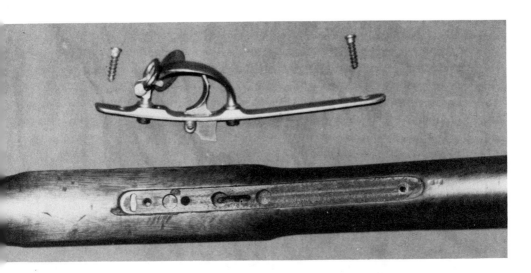

FIGURE 5.7b. Trigger assembly and its bed in the stock. When the trigger of a "cocked" musket is pulled, it pivots within its narrow slot in the stock, crosses into the deepest recess of the lock chamber, overcomes the resistance of the sear spring, and dislodges the sear from the notch of the tumbler. This releases the mainspring of the lock mechanism to fire the gun. For smooth action, the trigger needs an accurately cut slot; for safety it needs a well-placed guard. (M1855 Springfield rifle-musket, Springfield Armory Museum. Photograph by R. B. Gordon.)

By 1828 Blanchard had six machines in his production line that can be identified as inletting machines: those for "boring for the barrel" (#4), "milling the bed for the breech of the barrel and breech-pin" (#5), "cutting the bed for the tang of the breech-plate" (#6), "cutting for the tang of the breech-pin" (#9), "forming the bed for the lock-plate" (#12) and "forming the bed for the interior of the lock" (#13). In the second generation these machines were combined into various multioperation machines (figures 5.3b, 5.4b, 5.6b) that all used vertical-spindle cutting tools and dummy spindles for copying the shape of a metal pattern recess. Hence we can infer that the original 1820s counterparts also did so. The 1850s machines for bedding the trigger guard, ramrod, and bandsprings,

into position with a lever; with the crank shown he could tilt the stock while the cutter was operating. Air pipes communicating with the fan (E) blew away chips. Bedding for the guard required less than one minute. Blanchard did not make a machine for this purpose; it was in the "other half" of gunstocking. Cyrus Buckland presumably devised this "second-generation" machine. (From *The Engineer* 7 [April 29, 1859]: 295).

FIGURE 5.8. Second-generation Blanchard gunstock lathe. In this machine the cutting and tracing wheels (C) and (G), pivoting on the shaft beneath the bench, perform the "irregular" motion, while the model and gunstock traverse as they slowly rotate. At Springfield in the 1850s two such machines, [#10] and [#11] in table 5.1, were used for "finish-turning" the stock; at Enfield this type did the "first-turning" as well. As with all Blanchard lathes, the secret of its success is that the cutter rotates very rapidly while the model and workpiece rotate slowly. It "second-turned" a stock from butt to lock in 8 to 9 minutes or from lock to the first band in 5 to 6 minutes. (From *The Engineer* 7 [May 20, 1859]: 348.)

which were not included in the 1828 list, operated on the same principle (see figures 5.5a and b and 5.7b).

Blanchard left this feature of inletting by vertical-spindle cutters out of his patent. It bears a family resemblance to that feature of the earlier coaking machines at the Portsmouth block mill (c. 1805). It also, by inversion, so to speak, bears a family resemblance to James Watt's pre-1819 sculpture-copying machines, and to other carving machines of the mid-nineteenth century. These resemblances are discussed in chapters 6 and 7.

The machines that were non-traversing versions of the Blanchard

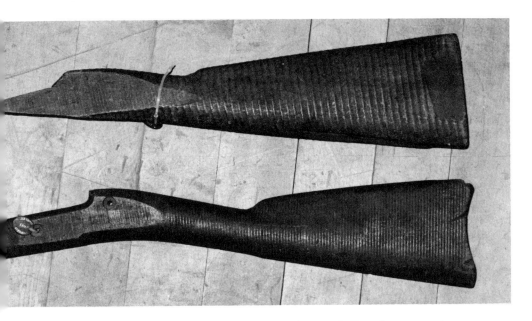

FIGURE 5.9. "First turning" and "second turning" of gunstock. By a slower traversing motion of the cutting wheel and the workpiece relative to each other, one could "finish turn" (see lower) an already "turned" (see upper) stock, lessening the need for further handwork. (Musket butts for 1842 model musket, Springfield Armory Museum. Photograph by Robert B. Gordon.)

lathe, for cutting the areas of the fore-end for the barrel bands and between them (figure 5.5c) were different in several respects from the patented lathe, and not self-acting. But into their second generation they seem to have been regarded as covered by Blanchard's (extended) patent, for they and the usual Blanchard lathes were the only pieces of the Ames Company machinery for which the English Ordnance Department had to pay patent fees in the 1850s.[40] They bore a distant resemblance to the earlier scoring machine at the Portsmouth block mill, and a closer resemblance to some of Blanchard's blockmaking machines, described in chapter 6.

## SKILL REQUIREMENTS

The concept of work skills is by no means unambiguous.[41] In two senses, however, Blanchard's machinery did not eliminate the use of skilled labor in making gun stocks. Firstly, it left undone "half" of the traditional hand-tool tasks of stocking, some of which required great skill, such as the boring of the long straight hole for the ramrod, a task that remained unmechanized until 1860. In the other sense, the operation of Blanchard machinery was not itself a totally "deskilled" task, for it usually required hand and eye coordination, dexterity, and judgment on the part of the operator. Only the irregular turning lathe was self-acting in the sense that its operator needed only to load and unload the machine. That operator ran the slabbing machine (#2) simultaneously, so his task was increased in complexity beyond the demands of the lathe alone.

Both of the other types of machine Blanchard designed for his production line were more demanding. The machine (#11) for bedding the barrel bands and smoothing the space between them required the operator to control by hand the rotation of the model and stock so as to prevent splintering when cutting against the grain, and to bring other cutters into play by foot action when one operation was completed. All of the vertical-spindle machines required the operator, during operation, to manipulate at least one, and frequently two at once, hand levers and crank handles during operation, to move a tracer pin around within a hollow pattern while the corresponding cutter cut the proper shape into the wood. To perform such actions well and quickly required a worker to develop skills other than those of a traditional gun stocker using hand tools, but skills nevertheless.

## TIMING AND PRODUCTIVITY

How long did it take to make a gunstock in Blanchard's production line, and how much was the productivity of the gunstockers improved with his machines over their previous methods? Blanchard gave a partial (and hardly impartial) answer to these questions in his petition to Congress in 1833 for an extension of the patent for his lathe:

> By this machine the government have been enabled to turn from the Block one hundred and fifty gunstocks complete in a day by the labour of one man whereas before the use of your petitioner's improvement the same work could not be done by less than one hundred men in the same time.[42]

In the same petition, Blanchard said gunstock turning in his machine was "an operation of a few minutes." Assuming he was tending one gunstocking lathe for a ten-hour average day, the "one man" to whom Blanchard referred would have to complete a gunstock every 4 minutes to produce

150 in a day. This agrees fairly well with the 4 to 4 1/2 minutes for "rough turning" that Whitworth and Anderson observed at Springfield twenty years later.[43] Blanchard's very first full-size stocking lathe at Harpers Ferry in 1819 took twice as long—9 minutes—to turn a stock,[44] either simply because it was slower or because it was taking a finer cut than did the Springfield lathe.

But these remarks concern the output of the Blanchard lathe alone, rather than the whole set of machinery and hand operations for making the gunstock really "complete." As Blanchard fully recognized, in order "that his invention may be useful to the extent above described it was essential that divers pieces of machinery should be constructed and put in operation in connexion with said turning machine."[45] Table 5.1 shows the times for operations by the gunstocking machines observed by Commissioners Anderson and Whitworth at Springfield Armory in the 1850s that correspond to the gunstocking production line listed in early 1828. It also indicates which machines in the earlier production line performed the same functions.

From the machine operation times in this table one can guess only approximately what the times of operation were for the earlier machines. Such guesses must be modified by recognition that some machines of the 1850s production line combined functions of two or three of the 1820s machines, as well as a general presumption that the Springfield machines of the 1850s were improved in performance over those of the 1820s.[46] For instance, the 1850s lock-bedding machine took less than one minute, while the machine that Blanchard mentioned to Lee in 1819 had taken a minute and a half.[47]

It looks as if Blanchard had apportioned the tasks of the other machines so that none of their operations took longer than did the lathe itself. In the 1850s, however, the Commissioners were troubled that the Blanchard lathes took so much longer than the other machines in the line. Smooth-turning lathes took even longer (5 to 6 minutes and 8 to 9 minutes) than did the rough-turning lathe (4 to 4 1/2 minutes). So after consulting Mr. Buckland and Mr. Burton, they ordered extra numbers of these machines for Enfield, in order "to keep a flow of work through . . . the plant . . . and . . . more than treble its yield."[48] They were seemingly untroubled, however, by the remaining unmechanized work on the gunstocks, which, as we shall see, was the major production bottleneck in both the 1820s and 1850s.

After Blanchard's machines were installed in the 1820s, the piece rate that the stockers on Armory Hill received for gunstocking dropped to 50 cents per stock, for now they were only completing "the other half" of the job. The operators of the "half-stocking" machines were paid piece rates for their various operations, too. Added up, the stocking piece rates came to a total labor cost slightly over 69 cents per stock in 1835.[49] After piece rates rose sharply between 1835 and 1837, this total was 89.5 cents per stock, which was actually a little higher than the cost before Blanchard began his half-stocking contract in 1823.

Some evidence suggests that there was attrition of the gunstocking machines after Blanchard left the armory, in which case the hand stockers would have had more to do than while he was still there with a full component of machines. Of the fourteen listed in 1828, machines (#1), (#7), (#9), and (#12) are missing from the identifiable gunstocking machines listed in the Springfield Armory inventory of 1834. The ten remaining range in value from $25.00 for the "machine for cutting stocks for upper bands" (#10) to $300.00 for the "machine for fitting on bands" (#11).[50] Their values totaled $1,425. The same ten were depreciated 3 percent and valued at $1,377.40 in 1838 and 1839. But in 1840 new stocking machines began appearing in the annual inventory; by 1842 there were sixteen. All but one of the "same" ten machines were valued substantially higher than in 1838; three of the obviously "new" machines had *very* much higher values in the hundreds of dollars each.[51] Retooling was clearly under way, and the stocking machines' value now totaled $4,950.50.[52]

After reorganization of work at the Armory and a replacement and augmentation of Blanchard's machines by the second-generation stocking machines, the labor cost per stock went down to 60 cents in 1843 and to 42 cents by mid-year of 1854, when the second group of English Commissioners visited the Armory.[53] These reductions in labor cost, thirty years in coming, reflect, of course, a reduction in the time needed to make a gunstock.

By Commissioner Joseph Whitworth's timing at Springfield in 1853, the total time of the machine operations for one gunstock was 28 minutes, 45 1/4 seconds, and of hand operations, 2 minutes, 17 seconds. After adding these together and subtracting 8 minutes and 58 seconds for "double simultaneous operations during turning," Whitworth concluded that a "Man's time given to the whole operations of making a complete musket-stock" was 22 minutes and 4 1/4 seconds.[54] A year later, Commissioner John Anderson similarly timed the machine operations totaling

29 minutes, 58 1/2 seconds, which is not far different from Whitworth's timing before taking simultaneous operations into account. But Whitworth had ignored about an hour of handwork that Anderson observed at Springfield, including "boring for the ramrod, filing off the sharp edges, and a general smoothing."[55] This is a 2:1 ratio of hand to machine work, compared to Whitworth's report of approximately 1:10.

A machine was devised by 1860 for boring the closed part of the channel for the ramrod, but the finishing operations resisted mechanization until a much later generation of stocking machinery. Decades later, Charles Fitch estimated that the amount of handwork necessary even in his day, the 1880s, still outweighed machine work by a ratio of 5:3. After recounting thirty machine operations, Fitch says "finishing with hand shaves, scrapers, and sandpaper, and oiling with linseed oil . . . require about five-eighths of the labor on the stock, all the varied and curious cuts made by machinery requiring only three-eighths."[56] Elsewhere in his report, Fitch says:

> The machining of stocks can now be done on a large scale at the rate of 28 per operative per day, and all the work, including shaving and sand-papering, which constitute the major part of it, at 10 per operative per day.[57]

That is to say, handwork persisting in 1883 was cutting down the daily output sharply, from 28 to 10 per operator.

Fitch also mentioned gunstocking productivity improvement that had been due to Blanchard's machinery:

> Before the introduction of Blanchard's machinery one skilled man was capable of making 1 or 2 stocks in a day, much of the work being in the fitting of the metal parts. With his earlier and ruder machines an output of 5 or 6 stocks per operative per day seems to have been attained at an early date.[58]

Expressing the same idea somewhat differently, Fitch estimated that the "early results" of Blanchard's machines enabled ten machine workers and seven hand workers to stock 100 muskets a day, where it had formerly required seventy-five hand workers to stock 100 muskets a day.[59] Either way, Fitch's figures imply that Blanchard's own "early" machines brought about a spectacular—approximately fourfold—increase of output per stocker. In making his estimate, Fitch used "data furnished by Mr. A. H. Waters," Blanchard's biographer. The Waters family armory had resumed contract production of military long arms in the Civil War, after a hiatus since 1845, and employed 200 workers during the war, but only in making rods and bayonets, not whole guns.[60]

It is difficult, at this late date, to guess how Fitch derived this estimate, which assumes, abstractly, production on a much larger scale than in fact existed in any single gun factory from the time when Blanchard's early machines were set up in the 1820s until they were replaced by Buckland's second-generation machinery in the 1840s. A rate of 100 a day implies a production of 30,000 guns in a year, but neither of the national armories at Springfield and Harpers Ferry reached that annual output before the Civil War, and the contract armories were smaller.[61]

Most of what has been written since 1883 about nineteenth-century armsmaking has relied on Fitch for information that has seemed unavailable otherwise. Fortunately, however, the Springfield Armory records that have survived include both monthly payrolls for the whole armory and work returns from the individual workshops at Springfield for the period of interest here. Analysis of the actual output of the gunstock hand-workers on Armory Hill plus the gunstocking machine operators at the lower water shop gives quite a different picture from Fitch's estimate.

Graph 5.1 shows the outcome of such an analysis: the average monthly output per gunstock worker at Springfield Armory 1817–40, calculated from a sample of one or two months for each year. It shows that the productivity increases for gunstocking with the benefit of Blanchard's machines, even in their second decade, after a generous breaking-in period, were definite, but never even approached a fourfold increase over the the pre-Blanchard level. For instance, the high point shown in this graph, representing an average per-worker monthly output of nearly 59 guns stocked in January and May 1834, is more than twice the low point of less than 27 guns stocked in those months in 1820. The more usual average output levels of about 39 guns per workman in 1836–38, however, represent an increase of only 47 percent, a little less than half, over the level in 1820.

Thus, a person could do each of several gunstocking operations very much faster with one of Blanchard's machines than by hand tools. But the overall output of the stockers with Blanchard's own machinery was only modestly improved. This is primarily explicable by the persistence of the handwork necessary to complete the job, as mentioned earlier. "The other half" of stocking that Blanchard's first-generation machines did not do was mechanized to a large extent by the second-generation machines by 1860 but the remaining handwork involved in the payroll's catchall term "completing" stocks still required a large proportion of the stocking workforce.

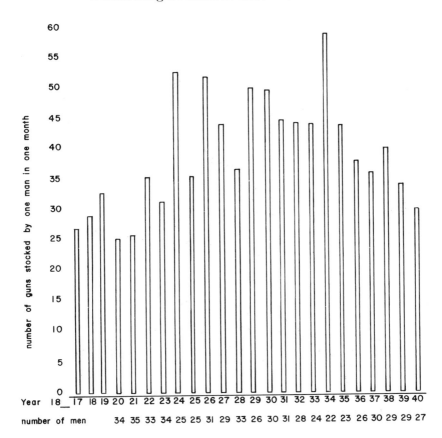

GRAPH 5.1. Average monthly output per gunstock worker at Springfield Armory 1817–40. Bars represent averages of January and May outputs, except for 1817 (February only), 1818 (April only), 1819 (January only), 1825 (January and July), and 1840 (January only). In addition to hand stockers, number of men includes stocking machine operators: six in 1829 and seven or eight thereafter; guessed as two in 1821, four from 1824 through 1826, five in 1827–28. (Work returns for stocking and lower water shops, Springfield Armory Records, National Archives.)

The Civil War closed the Harpers Ferry Armory and greatly expanded the workforce of the Springfield Armory. For the first time there was a scale of operation commensurate with Fitch's assumptions, that is, over a hundred gunstocks a day. The number of workers engaged in gunstocking there had shrunk from its pre-Blanchard tally of 35 to only 15 by July 1853, but ballooned to 180 in 1864, a more than tenfold increase.[62] But the Armory was producing sixteen times as many guns as in 1853, so the per-worker productivity had gone up, at a rough estimate, from almost four a day in 1853 to over five gunstocks a day in 1864.[63] Over half of the gunstockers in 1853, and at least three-fifths of them in 1864, were doing handwork, so the machines—even in the second generation —had clearly not eliminated handworkers.[64] But over the decades since 1820 the two generations of gunstocking machines machines, together with division of labor and other kinds of production rationalization, had made possible this immense expansion of scale in a wartime emergency.

## BLANCHARD'S REWARDS FROM MILITARY GUNSTOCKING

Since Blanchard's rate of payment from the National Armories was explicitly tied to the savings his machines produced, calculation of his rewards and the government's savings are intertwined. To answer either question is not simple. As mentioned above, Blanchard's initial royalty fee for the gunstocking lathe alone was 2 cents per stock turned, while the Springfield Armory paid 10 cents less to those stockers who used them, thus garnering 8 cents' savings. After about three years on that basis, Blanchard became inside contractor from mid-1823 through 1827, and was paid 37, then 32 cents per musket half-stocked by his machines, grossing somewhat over $18,500 for the whole period, from which he paid an unknown amount in wages to the four or five operators of his machines. After his years as inside contractor, he negotiated a royalty fee of 9 cents to be paid per musket produced in the national armories during his patent period. (This was in recognition of all fourteen machines for half-stocking, only one of which was patented.) If we were to assume he was indeed eventually paid royalties at 9 cents per gun for the years 1828 through 1833, we could derive, from the output of the national armories for those years, a total of $13,967, or an average of $2,328 annually, but that may well be a false assumption.[65] After his patent was renewed Blanchard attempted to collect royalties of 6 cents per musket from the United States for his second patent term of 1834–1848 and actually obtained a contract to that effect from the United States in October 1837,[66] but he met opposition in the government, and settled in 1839 for payment, as had supposedly been the basis of his original agreement with the War Department in 1828, of "one-half the clear . . . savings to the U.S. from the use of my improvements during the full period of 14 years," that is, his first patent term. The shortfall between what he should have received from the War Deparment and had actually received was calculated to be $6,653.44, which he was paid in July 1839, whereupon Blanchard declared the account settled.[67]

## THE MILITARY'S SAVINGS FROM BLANCHARD'S GUNSTOCKING

We may well ask, what *were* "the clear savings to the U.S." from Blanchard's gunstocking machines? Recent scholarship on the "armory system" of manufactures argues that the cost-savings rationale for new machinery that the Ordnance Department habitually used in appealing to Congress for appropriations was probably not justified by economic reality, and that the military's enthusiasm for achieving interchangeability through mechanization was an expensive luxury.[68] If so, was this true of the Blanchard stocking machinery? Did the military perhaps *lose* money by supporting Blanchard's "research and development" of this new technology? Unfortunately, to answer this question even in its narrowest sense at all accurately calls for information that is not available, and what is available is of dubious validity. The records of the national armories, although compulsively detailed on some topics, are sketchy or nonexistent on such topics as amortization of capital equipment. To judge whether Blanchard's machines saved or lost the armories money, one should balance the saving on the cost of labor, for which records do exist, as discussed earlier, against the expense of the machines themselves and the extra structures and power needed to use them. Since both national armories ran on waterpower, this calculation would require an estimate of the share of the flumes, waterwheels, and so forth that would be required by the gunstocking machines.

When Edward Lucas, the superintendent of Harpers Ferry Armory, was asked in 1839 to supply information of this sort, presumably in order to derive the amount Blanchard should be paid, he pointed out that such calculation "is after all mere guesswork." He nevertheless guessed that "The whole Waterpower of the Musket Factory must be worth something like one hundred and fifty thousand Dollars—And the Stocking operations require about one-tenth part, equal to Fifteen Thousand Dollars." He went on to report that the labor cost of stocking a musket at Harpers Ferry had gone down 28 cents, from $1.25 "previous to the use of Blanchard's machinery," to 97 cents. He estimated "without looking at the annual reports" that the annual output of muskets at Harpers Ferry had averaged eight to ten thousand, and stated that "the loss of stocks by the use of [Blanchard's] Machinery, over that of stocking by hand" was "Nothing."[69]

Lucas was not asked the cost of the machines themselves, but from other sources we may estimate Blanchard's machines at Harpers Ferry to have cost about $1,850.[70] Then, by multiplying the 209,820 muskets produced at Harpers Ferry 1820–39 by 28 cents saved per musket and subtracting $16,850 for the cost of the machines and waterpower, we could derive, very roughly indeed, a "savings" of $41,899 at Harpers Ferry by Blanchard's machines, or an average of 20 cents per musket produced in that time period.[71] Then, if we were still courageous (or foolhardy) enough, we might overcome our ignorance of waterpower costs at Springfield by assuming them to be the same as Lucas said they were at Harpers Ferry, and run through the same calculation for Springfield Armory.[72] This would give us a net savings of $47,340 or 16.7 cents per musket at Springfield, and a total of $89,239, or 18 cents per musket, for savings to the United States due to Blanchard's half-stocking machines 1820–39 at both armories.[73] From this we should of course finally subtract the unknown total amount that Blanchard collected from the United States between 1820 and their final settlement of accounts on July 18, 1839. If he was allowed on average 6 cents apiece for the muskets produced 1820–33, his total would be $21,361. If he was allowed, as Edward Lucas grudgingly recommended, only 3 cents per musket, Blanchard's total would be $10,680.[74] If he was allowed as much as 9 cents each musket, his total would be $32,042. Thus, by these very "iffy" calculations, we might guess that *after* paying Blanchard for his machines and their invention, the United States saved something between $57,197 (11.6 cents per musket) and $78,559 (15.9 cents per musket) during the time his own machines were in use at the national armories, before they were replaced in the 1840s by gunstocking machinery of the "second generation." Even by alternative calculations on less favorable assumptions, the armories did not lose money on Blanchard and his machines[75] By modest rather than spectacular productivity improvement, then, we can guess they had more than "paid for themselves." In the larger sense of their supplying the immediate model for the second generation gunstocking machines and less directly for other machinery and production systems at the armories, it seems even clearer that Roswell Lee's desire to "bring [Blanchard's] machinery to the most perfect state" had been an act of good long-term management, not an indulgence in government-subsidized "luxury."

## OBSOLESCENCE AND LONGEVITY

Superintendent Lucas remarked of Harpers Ferry in mid-1839 that "The Machines in use at this Armory have been considerably improved by the workmen, since they were first introduced by Mr. B. and I presume it is the same case at Springfield." As the inventories of Springfield Armory in the late 1830s suggest, Blanchard's own machines, with the exception of the lathe that was still working in the 1850s and is extant today, were indeed on the way out. By contrast, the Portsmouth blockmaking machines built in the first decade of the 1800s were unchanged and in full operation after a century, and in some few cases still used at the dockyard in the 1980s. The forty-five or so Portsmouth machines cost over £12,000 and were built to last; Blanchard's machines for both armories probably cost less than $3,500, and confirm the generalization that American machinery of that era was built for a relatively short useful life before becoming obsolete.

## THE ENGLISH PERSPECTIVE

Concerning the Blanchard lathe, Parliamentary Commissioner John Anderson wrote in his 1855 report, "It is most remarkable that this valuable labour-saving machine should have been so much neglected in England, seeing that it is capable of being applied to many branches of manufacture."[76] English neglect of Blanchard's invention was not from lack of early communication. In 1822 an English patent was taken out by one John William Buckle of Mark Lane in London for "Machinery for Shaping or Cutting Wood, etc," (Great Britain Patent #4652, March 2, 1822). Buckle did not claim it was *his* invention; it had been "made [over] to" or "communicated to" him by one John Parker Boyd of Boston, Massachusetts. It was a direct copy of the Blanchard lathe, although Blanchard's name was omitted and the specification was worded differently from that in either of Blanchard's versions of his patent. Buckle's patent was described in *The London Journal of Arts and Sciences* at the time, and its expiration was duly announced fourteen years later.[77] During hearings conducted by a Parliamentary Committee in the mid-1850s on the question of small arms manufacture, a witness testified that a model irregular turning lathe *had* been demonstrated in London and Birmingham about twenty years earlier, and that a Birmingham arms manufacturer—"a very extensive one"—had actually tried briefly to use a Blanchard lathe but had found it uneconomical.[78]

There are many possible explanations for lack of interest in the Blanchard lathe when it appeared briefly in England in the 1820s or 1830s. The usual economic explanation is that hand labor was so cheap in England, relative to the United States, that there was insufficient reason to adopt labor-saving devices.[79] With regard to gunstocking, Russell Fries has pointed out that the Birmingham gun trade was so decentralized in organization that no single private manufacturer would profit by investing in machinery for large-scale operation.[80] Another school of opinion blamed labor opposition: one visitor reported in 1849 that "Stocking machines have been made and put up in Birmingham, but the stockers have always prevented their use."[81] Regarding its general application, Nathan Rosenberg has suggested that the Blanchard lathe was among those American machines that were wasteful of wood in their early forms and therefore would have little appeal in England, where wood was so much more expensive.[82]

Yet thirty years later, the Blanchard lathe was especially prized among the machinery that the English ordered for their new Armory in Enfield. The economic, technical, and social reasons for the Blanchard lathe's initial rejection and later adoption in England are complex and beyond the scope of thorough discussion here. For gunstocking, however, one important reason for the difference in its appeal at the two times is that in the 1820s it appeared in England in isolation, and in the 1850s it was accompanied by the rest of the second-generation production line, on which its success at the Springfield Armory had depended. Furthermore, that success was real, but neither so soon nor so spectacular as contemporary puffery and subsequent historians have said it was.[83] It took those thirty years of experience and reworking of the machinery in its second generation to prove that it could indeed produce more than modest economy as well as uniformity in gunstocking.

## SYSTEM THINKING FOR PRODUCTION LINES

In his design of individual gunstocking machines, Thomas Blanchard was acting as a mechanical engineer; in coordinating them in his "half-stocking" production line, he acted as an industrial engineer, concerned with the machines as an overall system.[84] For maximum output in a given time, the smooth "flow" of the workpiece from machine to machine was of concern in such a production system, as was the sequence and timing of individual machine operations.[85] His early fame rested in large part not only on his ingenious invention of the irregular turning lathe, but also on his contribution of "system" to the American system of manufactures.[86] But having learned "system thinking" for producing gunstocks, Blanchard himself afterward applied it only to the manufacture of marine pulley-blocks and deadeyes, for which the Portsmouth machinery in England had already demonstrated the benefits of such systematization.

*APPENDIX*

A

# BLANCHARD'S PRODUCTION LINE FOR HALF-STOCKING MUSKETS

(Machines are numbered as in table 5.1, p. 95)

## Shaping the Stock

The black walnut gunstock blanks delivered to the Armory were thick planks cut roughly to the outline of a stock. Blanchard's first machine, which sawed the blank "to its proper length" (#1), is not described among the second-generation machinery. From it the blank went to a machine for "facing stock and sawing it lengthwise" (#2), which probably had, like the second-generation "slabbing machine" [#1], a circular saw that made two cross cuts and six lengthwise cuts to remove excess bulk from the fore-end of the stock, where the barrel was to rest, before it was shaped by later machines in the production line.[1] This slabbing machine for the fore-end was a "provider"[2] to the self-acting Blanchard lathe (3), in which the exterior contours of the rest of the stock were shaped. This means one man tended both machines at once, and completed both operations within 4 1/2 minutes.[3]

As mentioned in chapter 5, the Blanchard lathe for rough-turning—machine [#2]—that the English Commissioners saw at the Springfield Armory in 1853 and 1854 was the same old wooden-framed one (#3) with a "hanging lathe" that had been in operation for thirty years (see figure 5.2.) It turned the stock to shape from the butt to the beginning of the fore-end. Meanwhile, in 1843 Blanchard had patented an improved "rocking lathe" with a "back and under rest" feature that was useful for turning long thin objects. (See chapter 7 for a description of this improvement.) Blanchard wrote: "I never could . . . turn the whole length of the stock . . . until I made the . . . improvement of the back rest, which keeps the stock from springing."[4] In 1842 Blanchard was selling stocking lathes of his improved "rocking" type that were capable of turning whole gunstocks twice— rough and smooth—in the same machine.[5] For Enfield Armory, the English Commissioners bought Blanchard lathes of the "rocking lathe" type; nevertheless, each turned about half of the stock instead of the whole stock, presumably for the sake of production line "flow."

## Bedding the Barrel

After its thick end was shaped in the Blanchard lathe, the gunstock went to the machine for "boring for the barrel" (#4), which had a vertical-spindle cutter whose path was guided by a tracer moved along a slightly tapered model groove or "form." At the breech end of the barrel, the groove in the stock had to open into a larger cavity with straighter sides, to receive the "flats and ovals" of the

*125*

barrel breech and the end of the breech pin, or, in usual modern parlance, the breech plug. The tang of the breech plug also needed a shallow bed on top of the stock. Together with (#4), Blanchard's separate machines for "milling the bed for the breech of the barrel and breech-pin" (#5) and for "cutting for the tang of the breech-pin" (#9), were combined in the second-generation production line into one machine [#4], "for bedding the barrel and cutting out the space for the breech-pin."[6] This machine featured a row of vertical- spindle cutters, each coupled with a guide-pin by which the operator traced the interior of a steel pattern of the desired cavity in the gunstock: the slightly tapered groove in the fore-end for the barrel, the square bed for the breech end of the barrel, and the cavities for the end and tang of the breech plug[7] (see figures 5.3a and b). A barrel-bedding machine of this type is on exhibit at the American Precision Museum in Windsor, Vermont. Once the bed for the barrel was formed in the stock, it was used for positioning the stock correctly in several of the machines later in the production line: the stock fit onto a dummy barrel in those machines.

## BEDDING THE BUTT PLATE
In Blanchard's production line the gunstock next went to machine (#6), which cut out the bed for the tang of the butt plate (then called "breech" or "heel" plate), and to machine (#7), which bored holes for the butt-plate screws. These operations were performed by a single "butt-plate machine" [#7] in the second-generation production line.[8] In this machine vertical-spindle and horizontal-spindle cutters excavated a recess for the butt-plate tang and drilled and threaded two or three screw holes, depending on the model under production (see figures 5.4a and b).

## GAUGING FOR THE BARREL
Blanchard's machine (#8) for "gauging for the barrel" probably corresponded to the second-generation machine [#5] in which every stock was sawn, by circular saw, to precisely the same length and angle at the muzzle and butt ends.[9] His machine (#9) cut the shallow bed for the tang of the breech plug, and as we have seen, its function was combined in the second generation with two others in the barrel-bedding machine [#4].

## SHAPING THE FORE-END
### BEDDING THE BARREL BANDS
Blanchard's machine (#10) cut a depression or "concave" in the tip of the stock for the "uppermost" of the three barrel bands, as did part of machine [#8] in the second generation. Figure 5.5b shows the lower band. Machine (#11), for "dressing" the slim fore-end of the stock "for and between the [barrel] bands," was a variant of the Blanchard lathe, but operated somewhat differently. It had horizontal-spindle cutting wheels that did not move sideways, as in the Blanchard lathe, but were themselves as wide as the sections of the fore-end to be shaped. These

wheels or drums were fitted with plane irons and left a smooth surface. The operator of this machine slowly rotated the gunstock and the model by handwheel instead of by power. It was succeeded by two machines [#8] and [#9] in the second generation, one for bedding the bands themselves and one for the spaces between the bands, shown in figure 5.5a. In these machines, and by inference in Blanchard's machine (#11), the operator used foot pedals successively to bring the two pairs of cutters in contact with the work, and the corresponding tracers into contact with the iron cams shaped like cross sections of the stock fore-end, on one side and then on the other.[10]

### Bedding the lock

For "forming the bed for the lock plate" and for "forming the bed for the interior of the lock" (figure 5.6b), Blanchard's production line used two separate machines (#12) and (#13). But the production line of the 1850s combined these operations into one lock-bedding machine [#12] (figure 5.6a), which deployed a succession of five vertical-spindle cutters of different size, each following the action of a tracer pin that the operator moved around at different levels within a "steel copy of the recess." The cutters thus hollowed out a hole of different shapes at different depths in the stock, to accommodate the various irregularities of the lock mechanism. One such Ames Company lock-bedding machine survives at the Science Museum in London, another at the American Precision Museum in Windsor, Vermont.[11]

As mentioned above, Blanchard had told Roswell Lee in 1821 that he had devised "a method by which I can vary the jig and set it to every lock."[12] Charles Fitch wrote that Blanchard's original machine "for forming the bed of the lock-plate" used a pattern that was adaptable to varying shapes and sizes of lockplate. Its sides "were sprung inward toward a center, so that they would conform inside to any shape of lock-plate set in the interior . . . and thus every cut in wood was made by machinery to conform to the irregularities of the metal work." Thus, says Fitch, "Blanchard's ingenuity in making stocking machinery had outrun the facilities for making the metal parts [uniform]."[13] After 1840, when this compensatory ingenuity was presumably no longer needed at the Springfield Armory because the lock plates were by then sufficiently uniform, "the machinery was destroyed, and no official record remains of this curious invention, which was not in use at the private armories, where the lock-plates were at this time usually fitted in by hand."[14] The machines of the 1850s at Springfield and Enfield for bedding the lock and lock plate had nonadjustable patterns corresponding to the one and only shape and size of the interchangeable locks.[15]

### Boring holes for side and tang pins

Figure 5.1 shows two side pins above the side plate and the tang pin at the end of the breech plug. These threaded pins hold the working parts of the musket— barrel, lock, and trigger assembly—together on the stock, so their holes have to be drilled accurately, crosswise and vertically. In Blanchard's production line and in that of 1854, the final stocking machine (#14) and [#15] was "for boring side and tang-pin holes," that is, drilling for the side screws and the "breech-nail," or "tang pin of the breech plug."[16] It did so in less than half a minute. As in several of the other machines, the stock was clamped upside down over a dummy barrel that fit into its barrel groove, assuring accuracy of the stock's position relative to the cutting tools. The stock was repositioned between drilling the breech-nail and side-screw holes. No picture of the machine is available.

# 6

# THE
# BLOCKMAKING
# PRODUCTION LINE
# AT WINOOSKI
# FALLS

꙼꙼꙼꙼꙼

THE ten blockmaking machines for which Thomas Blanchard received
U.S. Patents #3–#9 and #17–#19 in August 1836 have been ignored
in history,[1] but they should be recognized as an early example of production line design. That is, they constitute a series of special-purpose machines for performing a sequence of operations to produce an object made
of uniform parts. As individual machines and as a production system,
therefore, they can be compared both with the blockmaking machinery
set up 1802–8 at Portsmouth Dockyard in England, and with Blanchard's gunstocking machinery of the 1820s at Springfield Armory. Those
production systems, however, grew out of military need, under the aegis
of the British Royal Navy and of the U.S. Army, respectively. By contrast, Blanchard's block mill design provides an early instance in which a
production line was developed for commercial purposes, under the aegis
of patent protection for the inventor's intellectual property.

## BLOCKS AND BLOCKMAKING
## BEFORE BLANCHARD

Pulley-blocks have been used for lifting or hauling heavy weights since
antiquity.[2] Until very recent times they were made primarily of wood.
Large numbers of pulley-blocks were needed on sailing ships, so blockmaking became a woodworking craft located near ports where ships were
outfitted. Many variations in shape and size of pulley-blocks evolved for
special purposes; some made by eighteenth-century English blockmakers
are shown in figure 6.1. Besides pulley-blocks for use in a ship's running
rigging, one-piece blocks called "deadeyes" were part of the ship's standing rigging. To shape the component parts of pulley-blocks, deadeyes,
and other items, blockmakers in the eighteenth and early nineteenth
centuries used hand tools and lathes, as shown in figure 6.2.

A pulley-block consists of a shell (also called "block") within which
one or more sheaves (or "pulleys") rotate, each within a chamber, or
mortise, on a central pin fastened through the shell (see figure 6.3). The
top or "head" end of a block's mortise is round for the passage of the rope
through it; the bottom or "arse" end is square. Around its periphery the

*131*

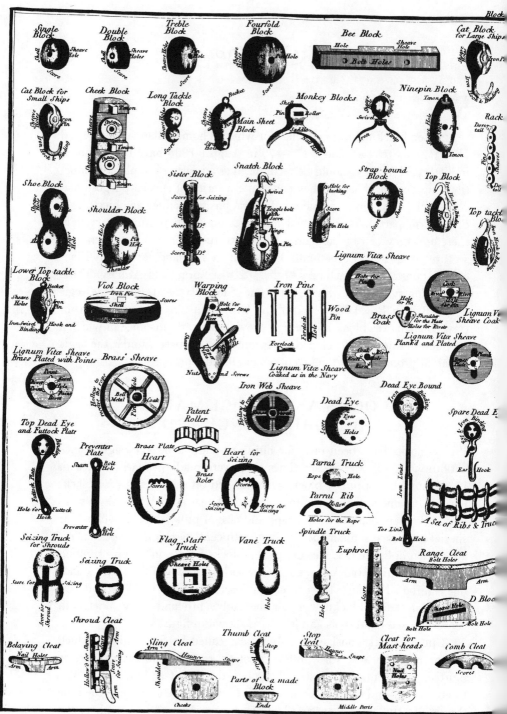

Single Block · Double Block · Treble Block · Fourfold Block · Bee Block · Cat Block for Large Ships
Cat Block for Small Ships · Cheek Block · Long Tackle Block · Main Sheet Block · Monkey Blocks · Ninepin Block · Rack
Shoe Block · Shoulder Block · Sister Block · Snatch Block · Strap-bound Block · Top Block · Top tackle Block
Lower Top-tackle Block · Viol Block · Warping Block · Iron Pins · Wood Pin · Lignum Vitæ Sheave · Brass Coak · Lignum Vitæ Sheave Coak
Lignum Vitæ Sheave Brass Plated with Points · Brass Sheave · Lignum Vitæ Sheave Coaked as in the Navy · Lignum Vitæ Sheave Plank'd and Plated
Top Dead Eye and Futtock Plate · Iron Web Sheave · Patent Roller · Dead Eye · Dead Eye Bound · Spare Dead Eye
Preventer Plate · Brass Plate · Heart · Heart for Seizing · Parral Truck · Parral Rib · Iron Links · A Set of Ribs & Trucks
Seizing Truck for Shrouds · Seizing Truck · Flag Staff Truck · Vane Truck · Spindle Truck · Euphroe · Range Cleat · D Block
Shroud Cleat · Belaying Cleat · Sling Cleat · Thumb Cleat · Stop Cleat · Cleat for Mast-heads · Comb Cleat · Parts of a made Block

132

sheave has a groove in which the rope (called "line") runs. In a wooden block, a groove or "score" of varying depth also ran lengthwise around the outside of the shell, to hold in place the rope (called "strap") by which the block was fastened in the ship's running rigging or elsewhere.

The shells were commonly made of ash or elm, and the sheaves of *lignum vitae,* a very hard tropical wood. The pins, also commonly made of *lignum vitae,* were more often made of iron from the late eighteenth century onward. By the end of the eighteenth century metal bushings (also called "coaks" or "bushes") were usually set into the pin holes of the sheaves in order to reduce friction on the pins. A pulley-block of the type used by the Royal Navy in the nineteenth century, as shown in figure 6.3, was cut from a solid block of wood and the coak in its sheave has a characteristic three-eared shape that was standard in British naval blocks. But there were other variants in the shape of the coaks set into sheaves; a few are shown in figure 6.1. An alternative to making the shell of a block from solid wood was to fasten separate side "cheeks," partitions, and end pieces together into so-called "made" blocks, as shown in figure 6.4 and also bottom of figure 6.1. Very large size blocks were thus "made" from planks; during the nineteenth century it became more common for smaller sizes also to be "made" or "plank" blocks.

For satisfactory performance, a pulley-block had to be reliably strong and its sheaves had to run freely on the pin. Free-running sheaves required sides exactly parallel to each other and to the sides of the mortises within which they turned, and exactly perpendicular to the pin on which they turned. To make a strong block of any given size it was important to maintain the prescribed proportions and dimensions of sheaves, shell, mortises, and pins, all of which were calculated relative to the thickness of the line to be reeved through the block. Accuracy in these matters was not easy to achieve using hand tools. In handmade blocks, according to one observer, the pin holes tended to be "so rough and so uneven . . . that the blocks and shivers often caught fire through the violence of the friction."[3]

FIGURE 6.1. *(opposite)* Variety in blockmakers' goods. In addition to pulley-blocks of many sorts, blockmakers made a great variety of other wooden fittings for sailing ships, including deadeyes (right of center). Note the iron and wooden pins (center), the different shapes of bushings or "coaks" in the sheaves (center right and left), and the parts for "made" blocks (bottom center). (From David Steel, "Blockmaking," in *The Elements and Practice of Rigging and Seamanship* [London, 1794], vol. 1. Judy Beisler photo, Mystic Seaport, Mystic, Connecticut.)

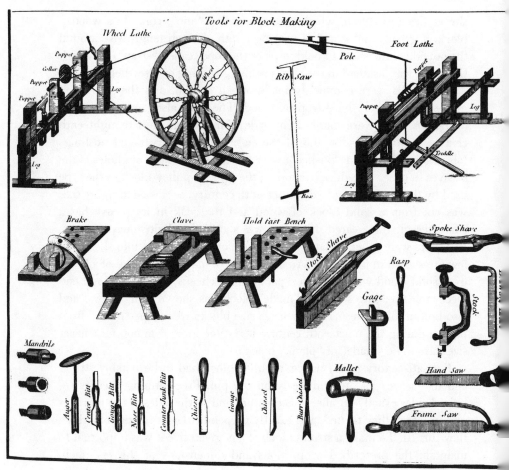

FIGURE 6.2. Hand tools for blockmaking, eighteenth century. Blockmakers shaped, bored, and mortised shells for blocks by using stock- and spoke-shaves, gouges, chisels, augers, saws, rasps, and drills as shown. Wheel and foot lathes helped them turn, bore, and groove the sheaves and wooden pins. They used the clave and brake to hold the shell and sheave, respectively, for working. (From David Steel, "Blockmaking," in *The Elements and Practice of Rigging and Seamanship* [London, 1794], vol. 1. Judy Beisler photo, Mystic Seaport, Mystic, Connecticut.)

Mechanization of blockmaking in England began in the 1760s under stimulus of contracts from the Royal Navy, and achieved a high point with the machines for blockmaking that were created by Marc Isambard Brunel, Samuel Bentham, and Henry Maudslay for the Portsmouth Naval Dockyard in the first few years of the nineteenth century[4] (see figure 6.5). The Portsmouth block mill made 200 sorts and sizes of blocks with

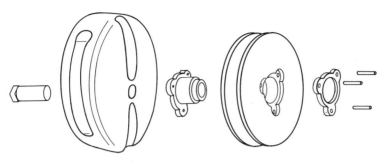

FIGURE 6.3. Parts of a British naval pulley-block, eighteenth to twentieth century. Left to right: iron or *lignum vitae* pin; elm shell, mortised for sheave, scored for strap, and bored for pin; half of cast bell-metal coak or bushing for pin hole of sheave; *lignum vitae* sheave with coak-shaped excavations around pine hole and groove for rope around rim; other half of coak; three copper rivets for securing coak in sheave. (Drawing by R. B. Gordon.)

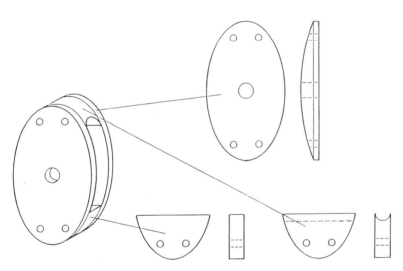

FIGURE 6.4. A plank block shell and its wooden parts, side and front views. A single-sheave plank or "made" block is made up of two cheek pieces and two end pieces riveted together as shown, to form a sheave chamber. Dotted lines indicate holes for rivets and pin, and the rounded groove for the top piece. Blocks with more sheaves would have an extra vertical partition and two more end pieces for each additional sheave chamber. (Drawing by R. B. Gordon.)

FIG. 6.5. (*following two pages*) Portsmouth Dockyard production line for pulley-blocks. At the block mill in H.M. Dockyard, Portsmouth, England, elm logs sawed into blocks of wood went through the machine and hand operations (in ovals) shown left to right in line (A) to become shells for pulley-blocks. *Lignum vitae* logs sawed into slices of wood became sheaves by the machine and hand operations shown in line (C). Iron rods became pins along line (B). All three elements were assembled into finished pulley blocks as shown at far right.

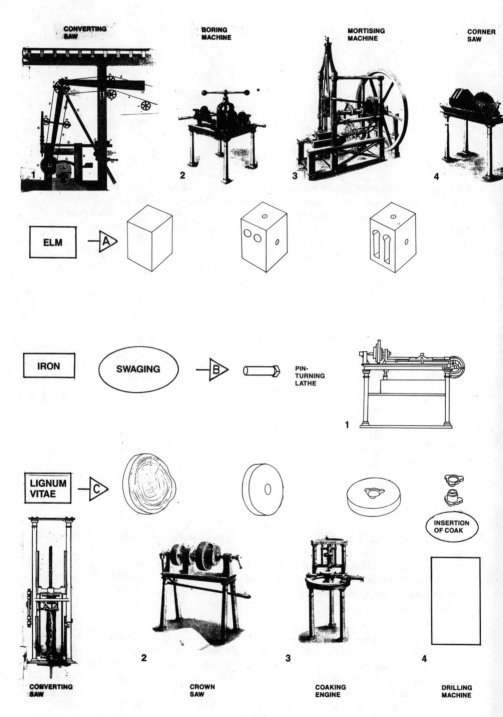

CONVERTING SAW

BORING MACHINE

MORTISING MACHINE

CORNER SAW

1

2

3

4

ELM → A

IRON

SWAGING → B

PIN-TURNING LATHE

1

LIGNUM VITAE → C

INSERTION OF COAK

CONVERTING SAW

2

CROWN SAW

3

COAKING ENGINE

4

DRILLING MACHINE

136

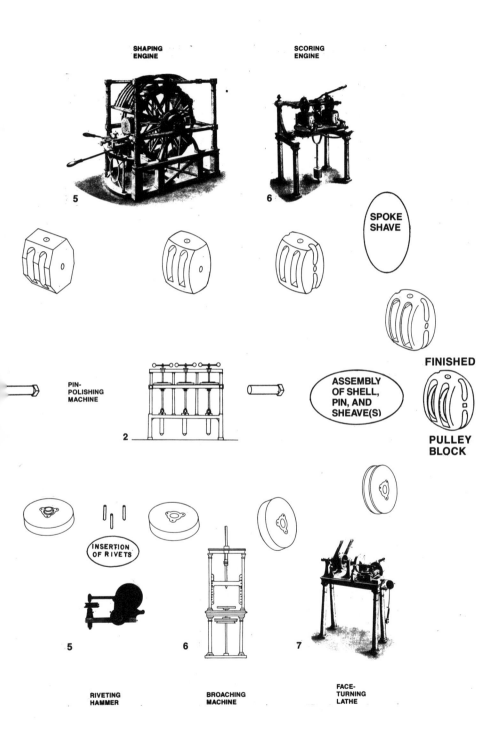

SHAPING
ENGINE

SCORING
ENGINE

5

6

SPOKE
SHAVE

FINISHED

PULLEY
BLOCK

PIN-
POLISHING
MACHINE

2

ASSEMBLY
OF SHELL,
PIN, AND
SHEAVE(S)

INSERTION
OF RIVETS

5

6

7

RIVETING
HAMMER

BROACHING
MACHINE

FACE-
TURNING
LATHE

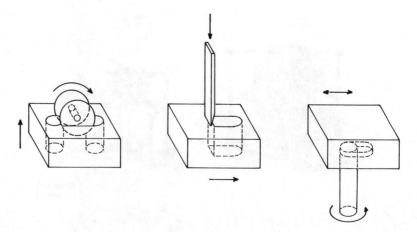

FIGURE 6.6. Three ways to mortise a "solid" shell for a pulley-block. Left: In the block mills of English contract blockmakers Dunsterville and Taylor c. 1800, mortises were cut into blocks by plunge-cutting with parallel circular saws half-way through from both sides, and removing the scraps by handsaw or chisel. Middle: At the Portsmouth block mill c. 1805, the mortising machine lengthened a previously drilled hole by a reciprocating chisel. Right: Blanchard's mortising machine of 1836 used a vertical-spindle rotating "spoon bit" cutter to rout the mortise from below and round off one end of it, then a reciprocating chisel to square off its other end. (Drawing by R. B. Gordon.)

capacity for a daily output of over 1400 blocks.[5] It demonstrated conclusively that blocks made by special purpose machines arranged in a rational production system were of higher average quality, as well as cheaper, than handmade ones. The block mill and its forty-five or so sturdy and accurate iron-framed woodworking machines represented a substantial capital investment by the Royal Navy, but it "paid for itself" in four years of operation,[6] and thereafter continued production for over a century.

The Portsmouth block mill immediately became a tourist attraction and was described in detail in articles in Abraham Rees's *Cyclopaedia,* the *Edinburgh Encyclopaedia,* the *Encyclopaedia Britannica,* and other encyclopedias and dictionaries throughout the nineteenth century. It was regarded as the epitome of mechanization.[7] The relevant volume of *Edinburgh Encyclopaedia* was reprinted in the United States in 1813,[8] so its detailed and illustrated description of the machinery and production line at the Portsmouth block mill was certainly available on these shores when Thomas Blanchard was inventing the irregular turning lathe.

American blockmakers had also begun incorporating machines into their operations to some extent. In 1796 English-born architect-engineer

Benjamin Henry Latrobe visited an "experimental" block mill in Alexandria, Virginia, where he noted mechanized augers for boring holes and drew pictures of two arrangements of circular saws for cutting off blocks to standard sizes and for cutting mortises in them. As pictured in his notebook, the mortising method resembled that of the contract blockmakers Dunsterville and Taylor in England[9] (see figure 6.6). In 1802, one E. Whiting received an American patent for a "blockmaking gang lathe," about which nothing more is known.[10] By 1812—after the Portsmouth block mill had been in operation for several years—Benjamin Latrobe designed a steam-powered block mill for the Washington Navy Yard, pointing out the advantage to be gained by the U.S. Navy from interchangeability of mechanically made pulley-block parts:

> that every block of a particular size & use . . . will take in exactly every sheave intended for that particular kind of block, tho' there were thousands of them delivered promiscuously . . . and that every sheave will run true and square with the block exactly filling up the mortice as it ought.[11]

Unfortunately this block mill, completed in 1813, was destroyed soon thereafter when the British burned Washington. We don't know to what extent it resembled the famous block mill in Portsmouth or less advanced one Latrobe had observed in Alexandria.

## A BLANCHARD—PORTSMOUTH CONNECTION?

As for Thomas Blanchard, whether or not he knew about the Portsmouth blockmaking machinery beforehand, he was certainly aware of it by the time he wrote the revised patent specification for his irregular turning lathe. Although it is absent from his specification of September 6, 1819, he mentions it twice in the revised version of January 20, 1820. In describing various forms of rotary cutters, he says "The cutters may be . . . formed and set into the cutter wheel like plane irons, as is used in the English machine for scoring blocks described in the Edinburgh Encyclopedia." However, he ends the specification by stating that "his machine or invention is different from" several others, including "the machinery described in the Edinburgh Encyclopedia for making Ships Blocks & Dead-eyes."[12] The machines for blockmaking that Blanchard patented in the 1830s were also very different from the Portsmouth machines, as will be shown.

Blanchard very early intended to apply his irregular turning lathe to blockmaking, for his patent specification of September 1819 (but not the revision of January 1820) identifies it explicitly as "a machine for turning gun Stocks, tackle and Shipping blocks, and may be applied to turning or forming wood, metal or other materials into any regular or irregular form."[13] In 1824 or 1825, while Blanchard was working at Springfield Armory, William Woodworth, "an agent for Mr. Van Rensselaer," called on him and asked to buy the right to use his irregular turning lathe to make ships' blocks. Subsequently Blanchard went in 1826 to "the Mills of Harmon Livingston Esq.," eight miles downstream from Hudson, New York, where Woodworth was the supervisor, and spent three or four months setting up blockmaking machinery there.[14] This block mill was the last of various waterpowered mills at its site, originally part of the Livingston family manor, near the mouth of Roeliff Jansen's Kill (now Livingston Creek). It operated for an indefinite period "about 1820 and thereafter" according to the local history.[15] Whether at that location or another, the Livingston Patent Block Company was apparently still thriving in 1833, when it was reported from as far away as Boston "that the use of the patent Livingston blocks has in a great measure superseded the manufacture of ships' blocks by hand."[16] The phrase "patent Livingston blocks" presumably refers to an unrecorded assignment or license by Blanchard to the Livingston Company for use of the machines he built for them in 1826. Of these machines we know only that they included a scoring machine in which William Woodworth injured his hand.[17]

After Blanchard moved from Springfield to New York City in the early 1830s—that is, after his careers as inside contractor at the Armory and as steamboat designer and captain on the Connecticut, Allegheny, and Kennebec rivers—he worked further to design machinery for pulley-block production. On December 29, 1835, while located at "Dry Dock" on the East River, he assigned to Neziah Bliss the rights to his renewed irregular turning lathe patent, specifying its use as "machinery for turning Ships Blocks and tackles . . . also to certain improvements contemplated as well as all further improvements which may be made."[18]

At the date of his assignment to Bliss, Blanchard had already begun the patent application process for at least some of his ten blockmaking machines: his affidavits for five of them are dated August 11, 1835.[19] The assignment's reference to contemplated improvements seems to cover the ten machines for which Blanchard received patents the following August 1836, for no assignments otherwise are recorded for these machines. After fire destroyed all Patent Office records in December 1836, someone soon took the trouble to restore the record of the assignment as well as the record of the ten patent specifications. This suggests that they were considered currently valuable property.[20]

Assignee Neziah Bliss (1790–1876) was a native of Hebron, Connecticut who had, earlier than Blanchard, also experienced a passion for building and navigating shallow-draft steamboats. Befriended by Robert Fulton and Daniel French, Bliss had operated his riverboats in Philadelphia, Cincinnati, Louisville, and New Orleans. In St. Louis he ran a steam-powered sawmill, and traveled far upstream in the lumber trade. Returning east, he joined forces with Union College president Eliphalet Nott in real estate and business ventures on both sides of the East River in New York. Together they established the Novelty Iron Works near the Dry Dock in Manhattan in 1831, of which Bliss became the manager, and they bought farmland across the East River on Long Island as a speculative venture, expecting the U.S. Navy Yard to be built there. This fell through, but Bliss married into the family (Meserole) from whom he and Nott bought other tracts of land, and became active in raising a family and in real estate development at that location in Greenpoint, and at Dutch Kills in Queens County, which became known locally as "Blissville." He was later described as a "live Yankee" who "with the proverbial energy and tact of his race" had developed Greenpoint into a thriving and populous "ward of the third city of the Union" (Brooklyn).[21] In 1834 Bliss promised Nott he would move "his block factory" to Bushwick on Long Island as one of several measures "conducive to settlement . . . and raising the value of the property" that they were contemplating buying there.[22]

That Neziah Bliss possessed a block factory and blockmaking rights to Blanchard's patent went unmentioned in the nineteenth-century biographical sketch of this "Patriarch of Greenpoint." It was, however, consonant with his previous sawmilling experience and his longstanding involvement with ships and steamboats, including the anthracite-stoked *Novelty,* for which the Novelty Iron Works was named. The dating is imprecise, but a block factory, containing a machine built by Blanchard "for the purpose of planing the cheeks of plank blocks," was located not far from the Novelty Iron Works.[23] Perhaps it belonged to Bliss; it was possibly also the Livingston block factory, relocated from Hudson. After Blanchard had developed the ten machines for which he obtained patents in 1836, the Livingston block factory (wherever it was then) sold out to the newly formed Winooski Patent Block-Making Company, which also bought Blanchard's patent rights.[24] We can therefore turn to the ten patent specifications for at least an approximate description of the production line in the block mill at Winooski Falls, outside Burlington, Vermont.

How can we tell that Blanchard in fact designed these ten machines to be operated together on a production line instead of individually in disparate workshops? A blockmaker might of course take a fancy to one or another of these machines and use it in his own context, filling in with handwork or non-Blanchard machines, but there are several reasons to believe that Blanchard intended them for coordinated use on a production line. First, the facts that he obtained patents for all ten machines within one month, and that they were his only explicit blockmaking patents, strongly suggest that he regarded them as a unit. Moreover, examination of the patent specifications shows that all together they do cover a sequence of steps in making pulley- blocks, and that they do not overlap with one another in function. They constitute not just an array of similar machines but a system for production.

Furthermore, phrases occur in the specifications that indicate a concern on Blanchard's part for the shifting of many workpieces through each machine—a consideration that is more characteristic of factory than of craft production. It is also presumably not accidental that he consistently uses the word "workman" for the operator of the machine, and never the term "blockmaker," which connotes the traditional craftsman. These various contextual hints support the interpretation of these ten machines as evidence that Blanchard regarded them as parts of a production system rather than discrete inventions. Finally, the machines were in fact bought together instead of separately and were set into operation in an early industrial-scale block mill, at Winooski Falls, Vermont.

Between 1819 and 1836 Blanchard's ideas about using his lathe for blockmaking must have undergone considerable elaboration because of his experience designing and operating a production line for half-stocking muskets at the Springfield Armory. As blockmaking machinery constituted a production line in the block mill at Portsmouth, so would Blanchard's patented machines constitute a production line when installed at Winooski Falls. They are, however, not copies of the Portsmouth machines. Collectively, they divide and combine the operations of blockmaking differently; individually they often use different means from those of the Portsmouth machines to achieve the same effects on the pulley-blocks.

Nor are they simply all variants of Blanchard's copying lathe, as Blanchard's single assignment to Neziah Bliss might suggest.

## BLANCHARD'S PRODUCTION LINE FOR PULLEY-BLOCKS

Blanchard's ten patented machines for blockmaking can be seen to comprise four sublines of production:[25] (1) for shells of solid wood, (2) for sheaves and pins, (3) for shells of plank blocks, and (4) for deadeyes. No instruction is given in the patent specifications concerning their sequential use, nor do we know how they were actually arranged at the Winooski block mill. The ten machines would, however, work together most efficiently if arranged as in the flow diagram in figure 6.7.

## MAKING SHELLS

Blanchard referred to "solid shell blocks" as the "common" type and designed three machines to make them, but he also designed three machines for making "plank or made blocks." Blanchard's machines for solid wood shells were granted U.S. Patents #5, to bore the block for its pin hole and mortise its sheave chamber (see figure 6.6), #4 to shape the shell's exterior contours, and #8 to score a groove in it for a strap (see figure 6.8).

Blanchard's patent specifications for making plank blocks describe machines for making side pieces or "cheeks" (U.S. Patent #19) (see figure 6.9); for end pieces (U.S. Patent #6), (see figure 6.10); and for riveting the sides and ends together (U.S. Patent #9). In a plank block, the extra chambers for double- or triple-sheave blocks require separate pieces for partitions, but Blanchard provides no special machine for making such pieces. Nor are any machines specified to drill pin holes or holes for the rivets holding the pieces of the block together. Implicitly, Blanchard has left these tasks to handwork or to unspecified uses of the other machines described for sawing and drilling solid blocks.

FIGURE 6.7. *(Following two pages)* Blanchard's production line for pulley-blocks and deadeyes. Blanchard's ten machine designs, patented August 1836, indicate workmen used special-purpose machines in sequence to make deadeyes and pulley-block shells of solid wood, to make and fasten together parts of "plank" pulley-block shells, and to make sheaves and pins to fit within either kind of shell. (Drawing by Lyn Malone.)

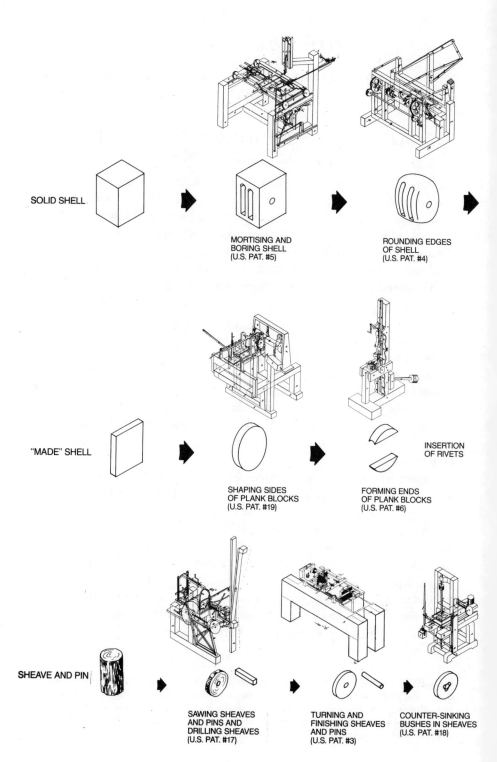

SOLID SHELL

MORTISING AND
BORING SHELL
(U.S. PAT. #5)

ROUNDING EDGES
OF SHELL
(U.S. PAT. #4)

"MADE" SHELL

SHAPING SIDES
OF PLANK BLOCKS
(U.S. PAT. #19)

FORMING ENDS
OF PLANK BLOCKS
(U.S. PAT. #6)

INSERTION
OF RIVETS

SHEAVE AND PIN

SAWING SHEAVES
AND PINS AND
DRILLING SHEAVES
(U.S. PAT. #17)

TURNING AND
FINISHING SHEAVES
AND PINS
(U.S. PAT. #3)

COUNTER-SINKING
BUSHES IN SHEAVES
(U.S. PAT. #18)

*144*

SCORING SHELL
FOR STRAP
(U.S. PAT. #8)

ASSEMBLY OF
SHELL, PIN, AND
SHEAVES

FINISHED PULLEY BLOCK

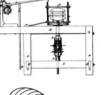

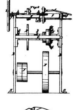

RIVETING PLANK
BLOCKS
(U.S. PAT. #9)

SCORING SHELL
FOR STRAP
(U.S. PAT. #8)

INSERTION
OF COAK

DEADEYE

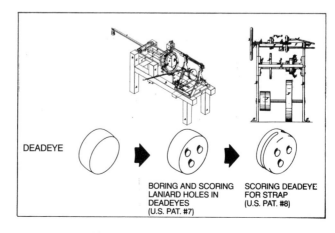

BORING AND SCORING
LANIARD HOLES IN
DEADEYES
(U.S. PAT. #7)

SCORING DEADEYE
FOR STRAP
(U.S. PAT. #8)

 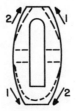 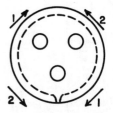

FIGURE 6.8. Scoring pulley-blocks and deadeyes. The score for a strap around a pulley-block or deadeye varies in depth, becoming shallow and disappearing at the head end, and when crossing the pin hole of the pulley-block. Scores and pin holes are indicated by dotted lines. Left: To avoid cutting against the grain of the wood, the Portsmouth scoring machine cut a shell in four operations, from the pin hole on each side toward each end of the pulley-block. Middle and right: The Blanchard scoring machine (U.S. Patent # 8) cut the score of a pulley-block or deadeye in two operations while the operator revolved it once on each side. To avoid cutting against the grain, the machine lifted the cutter away from the block for the second and fourth quarters of each revolution. (Drawing by R. B. Gordon.)

# MAKING PINS AND SHEAVES

In "solid" and "plank" pulley-blocks alike, the sheave is the critical moving part. It rotates within its chamber or mortise on a pin passed through both shell and sheave. To make a freely running sheave, the main considerations were to make sure its periphery was circular, its sides parallel to each other, and its pin hole central and perpendicular to its sides. The pin

FIGURE 6.9. *(opposite)* "Machinery for . . . shaping the sides of . . . plank or made blocks." Two pieces of plank already cut to the rough outline of a cheek and planed flat on their inward sides were held on plates in the "forked" holder shown enlarged at figures 2 and 3, in which they were fixed at an angle (figure 2) for successive presentation of the "lower and forward quarters of each pair of cheeks" to the curved cutting blades (q) jutting from the rotary cutter shaft (H). The brace or bent rod (r) fixed in rectangular stock (S) served to screw and unscrew the centers holding the cheeks on their plates. The apparatus for presenting the cheeks to the blades pivoted on the front corners of the framework (CCC). By the angled control lever (c), whose fulcrum is on frame (C) the workman pushed forward the apparatus holding the cheeks so that as the cutters cut, the guide board (w) slid against form board (u) (shown crosswise at Fig. 4). These motions resulted in "the proper curves both transverse and lengthwise" on one quarter of each cheek. He disengaged the machine three times to rotate the cheeks top to bottom and left to right without removing them from their plates. Thus he shaped all four quarters of both without cutting against the grain of the wood. (Patent drawing for U.S. Patent #19, National Archives, Suitland, Maryland.)

*146*

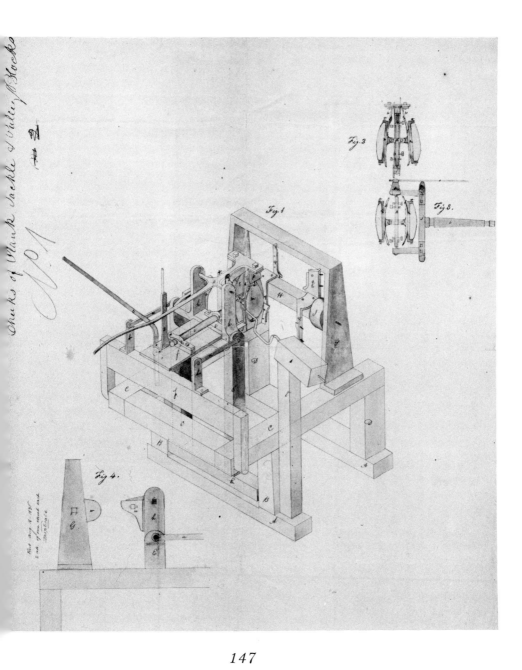

Chucks of Wank Jackle Fulley Hooks

Nº1

Fig. 1

Fig. 2

Fig. 3

Fig. 4

147

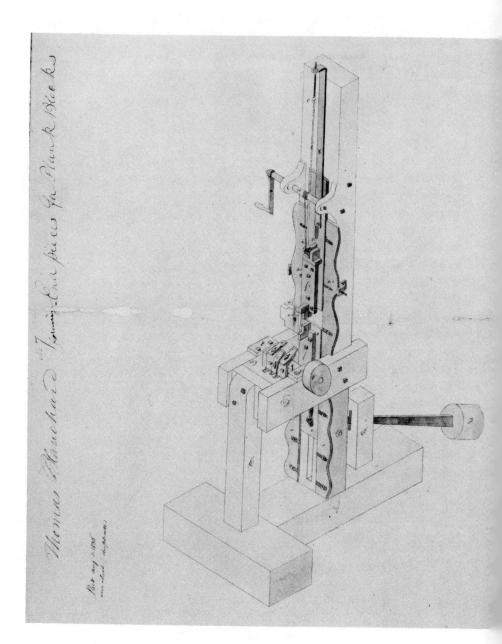

Thomas Blanchard's "Turning Cut pieces for Plank Blocks"

Patented aug.r 1806
enrolled deposited

had to be smooth and cylindrical. To reduce friction on the pin, the sheave pin hole was fitted with a bushing. The sheave also had to have a groove around its circumference in which the line would run. In Blanchard's production line, these operations on pins and sheaves were assigned to three machines: one rough-cut sheaves and pins and drilled pin holes (U.S. Patent #17), one turned pins and sheaves smooth (U.S. Patent #3), and one "countersank" or inlet for the bushing (U.S. Patent #18).

## MAKING DEADEYES

In the standing rigging of a ship, pulley-blocks are not necessary; the simpler and stronger blocks called deadeyes can be used to hold the rigging taut. According to David Steel in 1794, "Deadeyes are used when the strain is too great to trust a pin and sheaves."[26] Blanchard's patents omitted explicit machine-shaping of the fat-cheeked deadeyes. Since they are circular in outline, however, they could have been turned in any ordinary or Blanchard lathe. Blanchard's machine (U.S. Patent #7) bored and scored the three deadeye holes. Another machine (U.S. Patent #8) scored the groove for the strap around the outside. At Portsmouth, one machine both shaped and scored the circumference of the deadeyes (see figure 6.8).

To see what the overall differences were in the production systems of the Portsmouth and Blanchard block mills, compare figure 6.5 to figure 6.7. Appendix B discusses, step by step, the machines in Blanchard's blockmaking production line, comparing them to the ones at Portsmouth, and occasionally to Blanchard's own gunstocking machines at Springfield Armory. Both blockmaking systems made shells of solid wood, so we can compare the designs of their different machines for that purpose. One obvious difference is that Blanchard's production system includes fewer

FIGURE 6.10. *(opposite)* "Machine for forming end pieces of plank blocks for ships etc." These pieces determine the parallel sides and the curved top and flat bottom of the pulley block mortise. The operator cranked the winch to force a sliding clamp holding a piece of wood downward past three cutters rotating on a single axis. They cut three sides of the "head" (grooved) or "arse" (flat) end piece, as shown in figure 6.4. The middle cutter was retractable to present either a curved or straight blade for cutting the top or bottom end piece. The counterweight shown at the right resisted the descent of the slide and assisted its return upward for unloading. (Patent drawing for U.S. Patent #6, National Archives, Suitland, Maryland.)

machines than does the Portsmouth system. Another major difference is that Blanchard also mechanized the production of "made" or plank blocks, where the Portsmouth block mill left that to handwork.

## THE ASCENDANCY OF "MADE" BLOCKS

Nowadays all sizes of wooden pulley-blocks are "made" up of planks, but in the eighteenth century, only the largest were, for "solid" blocks were considered better. In 1794 David Steel wrote concerning "made" blocks: "Of this sort are large, treble, and fourfold blocks, for heaving down ships or other heavy purchase."[27] He said "smaller made blocks of modern invention" with patent rollers for bushings "are thought too complex for the Royal Navy and not so easily remedied in case of failure." The block mill at Portsmouth Dockyard in England made all of the blocks up through 18 inches long out of solid wood. Only blocks larger than that were "made," and except for "particular parts . . . as the sheaves, pin and cheeks," the workmen had to make them with hand tools.[28]

Over the nineteenth century, opinion on pulley-blocks shifted from favoring blocks whose shells were cut from solid wood to favoring "blocks made in pieces, filled in at the ends and riveted together." By the 1890s, such blocks received kinder mention in the *Encyclopaedia Britannica:* "It is questionable whether a block so made is not stronger than one cut out of the solid as in the latter case the short-grained wood at the ends of the mortises is very liable to give way."[29] This change in opinion may have reflected the increasing strength and reliability of metal bolts or rivets for fastening. As such fasteners became cheaper, it became more economical to "make" blocks of planks than to cut mortises into solid blocks of wood.

Blanchard's mechanization of "made block" production in the 1830s can be regarded as a benchmark in their improvement in quality relative to solid cut blocks. At Winooski, blocks as small as 7 inches long were "made" of planks. The Winooski Patent Block Manufacturing Company in 1836 advertised two size ranges of machine-made blocks. The smaller ones—5 to 9 inches long—were "solid, common and bushed *Ship's Tackle Blocks*," while the larger ones—7 to 16 inches—were "Plank Blocks."[30]

## THE MACHINES AS SYSTEM

Anyone designing a series of special-purpose machines for accomplishing a sequence of operations in a factory has to aim not only for the most accurate and efficient operation of the individual machines, but also for the overall efficiency and economy of the machines' acting together. Beyond making each machine as effective as technically possible, the designer has to consider the expense of constructing the machine and of the space they will take up on the shop floor. He has also to consider the "flow" along the production line—the timing and coordination of the various operations of the separate machines.[31] Bearing all these considerations in mind, the designer has to decide which operations to combine into a single machine and which to assign to different machines.

Implicit in the machine designer's decisions must be some assumption as to the scale of the factory for which the design is intended, and at least a rough idea of the number of machine operators that will be manning it. For a very large-scale factory, for instance, it might be more economical of the combined costs of operators' time, floor space, and purchase of machinery, to have a separate specialized machine set up for each and every small operation, while in a medium or small-scale factory, doubling-up of some operations might be more economical overall. In addition to scale of operation, the anticipated range of variety in the product is relevant. A greater variety within a given scale of output justifies more double-purpose machinery. These are industrial engineering concerns that influence the tasks of mechanical engineering.

In designing this set of ten machines for making pulley- blocks and deadeyes, Blanchard seems to have allowed for a smaller-scale operation and more variety of product than did the designers of the Portsmouth block mill. This can be inferred from the doubling-up of function in certain of the machines. The scoring machine could score both shells and deadeyes, by using different form boards. The machines for making sheaves and pins also doubled up on operations: U.S. Patent #17 specifies two different sets of equipment for sawing or for drilling, while U.S. Patent #3 describes removable equipment for turning sheaves and for turning pins. These two machines could easily have been designed as four machines, at the expense of floor-space and of initial cost, if it were assumed that a very great output of pins and sheaves would justify having four machines in readiness all the time, and avoid having to change the setup of two machines between producing one lot of sheaves and another lot of pins.

That Blanchard did not design four separate machines for the operations of these two suggests that he had in mind a factory in which the "flow" of production would be intermittent, and its pace would be tolerant of the time needed for changing the machines over from sheave production to pin production and vice versa. It suggests his recognition that construction cost of the machines and the space that would be needed for them might outweigh the need for smooth flow of a large number of sheaves and pins simultaneously along the production line.

A smaller-scale flexible factory would probably be more useful for a commercial blockmaker in an American port of the 1830s, in contrast to the large-scale production for the whole British navy, for which the Portsmouth block mill had been designed. It should be noted that the Portsmouth system was not readily adopted by commercial blockmakers in England either. As late as 1860, a Mr. Esdaile's commercial block manufactories in London were producing, presumably with different equipment, blocks twice as expensively as at Portsmouth Dockyard.[32]

Although Blanchard was certainly aware of the Portsmouth blockmaking machinery and had referred to it in his 1820 lathe patent, his blockmaking patents of 1836 do not refer to it. The prior state of woodworking art that Blanchard's patent specifications seem to allude to, by occasionally likening machine tool parts to hand tools—the "rebate plane," the "spoon bit," the "double-iron carpenters plane"—is handwork, rather than a block mill of either the Taylor-Dunsterville sort, as at Alexandria, Virginia, or of the more sophisticated Portsmouth variety. Blanchard's machines were touted at the time as the only ones of their kind, so handwork may indeed have been the predominant blockmaking technology in the United States when Blanchard undertook to mechanize it at Livingston Manor and then at Winooski Falls.

As individual machines, most of those shown and described in Blanchard's ten patent specifications for blockmaking are more complex and ungainly than the older elegant Portsmouth machinery for the same purposes. Comparison with Blanchard's own stockmaking machines is difficult, since only one of these—the gunstocking lathe—survives in illustrations or in reality, but it also seems more elegant in conception than its nearest blockmaking equivalents, the rounding machine (U.S. Patent #4) or the cheek-shaping machine (U.S. Patent #19) (compare figures 6.9 and 5.2). Certainly the 1850s second-generation stockmaking machines inspire (albeit as one would expect them to do) more confidence in their performance than do the pictures of these 1830s machines.

Taken as a whole, however, Blanchard's blockmaking machines, whose illustrations show frames "as of wood but may be made of iron,"[33] reflect a concern for adaptability to a variety of contexts that one might expect to find in a commercial environment. As discussed in appendix B, Blanchard's designs accommodated to a variety of bushing styles for the sheaves, to a variety of sizes of blocks to be made, to both solid-shell and plank-block construction, and to a smaller- as well as larger-scale production line. As we have seen, there are some gaps in the production line to be inferred from these patents, especially in the process for making plank blocks, gaps that would need to be filled by handwork or by machines not specialized for blockmaking. Blanchard's ten machines therefore do not constitute as complete a system for blockmaking as the Portsmouth machinery did. But his system may well have been the more "appropriate technology" for its time and place. Its initial application was on an ambitious scale for the United States of the 1830s; its flexibility allowed for an expected expansion that unforeseen disaster prevented, at least at its first location.

# APPLICATION

The Winooski Patent Block Manufacturing Company, incorporated in Vermont on November 10, 1835 with a capital stock of $200,000,[34] announced on April 1, 1836 that

> they have purchased the whole of the establishment formerly known as the Livingston Patent Block Machinery, with all the extension of the patent rights recently granted by Congress to Thomas Blanchard, Esq., the original inventor and patentee, together with all the late improvements made and patented by him.[35]

The directors of the company were New Yorkers and Vermonters: George P. Marsh, Guy Catlin, John M. Catlin, Uriah Bliss, and Peter Stuyvesant. George P. Marsh (1801–82), at that time a member of the Vermont legislature, owned property on the Winooski River outside Burlington and invested in a woollen mill there.[36] Marsh later became a famous philologist and diplomat. Peter Stuyvesant (1778–1847), whose mother was a Livingston, was also descended from his famous Dutch namesake. In Manhattan he owned property near Stuyvesant's Cove, for which Neziah Bliss and Eliphalet Nott had landfill and development schemes. Stuyvesant became president of the New York Historical Society.[37] Guy Catlin was a Burlington lumber merchant and businessman who had other Winooski manufacturing interests; John M. Catlin was presumably his relative.[38] Uriah Bliss has defied identification; perhaps he was Blanchard's assignee Neziah Bliss himself, whose Old Testament first name was subject to mistranscription.

At the time of its announcement in 1836, the Winooski Patent Block Manufacturing Company had already on hand "a large stock of machine made, solid, common and bushed Ship's Tackle Blocks . . . , and machine made Plank Blocks . . . , and other articles on reasonable terms." [39] The company moved the patented machinery, for which they paid $30,000, from New York City into the new mill that they "built expressly to receive it," at Winooski Falls. The mill, which cost $7,000 to erect, was powered by an 80–horsepower waterwheel. [40] The combined value of the machinery and mill was over fourteen times the $2,600 value reported for buildings and equipment at the average blockmaking establishment in Boston, and the machinery constituted a much higher proportion of the total. [41]

The company's initial capitalization of $200,000 was large, for they planned "to increase the machinery so as to meet the present and future demands of the blockmaking trade and maritime public throughout the United States." They maintained an office and store in New York City, whither they intended to send "a large, constant, and regular supply of these and other articles in the Block making line." [42] In 1837 the guide-book *New York As It Is* listed the company as of "Burlington and New York" with the local address of 40 and 42 Fletcher St. in New York. [43]

Thus, while shipping on Lake Champlain itself could be expected to generate some nearby demand for ships' blocks, the Winooski Patent Block Manufacturing Company was definitely aiming to supply not just the local market but the whole country. Low-cost water transport of the blocks to New York City was possible by way of the Champlain Canal, which had opened in 1823. The Winooski incorporators located their block mill at a waterpower site "in the heart of a country abounding with the finest and best of timber for their purpose," [44] that is, close to the source of the raw material instead of close to their customers at a seaport. At 80 horsepower, their waterwheel on the Winooski River gave them more power than was available to the Portsmouth Dockyard block mill in England, which from 1807 operated on two 30–horsepower steam engines. [45] With these advantages, plus exclusive use of Blanchard's machinery, "the only machinery of the kind in America" at the time, the Winooski Patent Block Manufacturing Company, by its own account, was within two years "doing a good business and would in a short time have driven all other blocks out of market. Such in fact was the case already," it was reported, "wherever they had been introduced." [46]

These aspirations went unfulfilled, however, for the block mill caught fire around 2 A.M. on December 21, 1838, "and in a short time the whole building together with the valuable machinery was entirely destroyed." The newspaper reported "there is little doubt that the fire originated from the gudgeons in the Blockmill."[47] The conflagration also consumed the adjacent "manufactory of machinery of various kinds . . . an extensive sawmill, paper mill, and Woolen Manufactory." Block-mill incorporators Marsh and the Catlins were also involved in these other enterprises. The well-capitalized block mill had only $7,400 worth of insurance,[48] and apparently did not arise Phoenix-like from its ashes. Four years later it was missing from the reconstituted industrial base for Winooski village, listed as "a sawmill, machine shop, sash factory, and an extensive woollen factory." Winooski (pop. 1739 in 1840) was reported to have "suffered very severely by fire."[49] We don't know whether Blanchard's machines reappeared elsewhere, but after such a vigorous start it seems likely that they were rebuilt, perhaps in the New York City area.

No further sale of rights to Blanchard's patent(s) for blockmaking purposes appear in the assignment records until the 1850s. After the second extension of the Blanchard lathe patent, from 1848, tackle-blocks and oars were the nautical purposes for which Newark carriage-maker James M. Quinby bought rights in 1851. That assignment also conveyed to Quinby broad rights "for the purposes of making and turning spokes, whiffle-trees, leading bars, springbars, shafts, carriage poles, saddletrees, hames, . . . gunstocks, ox yokes, last and boot-trees."[50] To these landlubberly preoccupations we next turn.

# BLANCHARD'S PRODUCTION LINE FOR PULLEY-BLOCKS AND DEADEYES

(Machines and blocks in process are shown in figure 6.7, pages 144–45)

# BLOCKS MADE OF SOLID WOOD

## MAKING MORTISES AND BORING THE PIN HOLE IN THE BLOCK [1]

In the late eighteenth century, English contract blockmakers Taylor in South-ampton and Dunsterville in Plymouth used blockmaking machines that partially performed the task of mortising by plunge-cutting with pairs of circular saws. The machine Benjamin Latrobe sketched at Alexandia, Virginia in 1796 was also of this type. But instead of circular saws, the early nineteenth-century mortising machines at Portsmouth Dockyard used a reciprocating chisel.[2] Blanchard's ma-chine (U.S. Patent #5),[3] however, differed from both earlier types of machine for this purpose; it achieved the same end by routing from beneath, using a rotating vertical-spindle bit (see figure 6.6). The "spoon bit" mortising cutter was rach-eted up to the block, which was held in a frame that moved back and forth a preset distance until the mortise was cut through. Mortising by vertical-spindle cutter had been described by Samuel Bentham in his English woodworking patent of 1793.[4] Unlike the Portsmouth machine, which could cut two or three mortises at a time, Blanchard's machine cut only one at a time. For blocks with more than one mortise, it used "index gauge plates," "index spring plates" and "studs" to reposition the block accurately for sequential cutting of mortises that would be the same length and width and parallel to one another.

This machine also bored the block horizontally for the pin hole during the time it was being mortised vertically from below: before the mortising cutter was halfway through the first mortise, the workman set in motion an auger on a sideways-working slide to bore the pin hole through the block. The combination of operations helped assure that the pin hole was at exactly right angles to the mortises, since the block did not have to be shifted to a different machine. In the Portsmouth block mill, the pin hole and mortises were cut in separate machines.[5]

There are several hints in this block-mortising specification that confirm the idea that the machines described in the separate patents were intended for use together in a production line. One such remark near the end is that "the workman . . . removes the block whose mortice is now so far finished to make room for others in succession to be mortised in the same way."

## ROUNDING THE BLOCK

After mortising a block and boring its pin hole, it was necessary to round off its sharp corners to bring it to an elliptoid shape. Blanchard's "stockshaving or rounding" machine for this purpose (U.S. Patent #4)[6] was a variant nontraversing Blanchard lathe. Unlike the gunstocking lathe, in which both the workpiece and the cutter were rotated by a power-driven belt, in the rounding machine the cutter was powered, but the workpiece and form piece to be copied were rotated by hand crank. In this it resembled Blanchard's machine for smoothing the fore-end of a musket between bands, described in chapter 5. It allowed the workman to vary the speed, and go more slowly "where the cutters act against the grain . . . to avoid stripping or splitting the wood, than is needful where the cutters act with the grain." The cutter wheel itself was different from the hook-bladed wheel of the gunstocking lathe, for it was fitted with "two cutters . . . precisely similar . . . to the cutting iron of a Carpenters double iron smoothing plane." Also resembling the machine for smoothing gunstock fore-ends between bands, the cutter wheel did not traverse along the block, for the plane cutters were wide enough to work on the whole thickness of the block at once as it was rotated end-over-end on a pin in its pin hole.

This machine was completely different from the Portsmouth machine for the same purpose. The Portsmouth shaping engine held ten blocks at once in a large chuck resembling a Ferris wheel, which whirled them past a gouge moved by hand-lever along a curved ruler, to shape one face at a time. The workman had to stop this machine for a quarter-rotation of the blocks on their lengthwise axes, and start it again to shape the second, third, and fourth faces of the ten blocks, while he made the gouge follow two different pattern rulers alternately to cut all four faces.[7] Blanchard's rounding machine, however, copied a "form piece" to shape a block shell exterior all in one continuous operation as the workman slowly rotated it once on its own pin-hole axis. Thus, it curved the block's ends and its mortised sides, but not the pin-hole faces, which implicitly remained flat. The finished block was "removed . . . to make room for another to be entered and operated on in precisely the same manner." Possibly hand rasping rounded the corners left by the machine.

## SCORING BLOCKS AND DEADEYES

The final machine operation for making either pulley block or deadeye was to score a groove around it for the strap to hold it in place. Blanchard's machine for scoring (U.S. Patent #8)[8] was another variant on Blanchard's irregular turning lathe. Since scoring was only cutting a groove of varying depth instead of a whole three-dimensional shape of varying contours, the pattern to control the action of the cutter was not a "form piece," or model of a whole block or deadeye, but only a "form board." Its undulating edge pressed against the dummy "friction wheel" while a rapidly rotating "hooked-knife" cutter wheel cut a groove around "that part of the deadeye [or block] which is with the grain of the wood." The form board was shaped so as to raise the cutting wheel frame away from the workpiece when it reached that part of the score where the cutters would have to cut against the grain, every other quarter of a rotation. By removing and replacing the block or deadeye the other way around, and repeating the operation, the workman completed cutting the score, with the grain of the wood, on the uncut segments of the path (see figure 6.8).

The form board shape was different, of course, for a deadeye score from that for a block; form boards would also be made in different sizes for different sizes of blocks or deadeyes. To rotate the workpiece and form board the workman turned a hand wheel around for each of the two operations per block. In this respect the machine was similar both to the rounding machine and to the machine for turning for and between bands on the fore-end of the gunstock, as discussed earlier.

Since Blanchard certainly knew about the Portsmouth scoring engine when writing the specification for his 1820 patent, he may have had it as his point of comparison when he wrote in 1835 that by his own scoring machine "a block or dead eye is made much cheaper and much better than in any other mode known to the subscriber." (Figures 6.5 and 6.7 show them both; figure 6.8 compares scoring in the two machines.) Blanchard's design to avoid cutting against the grain of the wood was different from the design of the Portsmouth scoring engine for that purpose, and more efficient. To score a block at Portsmouth, a workman had to perform four operations to present opposite sides and opposite ends to the cutter wheel. He had to stop the machine and turn the block over or rotate the table in between operations. Blanchard reduced the number of separate operations to two, by shaping the form board so as to lift the cutter completely away from the workpiece at the segments of its path that went against the grain. He made a point of claiming as his "invention and improvement" the arrangement "so . . . as to effect the scoring a block or dead eye by one change and two motions in which the cutters operate with the grain of the wood on all sides of the block or dead eye."

Although the Portsmouth scoring engine required twice as many "changes" and "motions" as the Blanchard scoring machine, it may not have been slower in output, for it worked on two blocks simultaneously, where the Blanchard machine held only one at a time. Blanchard's machine could score either a pulley-block or a deadeye, but at Portsmouth operations were assigned differently; one machine both shaped and scored the deadeyes.

# MAKING BLOCKS OF PLANKS

## SHAPING CHEEKS OF PLANK BLOCKS

The two pieces forming the outsides of a made block were called its "cheeks" (see bottom figure 6.1; figure 6.4). Blanchard's machine (U.S. Pat. #19)[9] was designed so that "cheeks are formed in the proper curves both transverse and lengthwise as the same are required to give a finished form to the sides of the block." Blanchard's "made" or "plank" blocks thus had traditional curved cheeks, while his smaller "common" blocks were left flat-cheeked. The machine held two cheek pieces, previously planed flat on one side, within a forked holder mounted on a conical shaft (see figure 6.9). Both pieces were moved against curved rotating cutters, in a compound curve controlled by the edge of a "form board" sliding against a "guide board," to cut one quarter-cheek on both pieces at a time. Thus in four passes all eight quarters of the two cheeks "are cut without being moved from the machine." This is an important consideration in a production line, not only to save setting-up time, but for keeping separate cuts in register and thereby promoting uniformity of product.

The action of this machine is much more complex than that of Blanchard's Springfield Armory machine for cutting the fore-end of gunstocks, since its blades are curved and its depth of cut is controlled by the motion of a sliding form board instead of a model of the end product. The Portsmouth block mill had no machine to cut cheeks for "made" blocks, so no direct comparison is possible. However, the Portsmouth shaping engine for solid-wood blocks cut the curves of their cheeks by moving a gouge along a curved path, unlike Blanchard's machine, which moved the cheek pieces while rotary curved blades cut them. In a sense Blanchard's machine is an elaboration of the Portsmouth scoring machine, in which blocks were also held in forked holders to allow repositioning without removal from the machine, and in which the rotary cutter, guided by a form board, operated on one quarter of the block at a time. But where the Portsmouth scoring machine cut a concave score along a linear path that varied in only in depth, Blanchard's cheek-shaping machine cut a convex surface onto an area that varied in breadth as well as depth.

MAKING END PIECES OF PLANK BLOCKS

Both of the two end pieces of a made block had to be cut "exactly to the thickness required by the mortice of the intended block," since in forming the head and arse ends of that mortice, or sheave chamber, they determined its width and the parallel spacing of the chamber's sides. In Blanchard's machine for this purpose (U.S. Patent #6),[10] a piece of wood is shaped on three of its sides at once by being forced down between two rotary straight-edged cutters and past a third that is optionally curved or straight (see figure 6.10). The wood is thus given two flat parallel planes and either a square or semicircular grooved edge, depending on its intended use at the rounded head end or the square arse end of the block's mortice. Then, "The workman reversing the operation at the winch . . . brings the piece up again and removes it, leaving the space between the center brackets open for other pieces to be successively formed in a similar manner." The shaping of the remaining curved outer edge of the end piece is left undescribed.

RIVETING PLANK BLOCKS

To complete the shell for a single-sheave plank block, a blockmaker sandwiched the two end pieces between the cheeks and riveted the whole block together at both ends. Like present-day tackle-blocks, Blanchard's plank blocks required only four rivets instead of the six illustrated for English "made" blocks in figure 6.1. His machine for this operation (U.S. Patent #9)[11] held a block on four small anvils, which adjusted to the right distances from one another, on a rotatable anvil plate. The machine compressed the block sandwich powerfully together between flanges, then its trip hammer riveted each of the four previously inserted rivets after the anvil plate was rotated a quarter-turn. After the riveting was completed "the workman . . . disengages the block to put in others in succession to be rivetted in a similar manner." Blanchard claimed that his mode of "rivetting plank Blocks while under a powerful pressure . . . by means of the above machine" produces "a plank Block . . . made much better and cheaper than heretofore, and . . . stronger and more durable."

After the end and cheek pieces—and partitions for double- or triple-sheaved blocks—were riveted together to form the block shell, it still required boring for a pin hole. Although unmentioned, this could be accomplished in the same machine (Patent #5) that bored and mortised solid blocks, even though the plank block did not, of course, need mortising. Then, we may assume, plank blocks could also undergo rounding in the rounding machine (Patent #4) and scoring in the scoring machine (Patent #8), as did the "common" or solid blocks, although in neither specification is this made explicit.

# MAKING PINS AND SHEAVES

### SAWING SHEAVES AND PINS AND DRILLING SHEAVES

This machine (U.S. Patent #17)[12] performed one of two operations at a time— sawing or drilling. In this machine, Blanchard allowed for using a variety of log sizes and for producing different widths of sheaves and lengths of pins. It was equipped with a circular saw mounted in a swinging frame for cross-cutting sheaves from a log of wood, or for sawing the rectangular blanks for wooden pins. It was also convertible to a sliding drill for boring the pin hole in a sheave. The saw had a "gauge slide" for regulating the "required thickness of sheave"; presumably different sized bits drilled holes for different sized pins. The drill was additionally capable of countersinking for a round bushing.

The operations that this machine performed were combined differently from the way in which the same tasks were assigned to machines in the Portsmouth block mill. At Portsmouth the "*lignum vitae* saws," held logs vertical instead of horizontal, to cross-cut the sheaves and saw pin blanks for powder-hold blocks;[13] then separate machines, the "crown saws," drilled the sheaves at the same time as they were cutting them perfectly circular. Blanchard's production line, however, requires the pin hole to be already drilled in the rough sheave in order to fasten the sheave to the machine (U.S. Patent #3) for cutting it circular and grooving its edge.

TURNING AND FINISHING SHEAVES AND PINS

From the machine for sawing and drilling, rough sheaves and flat-sided pin blanks would go to the machine for turning and finishing them (U.S. Patent #3).[14] Like the sawing and drilling machine, it had two distinct setups for two separate functions: making sheaves or pins. When the machine was set up for turning the sheaves, the workman fastened the sheave through its pin hole onto a mandril and as the sheave turned he cut it perfectly circular. From the front he advanced two cutters fixed on a slide at the desired diameter, plus one at the same diameter from behind. These cutters finished the edges of the sheave "square and clean." Then he operated a gouge on a cross-slide to cut the groove around the edge of the sheave "for the rope to lie in." With the alternative setup, the worker used the same machine to advance "a mill tool . . . whose hole is the required size of the pin" along a rotating pin blank to cut it cylindrical: "The teeth of the mill tool . . . strip off the angles of the pin . . . and finish it round and polished exactly to the required size."

Blanchard's two machines for preparing sheaves depart less from the block-makers' traditional use of a lathe than did the sheave-cutting and -smoothing machines at Portsmouth. Blanchard's patent machine cuts the sheave while it turns on a mandril, but in the crown saw of the Portsmouth block mill, a sheave is held stationary while the cylindrical saw cuts through it.[15] Blanchard's use of a slide for cutting the groove on the sheave's edge is, however, less traditional than the equivalent operation at Portsmouth, where the workman had to manipulate a hand-held gouge during the lathe's operation. Blanchard's sheave-making machinery simply omits the face-smoothing operation performed by that machine at the Portsmouth block mill (see figure 6.5 for the sequence of Portsmouth machines.)

For making wooden pins, Blanchard's provision of a powered lathe with a slide for carrying the mill tool along the *lignum vitae* pin was more mechanized than the simple lathe called a "whisket" that was applied to this task at Portsmouth. At Portsmouth, however, most of the pins were made of iron, in separate turning and polishing machinery.

COUNTERSINKING BUSHES IN SHEAVES

The final step in preparing a sheave for use in a pulley-block was to fit a friction-reducing bushing to its pin hole, so it was necessary beforehand to hollow out a bushing-shaped cavity around the pin hole on both sides of the sheave. The capability to countersink for an ordinary circular bushing was already built into Blanchard's machine for drilling pin holes (U.S. Patent #17), but for other shapes of bushing, such as three-eared or lozenge, a separate machine was required. (See figure 6.1 for bushing shapes.) Blanchard's machine for "countersinking for bushes" (U.S. Patent #18)[16] serves the same function as the Portsmouth "coaking" machine and operates in a similar manner, with a vertical-spindle rotary bit that cuts into the sheave a cavity of the desired shape and depth.[17] In both machines the sheave is moved around by hand-operated levers beneath the rapidly-rotating bit, whose spindle remains in one location. In Blanchard's machine, relatively easily removable templates or jigs for controlling the shape of the cut are added onto the platform, in contrast to the stops and curves that are built into the Portsmouth machine. This perhaps reflects a greater degree of expected variability in the style of bushing to be used in a commercial U.S. market, whereas the Royal Navy's sheaves were utterly standardized.

In fact, Blanchard's specification provides for the possibility not only of nonstandard bushings, but of downright nonuniform ones, even as his Springfield Armory machine for inletting lock plates in gunstocks made provision for nonuniformity in the shape of the gunlocks.[18] In both, there are devices for adjusting a pattern to the individual part itself so that the cutter will cut a customized shape and depth, but there is a significant difference. The lock plate-inletting machine at Springfield Armory was equipped with an adjustable hollow pattern to be copied by using a dummy tracing spindle to guide the cutting tool indirectly. Hence it was impossible to use a stencil or template for direct guidance of the cutter. But in this 1836 machine for countersinking sheave bushings, the actual bushing is lifted out after the "interior edges" of the "gig plates" are adjusted to its shape, so that the cutter can work through the resulting hole in the jig, directly on the sheave beneath. Thus it looks as if Blanchard solved the same problem, that of nonuniform gunlocks or sheave bushings, in two different ways in the two machines.[19] Another difference between the two machines is that in Blanchard's bush-inletting machine the workpiece (sheave) was moved around relative to the cutting tool, while in his lock-inletting machine, the cutter was moved relative to the workpiece (gunstock).

# MAKING DEADEYES

## Boring and scoring deadeyes

In deadeyes, David Steel remarks, "the edges of the holes nearest the resistance are gouged or sunk in to ease the strain."[20] In Blanchard's machine for this purpose (U.S. Patent #7),[21] a horizontal-spindle spoon-bit cutter was used both to bore the three holes through the deadeye and to rout out the scores for leading the lanyard ropes into the holes. The shape of the scores is traced by a "guide bar" moved within the "mortice" of a "form block." Thus the machine worked in part on the same copying principle as did the inletting machines in Blanchard's gunstocking production line at Springfield, but horizontally instead of vertically. The machine could be set up, "when the size of the dead eye admits it," to bore and score all three holes "at one operation by putting in two additional augers or bits . . . and by adjusting them to proper distances." Whether singly or by threes, the operator cut the scores on the opposite side of the deadeye by turning around "the swinging frame carrying the guide block and dead Eye with it" and repeating "a similar operation with the bit."

At Portsmouth, deadeyes were made differently. They were bored by the same machines that bored the pulley-blocks, and no provision was made for special machinery to score them for the lanyards, although they were scored by machine for the strap around their circumference. In Blanchard's production line design, this circumferential score around the deadeye was assigned to a different machine: after it left the boring and lanyard-scoring machine, and was turned to its round shape, the deadeye was scored by the same machine (U.S. Patent #8) that also scored pulley-blocks, as has already been discussed in that connection.

# DIFFUSION
# AND APPLICATION
# DIVERGENCE
# OF THE BLANCHARD
# LATHE

𝕏𝕏𝕏𝕏𝕏

**A**FTER the 1830s Blanchard did not continue to demonstrate "system thinking" in his design of machines. In order to exploit his irregular turning lathe fully for gunstocking and for blockmaking, Blanchard had transformed it into production lines of special-purpose machinery. There were several other important applications, however, for which the lathe could apparently be used profitably with little regard to the design of other machines in the production process, so he did not design those other machines. These applications were the turning of shoe lasts, handles for tools and agricultural implements, wheel spokes, and other parts for wagons and carriages. The products of the Blanchard lathe were in all these instances only intermediary to the end products for the consumer, namely, shoes, hand tools, agricultural implements, carriages, and wagons, but they were crucial intermediaries. Feeding into those industries, the Blanchard lathe provided the basis for enterprises that could and usually did exist independently from the enterprises that made those end products. By assigning and licensing the use of his machine, Blanchard abetted what may be called "application divergence," by which the same technology found use in otherwise disparate industries.[1]

During divergence of the Blanchard lathe out into these various applications, Blanchard and other users occasionally added features to it that helped them apply it to their particular needs. Some of these modifications were incorporated into patents; some were not, but became informally accepted as part of "the Blanchard lathe" whether or not Blanchard had included language in his patent that covered them. One such informal modification was a mechanism for making well-proportioned shoe lasts that varied in size, without changing the model. Another modification, the "back and under rest," was more explicitly recognized: Blanchard received a patent for it in 1843. It was a useful improvement for turning relatively long and thin objects such as ax handles and wheel spokes. Although separately patented, it was thereafter included in packages of patent rights to the Blanchard lathe that were assigned for use in the relevant industries. Blanchard also cross-bred his lathe with his unpatented inletting machine to produce a sculpture-copying machine, whose commercial use is undocumented. Blanchard's own use of it for showmanship, however, was important in his patent management.

Simultaneously with application divergence, the Blanchard lathe experienced geographical diffusion. Blanchard lathes underwent diffusion not only when Blanchard or other machine builders shipped the machines themselves, but also through his licensing and assignment of rights to build and use one's own Blanchard lathe. Particularly where distances were long or transportation difficult, this made diffusion of the lathes cheaper and easier than it would otherwise have been. Since Blanchard kept for himself (or for his Blanchard Gunstock Turning Factory) the rights for nonmilitary gunstocking and for lastmaking in eastern New England, the extent and timing of diffusion of Blanchard lathes for these purposes is less easily ascertained. But their spread westward for use in the carriage and wagon industry and the hand-tool and agricultural implement industries can be tracked through assignment records.

## SHOE LASTS AND BOOT TREES

According to Azariah Woolworth's own memory much later, he was prompted to develop a lastmaking machine in 1817–18 simply because

> One Augustus Turrell told me that I could not make a shoemaker's Last and that they would be quite an article for sale if I could make them. Well, Sir, I came to the conclusion at once that I should not undertake to make them by hand or by Guess—but should try to find out some rule; and concluded I could turn them after I had found some rule for it.[2]

Why did "one Augustus Turrell" consider lasts "would be quite an article for sale"?

In the evolution of the boot and shoe industry in the United States over the nineteenth century, "bespoke" or custom shoemaking by the town-based or itinerant cobbler was followed, particularly in New England, by a putting-out system in which upper parts of shoes and boots were sewn by women or whole families in scattered households, and the bottom parts were fastened to the uppers in small workshops called "ten-footers." Then the central shop of the putting-out shoe manufacturer grew, and took on more of the production processes, and the scattered operations were gradually centralized into factories, which increasingly acquired machinery after about 1855.[3]

Mechanization of shoe manufacture, then, followed a period of division of labor instead of initiating it. Shoemaking operations were mechanized only after the sewing machine was invented in the 1840s and adapted to shoe construction in the 1850s, first for uppers, and then, late in the decade, for soles.[4] Then further division of labor took place within the factories, as increasingly specialized machines were developed.

Even as feet vary in their proportions, so must the irregular forms vary on which boots and shoes are shaped. Hence for manufacturing boots and shoes, as distinct from custom-making them, lasts and boot trees require replication for three reasons: 1) to produce uniform copies of the same size and model shoe or boot, 2) to obtain various sizes of a given model of the shoe or boot, and 3) to obtain different proportions of depth, width, and length in the same sizes of a given model. In addition, since boots and shoes were (and are) very much subject to changes in fashion, frequent changes were made in the model itself, each time requiring replication of the new model in these three ways. For all these reasons shoe lasts and boot trees were needed in large quantities in the nineteenth-century boot and shoe industry. Those quantities also grew, of course, as the population of the country grew. In our period of study, irregular turning lathes for shaping wooden lasts and boot trees were rarely if ever incorporated into the factories for making boots and shoes, but remained the basis of independent woodworking enterprises that were suppliers to footwear manufacturers.

Whether by hand or machine, shoemaking required a last for the "lasting" and "bottoming" operations after the uppers were "bound" or sewn. The upper was stretched over the last and fastened to the sole while on the last, which was finally removed for the heeling operation. Before lasts were made by machine in quantities of sizes and shapes, a shoemaker would have a few of various sizes, which he padded out with leather when necessary to make higher insteps or wider toes.[5]

A shoemaker using hand tools or machines requires lasts for shoes and boot trees for boots. Lastmakers made both.[6] By hand-tool methods, a lastmaker could make three to six pairs of lasts a day.[7] Lasts were "assuredly the most important adjunct to shoemaking"[8] so one might expect mechanization of lastmaking to have gone hand in hand with the mechanization of shoemaking, but instead it preceded shoe machinery by several decades. There is no obvious reason, from the sequence of steps that took place in the changing organization of the shoe industry, why a need for quantities of uniform shoe lasts should have been suggested in 1817 to carpenter and clockmaker Azariah Woolworth in Waterbury, Connecticut.[9] Perhaps it was only the increasing number of shoes being produced by hand under the putting-out system that raised demand for shoe lasts and made them "quite an item for sale."[10]

Even though Blanchard invented the irregular turning lathe in the context of making gunstocks for military muskets, it is clear that he also had lastmaking in mind before the time of his January 1820 patent. Shortly after receiving his first irregular turning patent in September 1819, whose specification does not mention lastmaking, Blanchard put a model irregular turning lathe on display in Boston. Lastmaker Samuel Cox from Malden and shoemaker Nathaniel Faxon of Boston went together to look at it, and saw it turn a last in three minutes. Blanchard looked at Woolworth's machine in Waterbury, Connecticut that November, and then obtained a reissue of his patent in January. He mentioned lastmaking briefly in that specification, and submitted a patent drawing that showed a working model to make miniature lasts (see figure 3.2).

That winter Thomas Blanchard and Azariah Woolworth's assignee William Hovey each asked Samuel Cox to "stand skipper" over the manufacture of lasts by their respective machines. Each camp threatened to sue Cox if he signed on with the opposing faction, so he "concluded to stand neuter" until they had resolved their conflict over patent rights, as explained in chapter 3. Then he joined the Blanchard organization.

Blanchard's lathe was apparently not instantly successful for making lasts. Samuel Cox testified later that he had tried both kinds of machine without complete satisfaction, had resumed lastmaking by hand, and then had built a Woolworth-type machine with reciprocating cutter, modified by a Blanchard-type rotary motion of the model and workpiece and a feed screw. He used this hybrid machine for several years in the 1820s while under license for Blanchard's machine.[11]

Blanchard obtained the backing of Isaac Scott and James Clark and other stockholders, who were incorporated in Massachusetts as the Blanchard Gunstock Turning Factory on February 21, 1820; and he assigned all his rights to the corporation for all purposes and locations on June 29, 1820.[12] He must have been the chief agent of the corporation, however, for subsequent assignments of patent rights were still in his own name. Blanchard, or his corporation, had agents to license operators of the lathe. One agent, Colonel Henry Orne,[13] "sold rights . . . in Lynn, Danvers, and elsewhere," according to Charles White, an early lastmaking licensee. White said he had seen the Blanchard lathe put in operation by Scott and Clark, after which it "laid still for 3 or 4 years" until in 1823 White had bargained with Orne to use the machine free for a year's trial, and if it was successful, to buy it for $400 and pay a fee of $100 annually from then on.[14] White's successful use of the lathe induced Samuel Cox to try again after his initial difficulties with it.[15] From 1834 another agent-assignee was James Hendley of Boston, from whom lastmakers in New Hampshire and eastward in New England bought licenses.[16]

These agents were not completely effective at protecting the patent rights of the Blanchard Gunstock Turning Factory. While Blanchard was preoccupied with gunstocking and steamboating in Springfield in the 1820s and with designing blockmaking machinery in New York City in the 1830s, many unlicensed users began running Blanchard lathes, including lastmaker Chandler Sprague of North Bridgewater, Massachusetts. After getting his patent extended, Blanchard sued them in greater numbers than before. From the testimony of various lastmakers in these suits we can learn something about the economics of shoe last manufacturing in the decades of the 1830s through 1850s.

## LASTMAKING COSTS, PRICES, AND OUTPUTS

In 1838, after last prices had already been lowered by machine production,[17] a typical lastmaker sold finished lasts for about 63 cents a pair, with a discount of 5 percent to 20 percent for large and steady customers. The rough blocks of wood cost 2 to 3 cents each, or $20 for a thousand. It was not unheard of for one man to turn 200 or even 300 lasts a day by machine, but 120 to 130 was more usual. It was considered a fair day's work for three men with one machine to make and finish 125 lasts including handwork on the toes and heels after removing the lasts from the machines. Allowing for incidental delay, 120 a day was their estimated average over a month's time. Wages, ranging from $1.25 to $2.25, averaged $1.75 per day for a good hand.[18]

Thus, in an average day of operation, the lastmaker would pay $5.25 for three men's labor (perhaps including his own) and $2.40 for 120 rough blocks, which when finished into lasts he would sell for $37.80, or after, say, a 10 percent discount of $3.78, for $34.02. His remainder, after paying $5.25 for wages and $2.40 for raw material, would be $26.37 return from operating the one machine. From this he would need to pay for rent, amortization of his equipment and royalty fee, and fuel if his shop was steam- instead of waterpowered. If the lastmaker bought his machine from the Blanchard Gunstock Turning Factory, it would be well-made and relatively expensive; Charles White, for instance, had paid $400 for his. If he had one made locally or made it himself, using wood instead of iron wherever possible, he could cut the initial cost considerably. Estimates of the cost of such a machine built in 1834 ranged from $125 to $175.[19] Thus, if the lastmaker devoted as little as $1 out of his daily gross of $26 to paying for the inexpensive or the expensive version of the Blanchard lathe, he would have it paid for in, say, 150 to 400 working days—six to sixteen months. Even allowing that these calculations are incomplete and based on limited data, one can see that the margin between costs and earnings was fairly comfortable for the average productive lastmaker using an irregular turning lathe.

Since our average lastmaking team of three could produce only nine to eighteen pairs of lasts a day without a machine, but sixty pairs with it, it is not surprising to learn that by this time very few lasts were still being made by hand. Boston shoemaker Nathaniel Faxon, who in many years sold over 6000 lasts annually in addition to the ones he used himself, said in 1838 that less than a hundred in the last seven years were handmade.[20]

At that time, the two lastmaking establishments reported in an 1837 census of Suffolk County (Boston) manufactures had capital totaling $18,000, employed 29 persons between them, and were producing $40,000 worth of lasts annually. Thus the value of the output per employee was $1379. This was much more than the output for an employee in the manufacture of boots and shoes in Suffolk County at the same time, when 359 employees produced boots and shoes worth $102,641, or an average of $285 per employee.[21] This is perhaps a reflection of the relatively advanced state of lastmaking mechanization over shoemaking mechanization at the time. If we divide the value of $40,000 by 63 cents, the undiscounted price of a pair of lasts, we can estimate the output in Suffolk County in 1837 to have been 63,492 pairs, or, at 300 working days a year, almost 212 pairs per working day. Collins Stevens, whose factory was one of the lastmaking establishments in Suffolk County, said he was making 175 lasts,[22] or 87.5 pairs per day per machine. This was less than his reputed record-setting 300 lasts in one day, but well above the average lastmaking output of 120.

If some lastmaking establishments of that time were bigger than average, others were smaller and less prosperous. Chandler Sprague in North Bridgewater, for instance, began making lasts in mid-1836 with a second-hand machine and one helper, at a waterpower site that proved troublesome by going dry so that he had to move his shop and lost three months out of seven. Even on days when he could run the machine, his output was only twelve pairs of lasts a day instead of the average of sixty pairs. He was netting only $4.09 a day instead of our hypothetical average of

$26.37.[23] Yet Sprague survived losing a lawsuit to Blanchard for which he had to pay damages of $521.27 in 1838. According to the terms of the settlement, Sprague became a licensee for a fee of $50 a year for three years; then he was to be on the same terms as other licensees.[24] James Hendley was the assignee to whom he paid the fee. After 1847, when Blanchard obtained renewal of his patent and repurchased James Hendley's assignment territory (Maine, New Hampshire, Rhode Island and Massachusetts east of the Connecticut River), Chandler Sprague was still one of the licensees. They now began paying Blanchard 3 cents per pair of lasts actually produced, instead of a fixed annual fee. In autumn of 1847, the licensees held meetings to agree on a "tariff" or list of prices at which to sell different kinds of lasts, and Blanchard thereafter required his licensees to adhere to those prices[25] (see figure 7.1). Collins Stevens and three other lastmakers later attested to the Congressional Committee on Patents that they deemed "said tariff of prices fair & reasonable & of great advantage to the public generally," since its average increase over the immediately previous prices was only 1 1/2 cents per last, while the Blanchard lathe had reduced "the expense of Lasts to the consumer to about one half the price paid for them before said Invention."[26]

By 1858 Sprague's output had increased to about fifty pairs of lasts a day. He made 7757 lasts in the first quarter of 1858, and paid Blanchard $116.37 royalty,[27] which would amount to $465.42 annually. According to the "Tariff of Prices" used by Collins Stevens in 1856, the price of finished lasts had stayed the same since 1847, at an average of about 39 cents a pair.[28] At 3 cents per pair, the royalty was over 7 1/2 percent of this average list price. In 1857 Blanchard notified his licensees that he was raising the royalty to 4 cents a pair, that is, to more than 10 percent of the average list price. Blanchard said he intended to raise an additional $2,000 royalty per year from his thirteen licensees, assuming their output stayed the same, by raising the rate 1/2 cent per last.[29] From this we may infer that Blanchard's annual income from his lastmaking licensees at the old rate of 1 1/2 cents per last was $6,000. We may also derive a figure of 400,000 lasts for his licensees' total annual output, or a mean of 30,769 for each of the thirteen. At 31,028, Chandler Sprague's output had increased since 1838 to slightly above this average.[30] If he was selling at the average list price of 39 cents per pair of lasts, Sprague was grossing $6,050 annually at his lastmaking business in 1858. This may be an underestimate, for a local census of North Bridgewater in 1855, probably referring to Sprague's establishment alone, indicated last production of

# TARIFF OF PRICES.

| | | |
|---|---|---|
| MEN'S Block and Brogan, Right and Left Lasts, | 50 cts. | per pair. |
| "        "        "        "        Straight Lasts, | 25 " | each. |
| BOY'S    "        "        "        Straight, and Right and Left, | 42 " | per pair. |
| YOUTH'S Block and Brogan, Straight, and Right and Left, | 38 " | "    " |
| CHILDREN'S "        "        "        "        "        "        " | 36 " | "    " |
| WOMEN'S        "        "        "        "        "        "        " | 45 " | "    " |
| MISSES'        "        "        "        "        "        "        " | 40 " | "    " |
| MEN'S Pump and Slipper, Straight, Right and Left Lasts, | 45 " | "    " |
| WOMEN'S Straight, and Right and Left, Low Last, | 36 " | "    " |
| MISSES' Low and Bootee Last, - - - | 15 " | each. |
| CHILDREN'S Bootee Lasts, - - - | 14 " | " |
| MEN'S Right and Left Low Kip Brogan Lasts, - | 42 " | per pair. |
| BOY'S    "    "    "    "    "    "    "    " _ | 36 " | "    " |
| YOUTH'S Straight, Right and Left Low Lasts, - | 32 " | "    " |
| MEN'S finished Rubber Lasts, - - - | 50 " | "    " |
| "        "        "        "        with Block,    - | 52 " | "    " |
| WOMEN'S        "        "        "        "        - | 40 " | "    " |
| "        "        "        "        without Block,    - | 38 " | "    " |
| CHILDREN'S and MISSES'        "        "        - | 30 " | "    " |
| "        "        "        with Block,    - | 32 " | "    " |
| MEN'S Stoga Lasts, - - - - | 20 " | each. |
| BOY'S    "        "    - - - - | 18 " | " |
| YOUTH'S        "    - - - - | 15 " | " |

FIGURE 7.1. Price list for lasts. Thomas Blanchard's assignees agreed on these prices in 1847. Assignee Collins Stevens, a large-scale last manufacturer in Boston, submitted this as "Exhibit A" in one of Thomas Blanchard's lawsuits. From *Thomas Blanchard vs. Warren Wadleigh and Isaac N. Lane,* (From U. S. Circuit Court, New Hampshire District, 1857. National Archives, Boston Branch.)

40,000 lasts that year, valued at $10,000, or an average 50 cents a pair.[31] Nevertheless we may observe from the economics of lastmaking under Blanchard's patent in the 1850s that the patent rights for eastern New England earned about as much for Blanchard annually from thirteen licenses as the value of the output of one of his average licensees.

As mentioned in chapter 3, this group of thirteen lastmakers organized around Blanchard and his patent constituted a convenient pool of common "interest." Blanchard drew upon them for testimony in lawsuits, and for funds to help pay for a lobbyist in Washington to fight against the importation of lasts from the Canadian provinces. They also constituted a price fixing agreement. So long as Blanchard didn't issue any more licenses for eastern New England, they could be assured of a stable share of the market for lasts.

In 1857 (the wrong year for such optimism) Blanchard apparently came to the opinion that his licensees should collectively produce more lasts, in order to satisfy the demand for them, which would of course also increase his income from royalties. When this didn't happen, he warned them that if they didn't increase their output to "meet the market," he would issue licenses to more lastmakers in the area. This implies that he was refraining from issuing as many licenses as he could have done. Apparently disappointed in the results of this ploy, Blanchard next issued notice that in the following year's licenses he would raise the royalty from 1 1/2 cents to 2 cents per last. Some licensees paid the increased fee without protest, but the seven who had cooperated in financing the anti-importation lobby said Blanchard had promised them in return that he wouldn't raise their rates. They continued to pay Blanchard at the old rate. Chandler Sprague and Collins Stevens were among the seven who refused to pay the increased fee; so was another long-term licensee, Samuel Cox and Son, in Malden and Boston. Blanchard took Sprague to court, charging him with "patent infringement." After taking much testimony, Circuit Justice Clifford dismissed the bill of complaint as not being a case of infringement.[32]

## DESIGN ADAPTATIONS FOR LASTMAKING LATHES

In addition to paying fees, testifying in law suits, and helping to lobby Congress, Blanchard's licensees constituted a pool of innovative talent. Collins Stevens, one of the recalcitrant seven in 1859, had been a Blanchard licensee in Boston since about 1827, and was said to have made 300 lasts on one machine in a day. His was one of the two lastmaking establishments in the Suffolk County census in 1837, whose output was large for the time. He also made a valuable contribution to the design of the lathe in order to adapt it to the task of lastmaking. In about 1836 he devised an addition to the Blanchard lathe for varying the proportions on a given size last, and for making lasts of different sizes from the same model. He later called it a "fan board and lever."[33] It was an adjustable device that automatically pushed the swinging lathe, or frame holding the workpiece, a controlled distance farther out from the cutter than the model was from the tracing wheel, the distance varying in proportion to the contours of the model. This permitted the lastmaker to make proportional increases in last sizes from a single model, instead of having to use a different model for each size of last. Stevens normally produced lasts of about five sizes from a single model.[34]

Stevens later said that it was also possible to achieve the same results by other mechanical means and that before he had begun doing it mechanically, operators customarily controlled the swinging lathe for this purpose by hand, while the machine was in operation.[35] Some witnesses in 1838 said Blanchard's lathe could enlarge from a model, but not maintain proper proportions, so they regarded Stevens's device as a distinct invention.[36] But Stevens himself considered that his improvement was covered in principle by Blanchard's patent, although, he said, the patent specification did not describe the same "mode" of achieving this result.[37] Blanchard's patent specification of 1820 does say in very general terms how to make his lathe produce a "resemblance in form preserving the corresponding proportions with, but . . . smaller or larger than, the model," but does not specify any particular mechanical means for achieving this effect. Collins Stevens apparently did not attempt to patent his device, and its use spread informally among Blanchard lathe licensees for lastmaking. Over the years this informal adaptation of the lathe to lastmaking came to be accepted as a regular feature of Blanchard's invention.

Thomas Blanchard himself built a steam-powered lastmaking lathe at James M. Quinby's coach factory in Newark in 1843. It was the first Blanchard lathe the eminent machinist and inventor Seth Boyden had ever seen that produced different sizes from the same model. In the following three years Boyden built five Blanchard lathes in Newark on order from Amos K. Carter, using patterns from Thomas Blanchard's shop for the first one. Boyden testified that the machine patterns Blanchard sent from Boston "contained the principle of graduating and regulating and varying the width and length of the article to be produced" and that he, Boyden, understood that "principle and the peculiar mode of operation" to be part of Blanchard's "discovery" as described in his patent specification. "Altho'," Boyden added, "the various details of constructing the machinery . . . are not set out there at length." All but one of the Blanchard lathes that Boyden built in that period included "an index scale for graduating the width and length of the article turned, so as to produce different sizes from the same model," and that one was for making hatblocks instead of shoe lasts.[38]

Besides proportional variation of sizes, a feature important for lastmaking that a Blanchard lathe didn't need for other applications was the ability to make mirror images of the model for right and left shoes (see figure 3.4). This feature is mentioned in the 1820 patent specification as "resemblance in reverse . . . as in making a right shoe last after a left shoe last as the model." It was to be effected by causing the cutting wheel and tracing wheel to move laterally in contrary directions over the workpiece and model instead of the same direction. As with the preserving of proportions while changing sizes, Blanchard's specification states the general relation that the parts of the machine must bear to one another in position and action to achieve the desired effect, but does not specify exactly the mechanical means for making them do so. This was left to the discretion of "any artist skilled in the construction of machinery."

In the case of proportional variation in sizes, Collins Stevens' particular means for achieving this—his "levers and fan board"—gained a wide acceptance, although it was not necessarily the only solution to the problem. In the case of resemblance in reverse for right and left lasts, however, the mechanical problem was a simpler one of gearing to synchronize lateral motion in opposite directions, and no particularly identified "artist . . . in . . . machinery" emerges from the records as deserving even transitory credit for achieving the desired effect. Implicitly, the concept of right and left lasts was already a familiar one in 1820; otherwise Blanchard would not have mentioned it so casually in his specification. The machine Samuel Cox made for his own use in about 1824 was able to make both right and left lasts.[39] Yet we are told by several sources that "crooked" shoes instead of "straight" ones were not commonly made before the Civil War or even later.[40] If so, it was not for lack of earlier means to make matching right and left lasts by machine, which Blanchard's lathe made easy. The price list shown in figure 7.1 indicates production of straight as well as right and left lasts, and that rights and lefts were the same price as straight ones.

Design changes in the Blanchard lastmaking lathe after the period here discussed were small; the maximum output per machine did not increase strikingly although the average probably rose. Blanchard's lathe clearly prevailed over Woolworth-type lathes for lastmaking in the long run of experience, so twentieth-century pictures and descriptions of lastmaking lathes are not very different from the Blanchard lathe of the mid-nineteenth century. An American book of 1916 on the shoe industry says such a machine "turns out about 15 pairs of lasts an hour,"[41] which only matches the record highs of 300 lasts per (ten-hour) day reported for Collins Stevens in 1838. Yet an English book of 1936 says "The output from the [last-turning] lathe varies from 24 pairs of lasts per day when fine-turned to 45 pairs per day rough-turned."[42] Even allowing for a shorter working day, that output falls far short of the 1838 average of sixty pairs daily already noted above in New England.

## THE IMPORTANCE OF LAST UNIFORMITY

From the 1820s, one can argue, when the manufacture of shoes was decentralized but growing, the sets of machine-made, uniform lasts that were ordered by shoe manufacturers for a given model of shoe were the only means of preventing wide variations of size and shape of shoes. If the geographically scattered shoe makers working for any one shoe manufacturer were given uniform lasts, then they could produce uniform shoes even before shoe production itself was centralized or mechanized. Uniform lasts were in an important sense not only tools of production, but also the gauges for achieving uniformity of production. For right and left shoes of a given pair, this argument is obvious, but it applies also to the problem of keeping the variation tolerably low between different makers of two pairs of shoes nominally the "same" size within a given model of shoe, and also among different models.

Exactly how distribution to shoemakers of different models and sizes of lasts took place in the early period of the shoemaking industry is not mentioned in the records. I suppose that the entrepreneur shoe manufacturers, like Nathaniel Faxon, who sold over 6000 lasts a year, bought the lasts from lastmakers and resold them to the shoe makers to whom they "put out" work. This supposition is consistent with a few hints about "paying by lasts" in Blanche Hazard's book on the evolution of the boot and shoe industry in Massachusetts.[43] Whatever the mode of distribution was, the shoemakers used the lasts to make shoes of specified styles and standardized sizes. By making uniform lasts in quantity, the irregular turning lathe made it feasible, technically and economically, to abandon custom-made "bespoke" shoemaking, yet give customers some assurance of finding shoes to fit their feet in styles that they liked, even well before shoe manufacture itself was centralized into factories and mechanized.

## HANDLES AND SPOKES

From lawsuit records we know that Blanchard's lathe was applied to making ax handles and wheel spokes several years before 1840, by sale of machines and by license, but the earliest recorded (and restored) assignments for these purposes were made in September of that year, for New England and New York, and for Worcester County, Massachusetts, respectively.[44] Like the fore-ends of gunstocks, and unlike lasts, spokes and ax handles are long relative to their thickness. They had a tendency in the original Blanchard lathe to tremble or spring inward in the middle under the impact of the cutting wheel. After these initial assignments, and possibly in response to his assignees' experience with the machines, Blanchard invented an improvement to his lathe to remedy the problem, and obtained a patent for it in early 1843[45] (see figure 7.2). Thereafter, assignments for his lathe included this improvement, sometimes explicitly calling it the "back and under rest."

Several changes from the original 1819–1820 lathe are embodied in this patent specification. In the 1843 version of the machine the pivoting axis of the "lathe" holding the model and the workpiece is below the bench rather than above, so the specification calls it a "rocking lathe" instead of a "hanging lathe." It will be recognized that the underbench pivot was a reversion to the rocking motion previously known in ornamental turning lathes, discussed in chapter 4, and that it was also incorporated into the second generation of the gunstocking lathes described in chapter 5. Another change is that the "tracing" or "friction" wheel of the 1819–20 version was reduced to a wheel sector, named a "friction point." Unlike the 1819–20 version, which talks about equal sizes, this specification reflects the new position of the tracer *above* the cutter and therefore farther from their common "rocking" axis, by stipulating that the diameter of the pattern must be one-fourth larger than the article to be formed; similarly the "curve of the friction point" (i.e., wheel sector) is one-fourth greater radius than the radius of the cutting wheel. The major change, however, is the addition of back and under rests to steady the model against the friction point and the spoke or handle (or gunstock) against the impact of the cutters. The whole rocking stock with rests moves along with the sliding carriage that carries the cutting wheel and friction point past the length of the spoke or handle. The specification says the rests "should be faced with steel to prevent them from wearing by the pattern

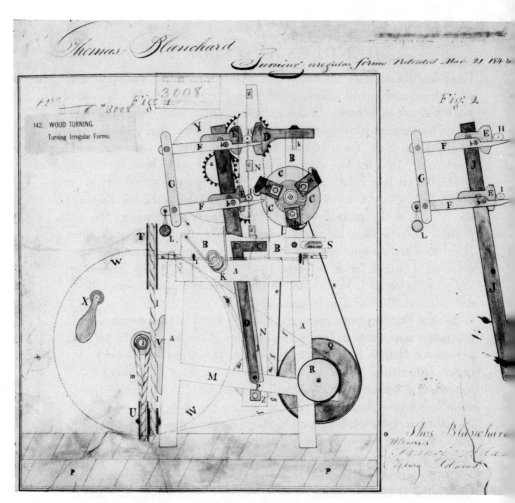

FIGURE 7.2. Patent drawing of Blanchard's improved lathe of 1843, end view. It was intended for making ax handles, spokes, or other long and thin objects. The "rocking lathe" (N-N) is shown in dotted lines. Between unshown centers it holds the workpiece (I) and model (H), which slowly rotate, causing it to rock on axis (P) below the bench, as does the "rocking stock" holding the "back and under rests" (E) and (F). These, counterweighted by weight (L) and pressed forward by spring (K), traverse along with the friction sector (D) and cutting wheel (C), bearing up under and behind the model and workpiece, to prevent their trembling during operation. (Drawing for U.S. Patent #3,008, March 21, 1843, from National Archives Cartographic Section, Alexandria, Virginia.)

and rough material" as these rotate on their axes. The patent drawing shows the familiar "crooked knife" cutters on the cutting wheel. Blanchard's patented modification of his lathe made it more attractive to makers of relatively long, thin wooden objects.

## TOOL HANDLES

The iron-and-steel heads of axes, hatchets, adzes, pickaxes, etc. were usually produced and sold separately from their "helves" or handles, so Blanchard's customers for this application of his lathe were not necessarily tool manufacturers, but more often independent woodworkers. The Blanchard lathes used for turning ax handles ranged from sophisticated metal-framed ones made in machine shops, including Blanchard's on Dover Street in Boston, to rather crude, homemade ones. In 1848 assignee Amos K. Carter showed a model Blanchard lathe in court, "to establish the principle of Blanchard's invention." The *Scientific American* described its back and under rest feature:

> On the back part of the machine, there is a curious but beautiful sliding rest, which is the subject of a patent in itself. It moves along after the cutter wheel and has two plane faces on which the pattern and cut helve rest. The pattern and helve roll upon the planes, while the rest has a rocking motion which accommodates itself to all the uneven turning of the patterns, etc. as they revolve. For turning long articles, this rest is a beautiful and positively necessary part of the machine.[46]

The illustration accompanying this article shows a neatly-made machine for cutting ax helves from a model (see figure 7.3). The cutting wheel appears to be of the crooked-knife type. A Blanchard lathe of this kind but with heavier cutters can be viewed at the Henry Ford Museum in Dearborn, Michigan.[47]

However, the irregular turning lathe that ax handle makers frequently used had a circular saw for a cutting tool instead of the crooked-knife wheel. Then, as the workpiece rotated, the machine cut a flat-bottomed spiral saw kerf that was the width of the set of the saw teeth, typically about 1/4 inch wide.[48] For example, the primitive wood-framed ax handle machine surviving at the National Museum of American History (see figure 7.4) is different from the one described and pictured in the 1848 *Scientific American* or in Blanchard's 1843 specification. Compared with those, it has a distinctly homemade appearance. Its component parts are

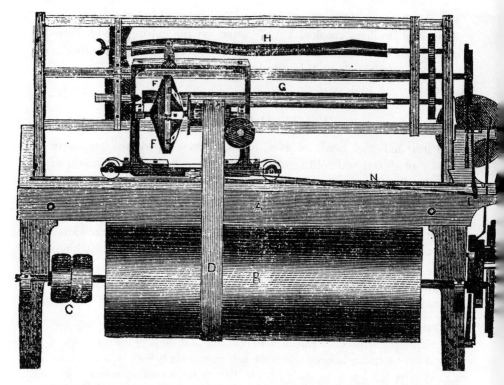

FIGURE 7.3. Blanchard's improved lathe of 1843, side view. The cutter wheel FF cuts
the workpiece G as the friction point above traces contours of the model H. Cord N pulls
the carriage of the cutter wheel and friction point from left to right along the length of the
bench. The back and under rests are not shown in this view. This drawing was "taken from
a model that has been before the Court to establish the principle of Blanchard's invention."
(From *Scientific American* 3 (September 9, 1848): 401.

reoriented, so that the model and workpiece are side by side on the same
axis rather than one above the other on parallel axes, and the friction
point presses up at an angle from below the model rather than in from the
side. Gravity, supplemented by the workman working a lever, holds the
model against the friction point and the workpiece against the cutting
wheel of this machine. The pivot for the rocking action of the workpiece
and model is a rocking beam behind them rather than a hanging lathe
above or a rocking lathe below. Lacking a "beautiful" back and under
rest, this arrangement of components belies the above quotation that "this
rest is a . . . positively necessary part of the machine" for turning spokes
or helves.[49]

FIGURE 7.4. Ax-handle lathe. In this primitive, mostly wooden machine, the model on the left and workpiece on the right rotate on the same axis. The rocking beam rocks up and down as the friction point presses up against the contours of the model. The cutting wheel, a rotary saw with side hooked cutters, shapes the ax handle accordingly. An attached cut-off saw is shown in left foreground. (Photograph from the National Museum of American History.)

The cutting tool of this Smithsonian ax-handle lathe is of a compound type: a circular saw with several crooked-knife attachments around the periphery. It leaves a flat-bottomed tool mark that is different from the round-bottomed spiral groove cut by the original Springfield Blanchard lathe, by its replica in the National Museum of American History, and by the Blanchard lathes of the second generation at Enfield Armory.[50]

## ROYALTIES, PRICES, AND OUTPUT OF TOOL HANDLES

Whether sophisticated or crude, and regardless of its cutter shape, if it was deemed to be a Blanchard lathe, the owner of an ax-handle machine was supposed to pay royalty. According to Abner Lane of Killingworth,

Connecticut, who had constructed and used Blanchard lathes from about 1838 and held a license from Blanchard's assignees in the 1850s, the royalty fee was 1/2 cent apiece for hatchet handles and 1 or 1 1/2 cents apiece, depending on length, for ax helves.[51] One ax-handle lathe in Norwalk, Connecticut had a daily output in 1851 of five to ten dozen ax and pick handles daily; three-fourths of this output was in ax handles, which were reported to yield 75 cents profit per dozen, while the pickax handles netted 50 cents per dozen.[52] The owners of this machine had understandably preferred not to reduce these figures by 12 cents royalty fee to Blanchard on each dozen handles, which would amount to 16 percent reduction of their profit on ax handles, 24 percent on pickax handles. Blanchard was therefore suing them for patent infringement. In an earlier infringement suit in Philadelphia the defendant, James B. Miller, said he and his workman ran his machine only two days a week, on each of which he made 20 ax helves and 40 hatchet helves.[53] If the fees were the same in Philadelphia as in Connecticut, Mr. Miller should have paid Blanchard's assignee Amos K. Carter 40 to 50 cents royalty per day's output to avoid being sued by the Blanchard Gunstock Turning Factory.

# WESTWARD DIFFUSION

We can infer that Mr. Miller's operation was a smaller one than that of Blanchard's first tool handle assignees, Gibbs and Boies, who agreed in 1840 to pay $200 per year in $50 quarterly installments for the assignment of rights for turning "handles of all kinds of tools now in use" for all the New England states and New York state.[54] Spelman Gibbs and Jarvis Boies were partners in manufacturing handles for axes, hatchets, etc., in Chester, Connecticut. Having set up their shop with Blanchard's machinery and conducted business for several years, enjoying the privilege of suing any competitors in New England who neglected to pay them for a license, Gibbs and Boies were aggrieved when Blanchard obtained the second extension of his patent in 1847 and wanted to charge what they regarded as an "exorbitant" price for renewal of their assignment. They went to court over the issue in May 1847.[55] We know that Boies, at least, continued in business thereafter, for he helped Blanchard sue two illicit ax and hatchet handle makers in Walpole and Alstead, New Hampshire, in 1853.[56] Boies joined with Josiah Leland of Union, Connecticut and the ubiquitous Amos K. Carter of Newark, N.J. to buy broader rights from Blanchard on May 9, 1849[57] and participated in selling the rights for Indiana, Illinois, and Missouri to one Henry M. Preston of St. Louis, in 1855. Preston paid them $2,000. The foreseen tool-handle applications of the lathe was expanding as the assignment moved west: Preston's assignment mentions not only "turning handles for all kinds of axes [and] hatchets [but also] adzes, smith tools, carpenters and joiners tools, and marble and stone cutter tools."[58] The drafters of this assignment probably had Indiana limestone quarries in mind. Five and one-half years later Preston sold his right for Missouri alone for only $100 to Woodburn and Scott,[59] who had previously bought rights to the Blanchard lathe in making carriage wheels in St. Louis, Missouri.

## PLOW HANDLES

Meanwhile, the application of Blanchard's lathe to handles of plows and other agricultural implements began later and followed a somewhat different path, which was linked to the path of Blanchard's woodbending machine applications. Implicitly, plows were not considered "tools" in the terms of the assignment to Gibbs and Boies, nor was the Blanchard lathe deemed suitable for shaping plow handles until Blanchard also devised a reliable way of bending them, at the behest of "the Boston manufacturers of Agricultural Implements," in the late 1840s. Plow handles were "peculiarly shaped, enlarging toward the ends deep in the vertical line as they lay on the plow, the vertical section forming an oval when finished."

The method plow manufacturers were using at that time "was first to make the handle broad across the bending line, then bend it, and afterwards reduce its width to the required degree by hand shaving."[60] Clearly the handles could not be put in the lathe for shaping after they were bent, and it is understandable that the manufacturers would not want to invest in Blanchard's lathe to shape the handles first, with the breakage rate they were then experiencing: two out of five handles broke during bending. Once Blanchard's method of woodbending was available, which dramatically reduced the breakage rate, it made economic sense to use both machines together. Blanchard's woodbending patent was granted December 18, 1849 (see chapter 8 on woodbending).

It seems likely that Blanchard himself licensed his lathe and bending machine to the "Boston manufacturers of agricultural implements" for a while, but three years later he assigned his rights for both machines for "all Plow, Cultivator, and Harrow handles and for no other purpose whatever, ... throughout all the States and territories of the United States" to A. V. Blanchard and Company. This was a partnership of his nephews Alonzo V., John D., and Franklin Blanchard, who ran the scythe factory that their father John B. Blanchard had set up in Palmer, Massachusetts. Over six years they paid their uncle Thomas $10,000 for the combined assignment: $8,500 for the lathe, and $1,500 for the wood-bending machine.[61]

As it had for other tool handles, the use of Blanchard's lathe and his woodbending machine for plow and cultivator handles spread westward. Beyond Blanchard's assignment to his nephews, we have little information on purchase or licensing of Blanchard lathes for such handles, but it seems likely that any plow-handle manufacturer who bought a Blanchard bender would also buy a Blanchard lathe. For instance, agricultural implement manufacturers Whittemore, Squier and Company, of Chicopee Falls, Massachusetts, made plows with "handles turned and bent by Blanchard's patent process."[62] In 1851 or 1852 James Coleman of Cincinnati, Ohio bought a woodbending machine from A. V. Blanchard and Company to make plow handles and by 1859 James Coleman and Company were turning out 150,000 pairs of plow handles annually.[63] In 1864 both a younger Coleman and the Colemans' woodbending machine had found their way into the large carriage-parts establishment of Royer, Coleman, and Company (previously Royer, Simonton and Company), and that company apparently branched into production of handles for agricultural implements. They paid A. V. Blanchard and Company $1,500 for an assignment of the patent rights in Ohio only for "turning, bending, and polishing plow and cultivator handles."[64] The persistence of the term "turning" in this assignment even two years after the Blanchard lathe patent had finally expired suggests a usual conjunction of the Blanchard lathe with the woodbending machine for making plow handles. Already owners of Blanchard lathes for carriage-making purposes, the Royers would have needed an additional license (had the patent still been in force) to use them for making plow handles.

## POLISHING HANDLES

The polishing machine alluded to in the A. V. Blanchard assignment to Royer's was presumably the one patented by Thomas Blanchard in 1854.[65] Polishing or sanding machines were usually solid rotating cylinders or cones coated with abrasive or polishing material.[66] To polish an object the operator of those machines would hold the object to the rotating cylinder and move it around to bring every part into contact with an abrasive surface. It would be difficult or slow to reach every part of irregularly curved objects with any such a machine. According to Blanchard's specification, however, his machine used an endless belt coated with "emery or some other suitable grinding, smoothing, or polishing material," and had a "feeding carriage" to hold the article to be polished. The belt ran over a set of pulleys and rollers so arranged that it came "in contact with and around the surface of the article to be reduced, smoothed or polished" as that article traversed in its carriage. The machine stopped automatically at the end of each traverse, whereupon "the attendant next moves the carriage entirely back, removes the piece of work from it and supplies it with a fresh piece." It could also be operated without its automatic feature: "Instead of employing the feeding carriage the article . . . may be held in the hands of an attendant and presented between the guide rollers or in any other proper way to the peculiar action of the reducing or polishing belt."

The flexibility of the belt presumably allowed it to conform better to the contours of the plow handle or other irregular object, but its other advantage over the usually depicted sanding machine was its automatic feed. Again, Blanchard's originality was in the machine's kinematics and not its components: for the way the belt was made to run in the machinery as described in the specification, and not for "the invention of an endless polishing or smoothing belt" itself. This machine was applicable to "various other articles" in addition to plow handles, and its fourteen-year patent did not run out until 1868, that is, six years later than the Blanchard lathe, but there is no further mention of it in the assignment record for plow handle turning or bending.

Thomas Blanchard's machine for polishing plow handles would make a helpful, though not essential addition to his machines for turning and bending them. For production of handles for plows and similar agricultural implements, then, it appears that three of Blanchard's inventions complemented one another and comprised a convenient package for sale and use, although they were not as closely interdependent in function as were the machines in his gunstock and pulley block production lines.

## WHEEL SPOKES AND CARRIAGE PARTS

A similar situation developed with regard to the use of Blanchard's inventions in making wheels and other parts of carriages and wagons. While in Pittsburgh in 1830, Blanchard submitted an estimate to Major

R. L. Baker of the arsenal there, for eight machines to be used in making gun carriages. They were for slitting and cross-cutting timber, turning flat or curved shapes, tenoning each end of wheel spokes, planing planks, mortising wheel hubs and flat pieces, smoothing wood, and sawing angles and curves. Except for the "self adjusting Laith" and the tenoning and wheel hub mortising machines, these were not special-purpose machines, but they were expected to save half the labor cost of one hundred dollars per carriage, and hence their own cost of $5,000 during the construction of one hundred carriages. "But," added Major Baker in reporting to the Chief of Ordnance, "what is more important than the economy which Mr. Blanchard anticipates, will be the attainment of an uniformity in our construction, which, by the present mode of work is as difficult, as it is desirable." [67]

We do not know whether this project was eventually carried out; it seems unlikely that Blanchard did so in 1830, in view of his steamboating activities that year. Blanchard neither followed through on this exercise to design machinery for making non-military carriages, nor even on a subline for making wheels. Yet his turning and bending machines were extensively used in the wheel and carriage-parts industry, sometimes in the same factories and sometimes separately.

Blanchard's first recorded (and restored) assignment for use of his lathe to turn spokes was to wheelwright Samuel G. Reed, of North Brookfield, Massachusetts, in September 1840. It cost $200 for the year, and allowed Reed to make and use one Blanchard lathe in Worcester County, Massachusetts for turning spokes to be made into wheels. It allowed him to sell his *wheels* anywhere, but not to sell *spokes* except in Worcester County. [68] At that time Reed employed only one man and an apprentice. [69] Eight months' experience with one machine apparently encouraged Reed to expand his sphere and scale of operation: in May 1841 he bought the right to build and use machines all over New England. He agreed to pay Blanchard "one-half cent for each spoke turned and sold" the first year, and thereafter to pay $250 per year plus 1/2 cent for every spoke sold or made above 50,000 spokes per year. [70] This assignment also included any improvements to be made, foreseeing Blanchard's back and under rest patent of 1843.

Reed, later credited with having pioneered the machine manufacture of wheels "as a separate and distinct industry," [71] expanded greatly as he mechanized, and was employing forty to fifty hands in 1844 and 1845. [72] His business survived a bankruptcy in 1848, at which time he was running two Blanchard lathes. Buying them back from an auction for

$50,[73] he continued to thrive at least into the mid-1870s. He moved his business to Worcester by 1856,[74] thence to Boston, and was living in Wellesley, Massachusetts at the time of the 1876 Centennial Exhibition in Philadelphia, where he exhibited a model of the apparatus he had invented for heating carriage tires with gas.[75]

We can suppose that use of Blanchard's machinery moved southward when Reed's apprentice, E. J. Whittemore, moved to Elizabethport, New Jersey in 1855, where he and two partners established the first wheel factory in that state. When the others retired from the business, the third partner moved it to Newark in 1860, where as Phineas Jones and Company, it grew into a large firm that in 1893 was locally proclaimed to enjoy "the reputation of making the best wheel in the world.[76]

## WESTWARD DIFFUSION

Meanwhile, carriage builders and manufacturers of carriage parts were spreading westward from the eastern seaboard centers of the industry, taking Blanchard lathes with them.[77] Sometimes the actual machines were shipped west; sometimes the license or assignment was sent and the machines were built locally. Samuel Reed himself made a variety of wheel machines as well as wheels, and from 1850 to 1855 he supplied, he later wrote, "some whole sets and some only part . . . to many now renowned wheel factories in Dayton, Ohio and some fifteen different States, and I generally sent a workman, who remained to operate them."[78]

In 1849 Charles G. Shane of Cincinnati, Ohio bought from Amos K. Carter his rights to the Blanchard lathe for producing "spokes for all kinds of wheels, swingle trees, poles for carriages, shafts, spring bars and bars for shafts, and all things appertaining to carriages" in a very large area: western counties of Virginia and of Pennsylvania, and the states of Ohio, Indiana, Kentucky, Tennessee, and Arkansas. He was to pay $4,000 for this assignment, in quarter-yearly installments over 8 1/2 years. But two years later, Shane sold this assignment, for "full consideration," to John Young, also of Cincinnati.[79] John Young was the "Company" of Royer, Simonton and Company, who became very prominent makers of carriage parts. By 1859 their factory was "undoubtedly the largest of the kind in the world":

> The yearly product of spokes is about one million; of felloes, one hundred and sixty thousand, and sets of shafts and bows in proportion. . . . Of the spokes, six thousand are made and finished daily.[80]

From the assignment record, it appears that the Royer company used the Blanchard lathes themselves, but had the machines built for others by Lane and Bodley, the larger of two woodworking machine firms in Cincinnati. Lane and Bodley produced machinery valued at $100,000 in 1859, and employed fifty hands.[81] Royer's gave power of attorney to Lane and Bodley in 1857 "to sell and dispose of rights for the turning of spokes in any of the above named states [in Royer's territory] . . . any sales by them shall be as binding and effective as if made by ourselves."[82] That fall, for instance, Lane and Bodley made two Blanchard lathes for Thomas B. Wing and William A. Richardson to use in Jefferson County, Kentucky, for which Wing and Richardson agreed to pay Royer, Simonton and Company $175 per year, and not to charge less for their spokes than Royer's company did.[83]

The *Scientific American* wrote twenty-three years later that Lane and Bodley were "the first Western manufacturers of the famous Blanchard lathe for turning irregular forms."[84] But another claimant for that honor is suggested by the assignment that Jacob Woodburn, a St. Louis carriage maker, bought for $2500 in 1850, for carriage-making applications in Missouri and adjoining territory and Illinois except for Cook County and its adjoining counties. Woodburn sold the assignment four years later, for the same price, to the owners of Gaty, McCune and Company, a major machine shop and foundry in St. Louis.[85] This company was later described as "one of the most extensive manufacturing establishments of its class in the whole Valley of the Mississippi."[86] Woodburn had already sold the assignment for *using* the machines to St. Louis carriage maker Joseph Murphy, but without the right to *make* the machines.[87] This suggests that the assignment to Gaty, McCune and Company was valued primarily for the purpose of making the machines rather than using them. Whether first in St. Louis or in Cincinnati, the assignment records show that Blanchard lathes were not only in use by the carriage industry, but also under manufacture in midwestern states for some years before the Civil War (see figure 7.5).

In contrast to these large operations in Cincinnati and St. Louis, small "shop rights" were still being sold in the 1850s. For instance, Richard E. Elie in Rochester, Wisconsin bought one in 1855 for $125, with the agreement that he use the Blanchard lathe only for his own manufacture of carriages, instead of selling spokes or other parts separately.[88] Western licenses were also being granted for smaller areas, as exemplified by the unrecorded user of Blanchard lathes in Cook County (Chicago) and adjacent counties in Illinois, which were excluded from Woodburn's assignment.

## OUTPUT AND PRICES OF SPOKES

Many early users of the Blanchard lathe for turning spokes were not wheelmakers themselves, but small one- or two-man shops with one machine. Some made ax handles, too. David Wooster, for instance, built a "spoke and helve machine" in Middlebury, Connecticut in the spring of 1834, and ran it in a rented shop with his assistant, Eldad Bradley, averaging 150 to 200 "setts" of spokes annually between 1838 and 1847.[89] Philo Beers of Hamden, Connecticut, who was turning handles for axes, hatchets, hammers, and sledges and spokes for wheels, was required by the court to report his output in 1848 and 1849. It varied widely month to month, perhaps partly because of waterpower variability, from a summer month's low of 43 spokes to an autumnal high of 2227, but in one month of medium output he turned out 1446 spokes,[90] which would be enough to outfit 30 carriages with twelve-spoke wheels. Beers's rate of output was exceeded in Naugatuck, Connecticut, where David Hull, with Joseph Wooster as helper, was making 400 to 500 spokes every two to three days in 1851.[91] Four-hundred-eighty spokes would be enough for 40 twelve-spoke wheels, or ten carriages with such wheels.

The market served by individual spoke makers included not only local smiths or wheelwrights who would need spokes for repairing broken wheels but also, more importantly, wheel manufacturers and carriage builders who would use the spokes for making new wheels for new carriages and wagons. A partnership in Bridgeport, Connecticut, for instance, bought a license from A. K. Carter in 1848 for one machine to make spokes and such other carriage parts as springbars, swingletrees, shaftbars and axlestocks. They were reported in 1851 to be producing spokes at a rate of 1000 a week. These they sold not only to carriage makers in Fairfield County, but also as far afield as New York City, Brooklyn, Philadelphia, Richmond and Petersburgh, Virginia, Augusta and Savannah, Georgia, and Montgomery, Alabama.[92] (This was a breach of their license, which cost a low $100 per year and had been for Fairfield County only.)

Some one-machine operations of this sort doubled in size, and overcame seasonal difficulties with waterpower by using steam engines. According to an estimate made in 1853 by one of Blanchard's licensees, a

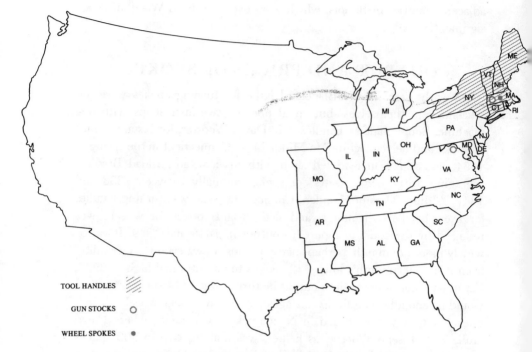

### BLANCHARD LATHE ASSIGNMENTS AS OF 1840

FIGURE 7.5a. Geographic diffusion of Blanchard's lathe 1820–1840. By 1840, after one renewal of Blanchard's patent, assignments for rights to Blanchard's lathe for making tool handles, gun stocks, and wheel spokes had remained, except for the Harpers Ferry Armory in Virigina, in New England and New York. (Map by Lyn Malone.)

two-machine spoke works could run on a fifteen-horsepower steam engine. It would cost $5,000, exclusive of land, to set up such a shop; $600 would buy the two spoke lathes.[93] By September 1853 the Bridgeport spokemakers mentioned earlier, named Seeley and Wheeler, had acquired an additional machine and were reportedly producing 2500 spokes per week, that is, enough for fifty-two carriages with 4 twelve-spoke wheels each. The second machine was not a Blanchard lathe, however, but a Philo Beers lathe.[94]

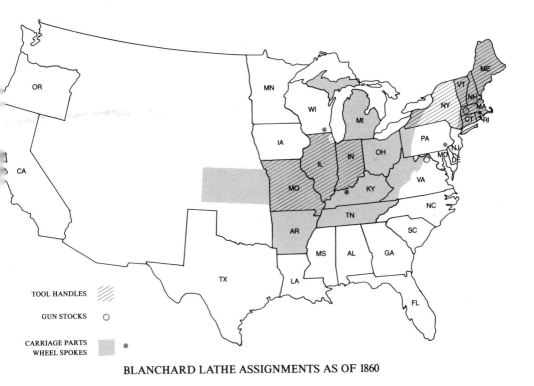

TOOL HANDLES

GUN STOCKS

CARRIAGE PARTS
WHEEL SPOKES

**BLANCHARD LATHE ASSIGNMENTS AS OF 1860**

FIGURE 7.5b. Geographic diffusion of Blanchard's lathe 1840–1860. By 1860, after two renewals, assignments for using the Blanchard lathe to make tool and implement handles, wheel spokes, and other carriage and wagon parts, had spread westward to the areas shown. The only assignee for gunstocking was the United States at the national armories, but private arms makers licensed lathes from Blanchard. Lastmaking, largely licensed rather than assigned, does not appreciably appear in the assignment records, but was an important application. (Map by Lyn Malone.)

## COMPETITOR MACHINES

Blanchard and his assignees sued Joseph and David Wooster, David Hull, Philo Beers, his brother Smith Beers, and over two dozen other makers of ax handles or spokes in Connecticut in the late 1840s and early 1850s, on the grounds of patent infringement. Frequently the defendants were using irregular turning lathes that had been built or designed by Smith Beers of Naugatuck, Philo Beers of Hamden, or Timothy Clark of New Haven. Timothy Clark received a patent for his irregular turning lathe January 19, 1847; Smith Beers and Philo Beers did so in 1850 and 1851.[95] Their machines were variants on Azariah Woolworth's Waterbury lastmaking machine of 1819,[96] having intermittent rotation of the workpiece and lengthwise motion along the grain by a cutter that usually consisted of a gang of circular saws. In Clark's machine, which was referred to informally as "a scooter" from its action, the pattern was not a model in the round but was like the edgewise "form boards" of Woolworth's very earliest "machine #1." A set of wavy grooves "scooted" along the tracer while the cutter rapidly traversed the length of the spoke, reproducing the waves of the grooves.[97] The spoke rotated between "scoots" while the next groove was lined up with the tracer. According to Clark, his machine was intended for ax handles and spokes, but was not suited for making objects—for example, lasts—as highly irregular as Blanchard's could make.[98]

How would someone setting up a spoke works in the 1840s or 1850s decide whether to buy Blanchard lathes or another kind of spoke machine? Quality considerations went into the decision, as well as considerations of fuel and manpower economy, speed of output, and spoilage rate. Jesse Duncan, superintendent of Lathrop and Son, a spoke and wheel shop in Bridgeport, Connecticut, made a comparison in 1853 between the spoke lathes of Blanchard and Philo Beers. He said his shop had both kinds but had discontinued using Beers's machine because Blanchard's "does better work than the Beers' machine and does the same amount of work at less expense." Lathrop and Son were producing 4500 spokes a week with two Blanchard machines. The Beers machines in Duncan's acquaintance had averaged 600 spokes per ten-hour day to Blanchard's average of 400, but a Beers machine required as much power as three Blanchard machines, and two men to attend it, instead of the one needed for Blanchard's. He said the Blanchard-made spokes were worth 50 cents more per hundred than Beers-made ones, for they were better turned and easier "to fit up into wheels," so that the carriage makers had to allow 50 cents more per hundred to a workman putting up Beers-made spokes into wheels than to one working with Blanchard-made spokes.[99] He said there was no appreciable difference between the Blanchard and Beers machines in loss of stock from improper centering of the workpiece, whether using defective or perfect wood.[100]

We don't know how widely shared this assessment was of the relative merits of the two machines for spokemaking, but we may note from the assignment records that usage of Philo Beers's machine remained local to the New Haven area, while Blanchard's assignments spread widely across the country. By August 1852 Philo Beers had assigned away all his "right, title, and interest" to his 1851 invention; by October 1853 his patent was wholly owned by the New Haven Wheel Company, one of the major wheel makers in the country, and its assignment record ended.[101]

The irregular turning lathe of his brother, Smith Beers, had a longer assignment record, lasting until mid-1859 and indicating the diffusion of his machine to locations in other eastern states—New York, New Jersey, and Virginia in addition to Connecticut—and westward into Pennsylvania, Ohio, Michigan, Illinois, Missouri, Wisconsin, and even Texas (see figure 7.6). Compared to assignments of Blanchard lathe patent rights, those for Smith Beers's lathe look smaller, usually covering individual towns and counties instead of multistate territories like Blanchard assignments, but they nevertheless suggest that Beers had a viable machine that survived in the marketplace beyond litigation by Blanchard.

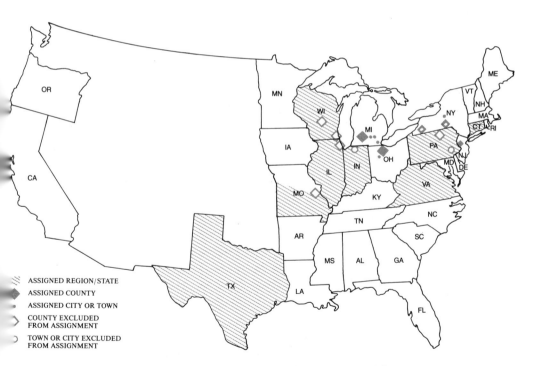

SMITH BEERS LATHE ASSIGNMENTS AS OF 1860

FIGURE 7.6. Geographic diffusion of Smith Beers's lathe by 1860. The assignment record for the irregular turning lathe patented in December 1850 by Smith Beers of Naugatuck, Connecticut indicates a widespread coverage, but spottier than that for Blanchard's. (Map by Lyn Malone.)

## LONGER-RUN DEVELOPMENTS

The design features of the Blanchard lathe seem to have survived the test of experience more successfully than its competitors for making spokes and tool handles. Decades after the Blanchard lathe patent had expired, ax-handle and spoke lathes operated on its principles instead of those of the Woolworth-type machines. One is shown, for instance, in the 1899 catalog of the Trevor Manufacturing Company of Lockport, New York. Except that it is iron-framed and neatly finished instead of crudely made of wood, it is very similar to the ax-handle machine at the National Museum of American History, having a rocking beam rather than a rocking or hanging lathe, continuous rotation of the workpiece and model, and a rotary cutter that cuts across the grain instead of lengthwise. It cost only $220, which was less than the price of $300 in 1853 for a spoke lathe in New Haven,[102] and a third of the price Blanchard had asked for the gunstocking lathe he sold to Eli Whitney, Jr. in 1843. As with Blanchard's earlier lathes, the Trevor lathe of 1899 came with a separate machine "included in the price . . . for smoothing the articles, as they are left more or less rough by the cutters." It is a nonautomatic belt-sanding machine, much simpler than the one Blanchard patented in 1854. At "200 to 400 spokes and 200 axe handles per day"[103] the Trevor lathe's rate of output did not exceed that of Blanchard lathes at Bridgeport and New Haven, Connecticut nearly a half-century earlier.[104]

## SCULPTURES AND DECORATIVE CARVINGS

The applications for which the Blanchard lathe was most suitable—to the production of gunstocks, shoe lasts, axe handles, and wheel spokes—supplied objects for which American demand, private as well as public, proved to be particularly large and sustained. Another frequently mentioned use for Blanchard's lathe was the copying of sculptures,[105] but no evidence for such use commercially has emerged from Blanchard's assignment or litigation records. This would be a less utilitarian application, for which one might expect to find smaller demand.

There were, however, also technical limits to the capabilities of a Blanchard lathe in copying irregular forms with fine and undercut detail, such as statuary, which would preclude its use for these purposes. Such tasks were much better handled by a different type of machine, which was developed in England at about the same time, in which the powered rotary cutter was much smaller and was not held in bearings on a horizontal axis, but rotated at one end of its axis, like a drill or router bit. James Watt, of steam-engine fame, used this type of vertical-spindle cutter in two sculpture-copying machines that he devised before 1819, in the last dozen years of his life. Watt is supposed to have seen Hulot's medallion-copying machine in Paris, and, as he diffidently wrote to a friend, "thought of some improvements on it which somewhat extend its uses."[106] The major difference of Watt's from Hulot's machine was the use of a separately powered cutter, which much more than "somewhat" extended its capability to cut deeper relief. Watt used his "equal" and "diminishing" machines not only to copy relief carvings on surfaces that were flat or convex up to about 90 degrees of arc, but also for copying free-standing sculptures one segment at a time[107] (see figure 7.7).

Thus Watt and Blanchard at roughly the same time both initiated the use of powered high-speed rotary cutters for copying irregular forms, but with a significant difference in the axis of rotation. Watt's machines were different from Blanchard's in several other respects as well, most importantly in that they could not complete the work all around in one operation, but only in several stages. With their vertical instead of horizontal spindles, and cutters like drill bits instead of crooked knives around a wheel rim, they acted more like Blanchard's gunstock inletting machines than like his lathe.

Subsequent British inventors, such as Benjamin Cheverton (1826), Joseph Gibbs (1829), and Thomas B. Jordan (1844 and 1845) made modifications on Watt's machines—all with vertical-spindle rotary bits—for copying sculpture and carving plaques or cylinders.[108] Such machines quickly found application in the decorative arts in England. Carving machines very similar to the English machines were also developed in the United States by mid-century, by inventors Hezekiah Augur (1846 and 1849) and Isaac M. Singer (1849), but with less immediately successful application to the decorative arts than their counterparts in England had.[109] Figure 7.8 shows Augur's 1849 machine. Thomas Blanchard also developed a machine for copying sculptures and bas-reliefs. It has hitherto been assumed to be an application of his lathe, but it was instead a modification of his unpatented inletting machines.

Watt's copying machines or Cheverton's would be impractical, though not impossible, for use in producing gunstocks, shoe lasts, or the like.

200

They were too slow in operation to have made it worthwhile, required constant attention and manipulation by the operator, and were capable of unnecessary refinements. Conversely, however, copying statues was commonly cited as an application of the Blanchard lathe. One reporter in 1847 said Blanchard's machine for turning out "busts of the human head" was "now in full and successful operation in Boston," and invited his reader to visualize "a bust of Daniel Webster rapidly revolving in one end of a lathe, and at the other he will see *fac simile* heads of the great expounder, of any desired sizes, turned out from marble, by machinery."[110] This is puzzling, for the usually depicted Blanchard lathe, with its relatively large cutting wheel on a horizontal axis, was not capable of making the delicate undercuts that would be necessary for sculpting such details on busts as eyes, nose, lips, or hair. (Nor, of course, was the rotation *rapid* of the model and workpiece in a Blanchard lathe.)

If, however, the diameters of the horizontally mounted cutting and tracing wheels on a Blanchard lathe were made very small, could they then conceivably be used for copying the small features of sculptures? Blanchard's 1820 patent specification seems to covers this contingency, but does not spell out the practical details. Not mentioning sculptures, it says

> any form however irregular may be exactly imitated provided every part and portion of the model can be brought in contact with the periphery of the friction and cutting wheels. Whence it results that in cutting an article which is concave . . . the diameter of the friction wheel and of the cutter wheel . . . must be diminished so that both can operate freely within the cavity proposed to be formed.[111]

The difficulty with using a very small horizontal-axis cutter, however, is not only that it would take longer to complete the work. A more serious difficulty is that even with a *very* small-diameter cutter, the clearance

FIGURE 7.7. *(opposite)* James Watt's "diminishing" machine c. 1818. Powered by the treadle and flywheel, a vertical-spindle rotary cutter and a tracer are mounted on a hollow bar above a smaller workpiece and the larger model, respectively. The bar is supported in a universal joint by an upright at the left end of the machine and counterweighted through chains, bars, and weights at the right. The operator guided the cutter and tracer forward and back and up and down by hand. The model and workpiece, mounted on carefully indexed circular plates, were moved proportionate distances laterally by pantographic levers not visible in this view, and intermittently rotated by hand through equal angles so as to carve a new segment of the statue. The machine also carved basrelief plaques. (Photograph from Science Museum, London.)

FIGURE 7.8. Hezekiah Augur's carving machine of 1849. It could cut smaller or larger copies than the model, by proportional lateral and transverse motions of the two sets of tables to which the workpiece and model were fastened. The tables also tilted at the same angles. Sets of pantographic rods for all three dimensions imparted proportional motions to the tables and to the vertical-spindle rotary cutter and tracer, which moved up and down according to the model's contours. (Photograph of model at the New Haven Colony Historical Society, New Haven, Connecticut.)

needed for bearings and the horizontal shaft holding the cutter as it traverses would interfere at some point noticeably short of completion, and one would have to finish the job by hand tools or with end-cutters on a vertical-spindle machine. All in all, it would be more awkward than using vertical-spindle cutters from the start, and rotating the work intermittently. The horizontal-spindle cutter of the Blanchard lathe simply couldn't do the job that a vertical-spindle cutter could for copying sculptures.

Blanchard himself, however, designed vertical-spindle machines in the 1820s—his various inletting machines for cutting small concavities for lock, barrel, and fittings into gunstocks at the Springfield Armory, which are described in chapter 5. Although he did not obtain a patent for his inletting machines, he seems to have regarded the inletting capability and his irregular turning lathe as part of the same machine, at least initially. Where Blanchard's vertical-spindle inletting machines were used for copying cavities into a workpiece, thereby creating an irregular space in a solid, Watt's and Cheverton's vertical-spindle machines were used for doing the opposite task—copying an irregular solid in space. But the use of the vertical-spindle cutters and tracers following a model was in principle the same. Blanchard could modify his inletting machine to make a sculpture-copying machine with less trouble and more success than attempting to use a very small-wheeled Blanchard lathe for the job. Blanchard's sculpture-copying machine is mentioned in several reports, but never described in detail before its patent in France in 1855, to be discussed. It seems very probable however, that the machine with which Blanchard "turned the heads of Congressmen" when lobbying for patent extension in 1848 was not an irregular turning lathe, but actually a vertical-spindle machine, as in his French patent.

Blanchard used a sculpture-copying machine, or its products, for persuasive or showmanship purposes on more than one occasion. During a patent lawsuit in Philadelphia in 1846, Blanchard or an agent informally passed small marble busts around among the jurors. They were 4 to 8 inches long, and "represented to have been turned by the patented lathe in question." One observer remarked—correctly, I believe—"that it was very unfair to exhibit them, for from the knowledge I had of the lathe for turning lasts, it [turning sculptures] could not be done." [112] The defendant was later granted a new trial. Blanchard also used his machine to make busts of Henry Clay and Zachary Taylor that were much admired when he visited Washington during Taylor's Presidential inauguration in spring 1849. A reporter wrote that "Some of the ladies in Washington pressed their glowing lips to the marble from love to the originals, and this was certainly a great compliment to the inventor of the machine."[113]

Blanchard took his machine to the Paris Exposition of 1855, where he demonstrated it in public and used it to sculpt a marble copy of a bust of Empress Eugenie. His machine won a prize.[114] A short French account of the event in Paris uses the term "burin" for its cutting tool, which implies a vertical-spindle machine rather than a lathe with a horizontal-axis cutting wheel.[115] It was reported to work with such speed that it produced objects for 4 francs that competing machines could produce at best for 12.[116] Next to his machine for copying sculptures in the round, Blanchard exhibited and demonstrated a relief-copying machine in which he made reduced-sized copies in ivory from a bronze medal of Emperor Napoleon III's head, "at the rate of one every twenty minutes, with band power."[117] Blanchard's use of a pair of machines on this occasion is reminiscent of James Watt's sculpture-copying machines, which also could make either bas-relief medallions or sculptures in the round.

While in France, Blanchard apparently applied for a patent "pour un machine à reproduire les bustes en marbre ou autres objets de sculpture avec réduction," which he received August 28, 1855.[118] Figure 7.9 shows it to be indeed a vertical-spindle machine, with a pantographic feature that allows variable-sized copies to be made of the original. Unlike Watt's or Cheverton's machines, however, in Blanchard's the model and work-piece rotated continuously and mechanically instead of intermittently by hand. This rotation was slow, while a rapidly rotating router bit ("burin")

FIGURE 7.9. *(opposite)* Thomas Blanchard's self-acting sculpture-copying machine, 1855. (Figure 2 is view from above; figure 1 is from the side.) A workpiece fastened at (R) (at right in figure 2) would slowly rotate with shaft (m) and move laterally in its carriage (C) while carved by a rapidly rotating vertical-spindle burin (not visible) powered through a complex of pulleys (x). The workpiece rotated together with the larger model (P), which moved laterally in carriage (B); the stylus (S), (figure 1) feeling the high and low points of the model, caused the burin to rise and fall while cutting the workpiece. The rotating burin, pantographically connected to the stylus, made cuts vertically proportional to the size of the workpiece; the lateral movements of the carriages (C) and (B) were also proportional, controlled by the rotation of the cam (N) moving against post (O) at the left. Another cam, viewed end-on at (d) (lower right of figure 1), controlled the transverse progression of the stylus and burin over the surface of the model and workpiece. As shown, the machine would make quarter-sized copies of the model, but it could be adjusted to other proportions. (From . . . *Brevets d'Invention [Paris: Imprimerie Royale, 1855]*, series 2, vol. 51, plate 42, "Machine de Sculpture, par M. Blanchard.")

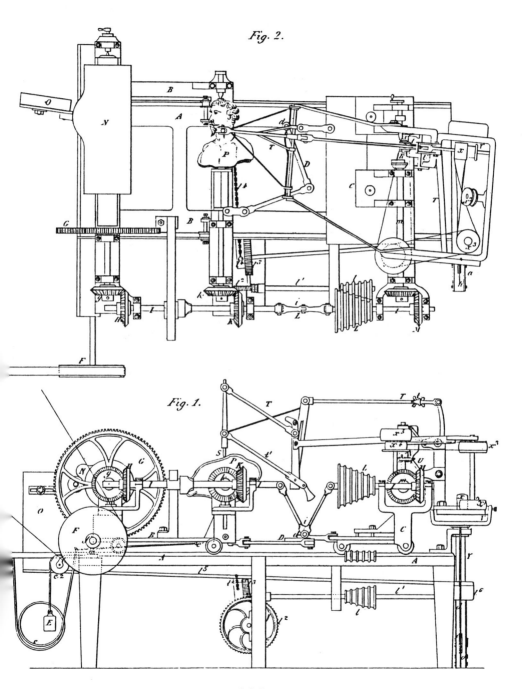

Fig. 2.

Fig. 1.

205

carved out features on the workpiece, guided by a feeler or stylus raised and lowered by the rotating model bust. This machine departed from both the Blanchard lathe and the usual sculpture-copying machines of the day by its use of a large cam rotating in unison with the workpiece and model. This cam, the same general size as the model, operated against a weight and a spring to move the carriages laterally, holding the model and workpiece at the correct proportional distance from each other. Another cam controlled the transverse motion of the stylus and burin over the model and workpiece. These cams allowed the model itself to operate as guide for the finer details only.

Perhaps this machine, with its rotation of model and workpiece and its vertical-spindle cutter and tracer, should be thought of as a cross-breed between Blanchard's lathe and his inletting machines. Since it was not the subject of assignment or litigation, we have no records of its commercial use. Blanchard himself, reported in "full operation" in Boston in 1847,[119] did turn out, "for years and years," marble statuettes and "cameos and intaglios from shell, with the precision and beauty of Italian hand work." Blanchard's small busts of Daniel Webster, Henry Clay, Zachary Taylor, Judge Woodbury "and other gentlemen" were on display at his Boston "factory" and at Amos K. Carter's office in Newark, but we are not told how many he produced, nor to whom, if anyone, he sold them. The *Scientific American* remarked that "In its application to the fine arts Mr. Blanchard's name has not been so extensively known only because the fine arts are so much less profitable in our country than the useful."[120] The only consumer mentioned in these reports was Daniel Webster himself, to whom a bust had been presented.

A possible indirect use for such small sculptures was to serve as master models for moulds in which to make ceramic statuettes. In England Benjamin Cheverton's machine was used this way, to reduce popular sculptures such as Hiram Powers's "Greek Slave" to household-size models for "Parian ware" reproductions.[121] In this country a few porcelain manufacturers produced such statuettes in the 1850s, including, from 1848 to 1856, Charles Cartlidge and Company of Greenpoint, New York, (again, Neziah Bliss's territory), whose output is thought to have included "biscuit porcelain busts of . . . Daniel Webster and Zachary Taylor."[122] It is tempting to speculate whether Thomas Blanchard supplied the models for this venture into mass-produced art.

Meanwhile, the bust of Blanchard himself has disappeared from Blanchard's monument in Mount Auburn Cemetery, but the two carved marble plaques on the sides remain as mute testimony to an intrinsically individualized use for his relief-carving machine. Blanchard's "useful" rather than "fine" arts are commemorated in these plaques, however. One shows his last-turning lathe, the other, his woodbending machine. We now bend our attention to the latter.

# BENDING
# WOOD

꒝꒝꒝꒝꒝

As shingle splitters know, wood breaks more readily along the grain than across it. A curved wooden object is therefore stronger if it can be bent instead of cut to shape, for it will offer fewer places for splitting along the grain. The technique of softening a length of wood in moist heat to make it flexible and then bending it into a curved shape was in practice long before Thomas Blanchard's era.[1] If the wood was held in the curved position by a form or mold until dry again, it retained its new shape. Hand methods for doing this persist today for some purposes.[2] However, the outer edge of the curve frequently broke during bending, since it had to stretch, while the inner edge less often suffered from being compressed during bending. Samuel Bentham, in his compendious woodworking patent of 1793 in England, advised that

> In the operation of bending a very material caution is, that as fast as you forse any peice to adapt itself to the curvature of the mould to which you are bending it, you apply a pressure, by means of wedges or skrew, &c. to that very part, and so all along the peice, particularly at the sharpest convexities . . . to . . . prevent the exterior fibres from starting out.[3]

Thomas Blanchard's method sixty years later adopted Samuel Bentham's "caution" of applying pressure "all along the piece" of wood during bending, but also applied endwise pressure before bending. This made it much stronger and solved the breakage problem. Blanchard's bending machine was originally designed for bending plow handles, but he went on to adapt it to the production of wheel felloes (rims) and other carriage and wagon woodwork, furniture, and even large ship timbers. The ship timber enterprise failed commercially within a few years, but Blanchard's bending machines spread westward with the manufacture of agricultural implements and of carriages and wagons, even as did his irregular turning lathe (see figure 8.1). His bending machine earned him more money than his lathe, but less enduring fame. In both instances, however, his patent required management through application, reissue, litigation, and extension as well as through assignment to a network of assignees and licensees.

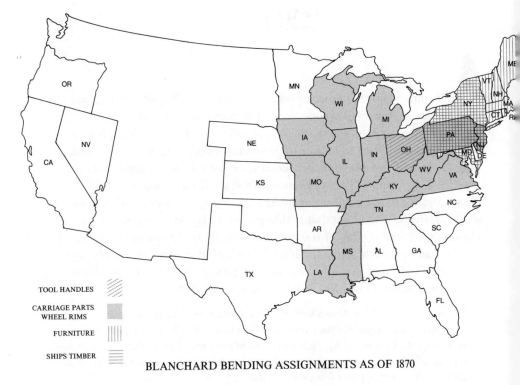

TOOL HANDLES

CARRIAGE PARTS
WHEEL RIMS

FURNITURE

SHIPS TIMBER

BLANCHARD BENDING ASSIGNMENTS AS OF 1870

FIGURE 8.1. Diffusion of Blanchard bending machine assignments by 1870. When Blanchard's woodbending patent of 1849 expired, assignments for making, selling, or using his machine for various purposes had spread to the territories shown. Compare with Figure 7.5b to see where both of Blanchard's major inventions were used in the manufacture of tool handles and parts for carriages and wagons. Map by Lyn Malone.

# BENDING BEFORE BLANCHARD

In his patent of 1793 Bentham alluded to two English patents of his day for applying woodbending to wheels and to structural woodwork such as stairway railings.[4] In the United States the earliest listed patent that implied a bending process was granted in 1818 to Simeon Stedman of Hartford, Connecticut for his "Bentwood handle and socket." Four years later E. Green and M. Blackslee of Litchfield, Connecticut obtained a somewhat more general patent for their method of "Bending timber for sleighs, etc."[5] These were apparently hand methods, for the first two woodbending patents later cited in lawsuits as machine patents were those granted in 1835 to Edward Reynolds of Haddonfield, New Jersey for a "Machine for Bending or Setting Felloes for the Wheels of Carriages and Waggons," and to Jonathan Mulford of Northern Liberties, Philadelphia, Pennsylvania for "a Machine for Bending Mast and Truss Hoops"[6] (see figures 8.2 and 8.3).

In the machines of Reynolds and Mulford, the stick of wood is wrapped, beginning at one end, around a rotating circular form. In Reynolds's machine, but not in Mulford's, an iron strap along the outside of the stick is intended to keep it from bursting outward during bending. Nevertheless, according to later report, Reynolds's machine wasted about 30 percent even of "good material."[7] A decade later, in 1845, one David Gans of New Detour, Illinois constructed a woodbending machine that he used for about three years without obtaining a patent for it, to make plow

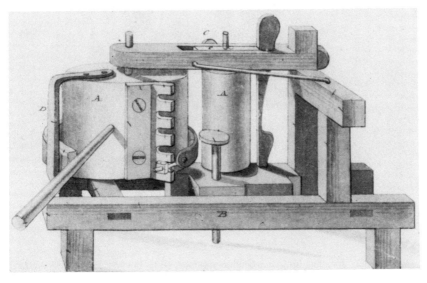

FIGURE 8.2. Edward Reynolds's bending machine, 1835. Wooden sticks or iron strips were bent around either of two wooden cylinders (A, A) for two sizes of wheel or hoop. After "boiling or steaming in the usual manner," the operator placed one end of a wooden stick under the "stationary clevis" (D), together with a piece of hoop iron to hold it in place while bending. The other end of the hoop iron is shown held in place by a nut. He turned the cylinder by the "hand spike" shown inserted in a hole. For wooden wheels "the felloes are to be semicircular." The machine was also intended for "iron tires, coopers sett hoops, mast hoops, etc." (From Edward Reynolds, patent for "A Machine for Bending or Setting Felloes for the Wheels of Carriages and Wagons," July 17, 1835, National Archives, Cartographic Section, Alexandria, Virginia.)

FIGURE 8.3. Jonathan Mulford's bending machine, 1835. Intended for bending mast and truss hoops, this machine wrapped a "hoop pole," secured by a wedge at one end, around the rim of the large wheel shown at right. The small roller just above was to keep the hoop pole from departing from the rim while bending took place. Power was supplied by hand crank at left. (From Jonathan Mulford, specification for "a Machine for Bending Mast and Truss Hoops," patented January 16, 1835, National Archives Cartographic Section, Alexandria, Virginia.)

handles for John Deere and Leonard Andrus.[8] His machine, too, wrapped the end of a stick, together with a metal strap, around a rotating form. In 1849 Abel Gardner of Buffalo, New York obtained a patent for his "Improvement in Apparatus for bending Hames," in which an iron strap pressed a stick against a curved block of wood, but the block did not rotate (see figure 8.4). In both Gardner's and Gans's machines, but not in the earlier ones, devices at both ends of the stick prevented it from elongating during bending. Gardner said one advantage of his invention was "an almost certainty of loosing [sic] no hame wood which is sound from breaking or fracture."[9]

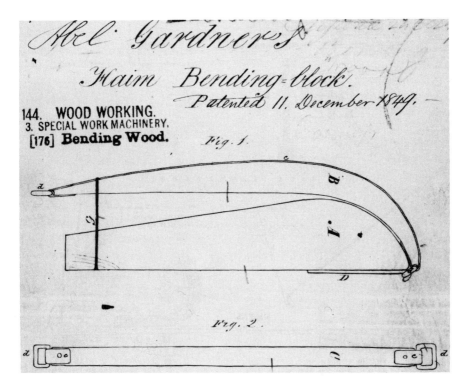

FIGURE 8.4. Abel Gardner's hame bender, December 1849. Specifically for bending horse collar hames, this apparatus used an iron strap (C) secured on the wooden stick (B) at both ends by rivets "if necessary" and by hook (D) through one of the links (d,d) at the ends of the strap. After the soaked or steamed wood was bent sufficiently over block (A) it was held in position by cord (G) until it was dry. (From Abel Gardner, specification for "Improvement in Apparatus for bending Hames," U.S. Patent #6934, December 11, 1849, National Archives, Cartographic Section, Alexandria, Virginia.)

# BENDING BY BLANCHARD

Very shortly after Gardner's patent, Thomas Blanchard obtained a much more widely applicable patent for "a new and useful Improvement, being a Method of Bending Timber and Other Fibrous Substances"[10] (see figure 8.5). According to Blanchard, the bending methods in use for

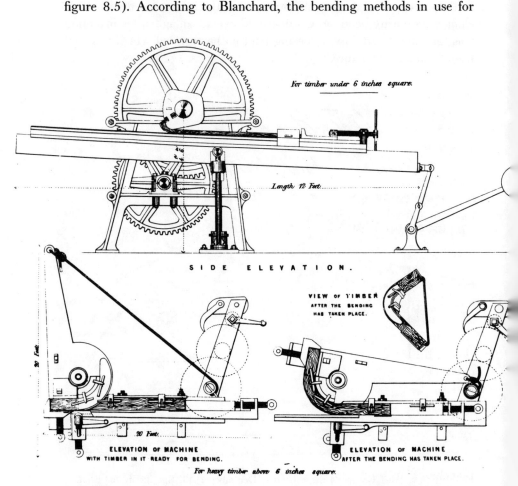

FIGURE 8.5. Two versions of Thomas Blanchard's bending machine. After devising his machine in 1849 for bending the ends of plow handles about 90 degrees, Blanchard later developed it for bending small timbers into completely closed loops (upper view) for slate or picture or chair seat frames, and large timbers at about right angles for ships' knees (lower view). In both versions, the screw on the right applied pressure endwise before bending began, and the form was rotated to bend the wood. (From *The Artizan* 15 (February 1, 1857): 28.)

making plow handles before he invented his machine suffered from a serious difficulty: the wood broke about two times out of five during bending.[11]

Blanchard's attention was drawn to the problem by the "Boston manufacturers of agricultural implements," who were interested in using his lathe to turn plow handles if they could afterward bend them safely. The current method was to bend them and then shape them at the ends by hand-shaving, but only about three-fifths of the handles survived the bending. Blanchard "immediately went to work investigating the properties of the wood and the laws that govern the breaking thereof." He made "many experiments" on the ability of wood to withstand tension and compression, and found that it was "compressible in both the length and breadth of its fibre; that by such compression it became much stronger without detriment to its other qualities."[12] He concluded that he could overcome the breakage problem if he first compressed the piece of wood endwise before bending it. Borrowing a term from metalsmithing, Blanchard called this compressing process "upsetting" the wood.[13] The wood fiber at the outer edge of the curve would then be only expanding within its natural limits during bending, instead of stretching beyond them. The machine he designed to do this, similar to that shown in the lower section of figure 8.5, allowed the stick of wood for a plow handle to slide along a groove. The operator applied end pressure by a screw. The other end of the stick was clamped to a rounded form or "mold" on the pivot end of a lever by which it was rotated. A chain with hollow links, also wrapped along the exterior of the curve, provided inward pressure on the wood, while maintaining the end pressure. As the operator rotated the form by closing the lever end of the mold, and the wood was wrapping around the mold, the operator gradually eased off on the compressing screw, "to prevent the timber on the inside of the curve from crippling or overlapping."[14]

## PLOW HANDLES

Blanchard's method proved successful and was put into operation for bending plow handles before he applied for a patent.[15] Since he didn't make a recorded assignment of his rights at that time, it is likely that he licensed them to the Boston manufacturers of agricultural implements. A few years later, he sold all his rights to his invention "so far as the same relates to bending plow, harrow, and cultivator handles" to A. V. Blanchard and Company, his nephews in Palmer, Massachusetts, for $1500.[16]

This was in conjunction with their purchase of rights to his irregular turning patent. They in turn licensed and sold machines for plow-handle bending to others in various territories. They sold one in 1852, for instance, to James Coleman and William F. Mitchell in Cincinnati, Ohio, who used it to bend an average of 400 handles a day with a spoilage rate of about 5 to 10 percent.[17] For comparison, we may note that this was a rate of 120,000 handles a year, while David Gans had made only one to two thousand handles per year for John Deere and Leonard Andrus, on his unpatented machine in 1845–48.[18]

## WHEELS AND CARRIAGE PARTS

Continuing to experiment with his woodbending invention for other uses, Blanchard found a vigorous market for it in bending felloes (rims) for carriage wheels. Rims of wheels for ancient chariots and medieval carriages were made of a single piece of wood bent into a full circle, and such wheels continued to be made in Estonia in modern times.[19] But traditional English wheelwrights sawed curves into several—say, six or seven —pieces of wood called "felloes" and fitted them together into a wheel. Each felloe was connected to the hub by two spokes, and fastened around the outside by short pieces of iron called "strakes," overlapping the felloe joints, or by a single hoop of iron "shrunk" on to serve as tire.[20]

Although heavier wagon and carriage wheels continued to be built of such sawn felloes in America, the nineteenth-century American bentwood wheel, made of two semicircular felloes, allowed wheels to be much lighter with the same strength. One of Blanchard's biographers says his bending machine could make one-piece wheel rims "in one straight-grained strip bent to a circle,"[21] but Blanchard's machine was ordinarily used to make semicircular felloes. For bending felloes, the form was somewhat more than semicircular, as is shown in figure 8.6, and the felloe ends were cut off after drying, to make each one 180 degrees of arc.[22] The inside of a semicircular rim for a wheel, say 42 inches in diameter and 1 1/2 inches thick, measured a little less than 66 inches, but the outside measured over 70 1/2 inches. So Blanchard's machine compressed a stick originally 70 1/2 inches long endwise by 4 1/2 inches. When bending, it stretched only partway out again around the outside, in a "slight elongation, caused by relaxing the screw during the revolution of the 'form.' "[23] For "bending large curves with flat sides such as felloes for wheels," Blanchard's machine used a metal strap to press inward on the

FIGURE 8.6. Blanchard-type felloe bender. While plow handles needed bending only about 90 degrees, wheel felloes required somewhat more than 180 degrees. (B) is the felloe after bending around form (D), which has been rotated by the cog wheel. (A) is the "upsetting" screw. (C) is the sliding bed upon which (B) rested before being bent. A man sitting on the end of the weighted lever added extra upward pressure of the bed against the felloe and form during bending. (From *The Hub* 20 (November 1, 1878): 388.)

outside of the curve.[24] In his 1849 patent specification he suggested that the bending of several felloes could be done at once by clamping them together in the machine, or even by bending a plank as thick as one felloe but as wide as several, and sawing them apart afterward. Although its drawing depicts a lever-operated machine for plow handles, Blanchard's patent description of 1849 also specifies that "instead of a lever to move it, cog wheels may be used and any power applied." Figure 8.6, an 1878 illustration of a Blanchard-type machine used for felloe-bending, shows a large cog wheel instead of a lever, as did the Blanchard-type machine photographed at Hoopes, Brother, and Darlington wheel works in 1969.[25] By dramatically lowering the rate of breakage during bending, Blanchard's machine helped make manufacture of bentwood wheels an economical proposition in nineteenth-century America.

Blanchard's first recorded sale of his bending machine rights for making carriage wheels was in 1852 to Simeon Bedford and Samuel O. Crane in Newark, New Jersey, who paid Blanchard $1,000 for exclusive rights to use three machines for bending felloes in New Jersey.[26] Crane was later called "the founder of . . . Newark's . . . industry of bending woodwork for carriage builders."[27] At the end of 1852 Blanchard's nephews, A. V. Blanchard and Company, paid Blanchard $8,000 for a broader range of applications than Crane's, including not only the bending of felloes, but also bending "shafts for carriages, handles for trucks, wheelbarrows, shovels, hand carts, frames for slates, and springs for carriages." This assignment was for all of the United States except New Jersey, so it didn't conflict with his assignment to Bedford and Crane.[28] A month later A. V. Blanchard and Company sold their right in over a dozen midwestern and southern states to Royer, Simonton and Company, of Cincinnati, Ohio, "for the sole purpose of bending fellys or rims of all carriage wheels."[29]

As might be guessed from the size of their territory, Royer, Simonton and Company ran a large operation, manufacturing "the various component parts of carriage wheels etc." The company had already acquired the right to Blanchard's spoke-turning lathe for a territory west of the Alleghenies in seven states.[30] As mentioned in chapter 7, in 1859 their factory, described as "undoubtedly the largest of the kind in the world," was reported to employ eighty hands making a million spokes and 160,000 felloes annually, "and sets of shafts and bows in proportion," having a manufactured value of $125,000.[31] In addition to wheel felloes, the woodbending machines at the Royer establishment bent bows for buggy tops and curved backs and arms for seats, as well as shafts, side bars, and other carriage parts (see figure 8.7).

In 1856 John C. Morris, also of Cincinnati, obtained a patent[32] for a woodbending machine, and thereafter engaged in prolonged infringement litigation with the Royer and A. V. Blanchard companies. While Blanchard's machine used a rotating form on which to bend wood from one end, Morris's machine used a stationary form to which wood was bent from the middle (see figure 8.8). Both types of machine used end pressure to prevent the wood from stretching during bending, but Morris's did not apply extra pressure before bending commenced, nor, or course, did it provide for relaxation of the pressure during bending. Thus, a stick of wood in Blanchard's machine was in uniform compression when bending began, but Morris's machine prevented expansion of the fibers only after bending began. One expert in wood technology wrote in 1878 that the "upsetting" action in the latter type of machine "takes place at the extreme ends, as there is no pressure when the levers first move," resulting, during drying, in differential shrinkage of the wood, and in use, a tendency toward flattening of the wheel on opposite sides. His opinion was that "It

FIGURE 8.7. Bentwood and irregularly turned carriage parts. Besides wheel rims, the Blanchard woodbending machine supplied the carriage industry with numerous other bentwood parts shown here. In addition, the Blanchard lathe supplied spring bars, whiffle-trees, and poles. (From the Dover Publications' 1970 reprint of G. and D. Cook and Company's *Illustrated Catalogue of Carriages and Special Business Advertiser,* New Haven, Conn. [New York: Baker & Godwin, 1860], p. 98.)

is an impossibility to make a rim of this kind stand the ordinary hard usage of city streets," but that a Blanchard-type machine "in the hands of a skillful operator," rendered the upsetting "very regular and uniform."[33]

We may perhaps surmise that the Blanchard machine required more judgment by the operator in the easing off of pressure during bending, and made a somewhat higher quality wheel than did the Morris-type machine. This quality difference was probably not decisive in the market, for both kinds of machines were used with apparent success in the American wheel trade. American wheelmakers exported large numbers of bent-

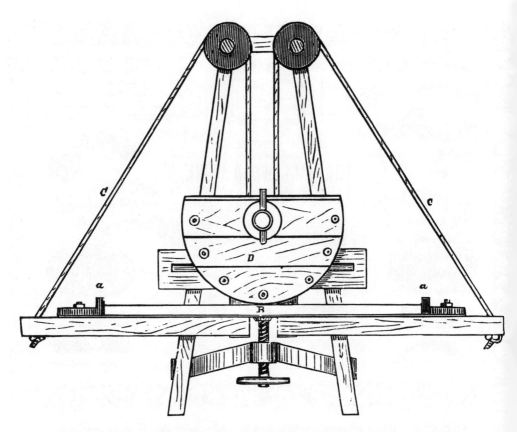

FIGURE 8.8. Morris-type felloe bender. The straight stick (B) is the felloe before bending around the stationary form (D). It is constrained by stops (a,a) at its ends, but no additional end pressure is applied. A windlass unseen behind the form lifts the split bed on both sides by the ropes (C,C) in order to bend the felloe to the form. (From *The Hub* 20 (November 1, 1878): 388.)

wood wheels abroad as well as supplying the rapidly expanding domestic market as the population of the United States spread westward across the Great Plains. In 1870 Blanchard's patent expired, but Morris obtained an extension for his. Machines of both types survived thereafter, but the Morris-type felloe-bender seems to have become predominant, for it is more often shown in trade catalogs that survive from the late nineteenth century, such as those of woodworking machine companies in Ohio: J. A. Fay and Egan Company of Cincinnati, or Defiance Machine Works, of Defiance. Richardson, Merriam, and Company of Worcester, Massachusetts, however, was one commercial producer of Blanchard-type felloe benders after 1870,[34] and both types continued in use at the Hoopes, Brother, and Darlington wheel works in Pennsylvania until recent years.[35]

## CARRIAGE-MAKING MECHANIZATION

As we have seen here and in chapter 7, both of Blanchard's woodworking machines were used in making wheels, which was a subindustry in itself, and both were used in making other parts of carriages and wagons. Besides the spokes for the wheels, the shafts, springbars, axle-stocks, whiffle-trees, etc., all needed turning, and besides the rims for the wheels, the buggy bows, seat rails, shafts, sleigh runners, etc., all needed bending. The assignment and litigation records for Blanchard's patents indicate that such turnings and bendings were being done by machine in the 1840s and 1850s. Revision is therefore needed in the idea, as in the following quotation, that mechanization in that industry first took place after the Civil War:

> Beginning in the 1870s mechanization led to a radical transformation of production techniques . . . In 1865 every step in buggy-making was done by hand. Within thirty years most steps were done by machine. Such a leap in the use of power occurred primarily because of developments in metal working.[36]

Mechanization of *woodworking* for making carriages had already taken place well before the Civil War. As his lawsuits show, Blanchard's machines were not the only ones to be used for irregular turning and woodbending in the carriage industry before his patents expired in 1862 and 1870. Nor was mechanization confined to these two operations in making wagon and carriage woodwork; future research into the assignments of patents for mortising, tenoning, and planing machines in the carriage industry may well reveal a similar timing and geographic spread.

## SHIP TIMBERS

Besides bending plow handles, wheel felloes, and carriage parts, another use for Blanchard's machine was to bend timbers for ships. In order to shape wooden ships' futtocks and knees, ship builders traditionally preferred to search out and hoard a variety of naturally crooked-branched timbers, so they could cut pieces having the grain run along the curves.[37] This achieved greater strength with less weight than would be necessary if they sawed straight timbers into curved shapes. Live oak grown in Georgia and Florida swamps produced "all the queer shapes which delighted a shipwright's eye," but in New York shipyards it cost more than twice as much as white oak from closer sources, and was heavier.[38] If straight timbers could be bent, however, it would no longer be necessary to rely on "angular-shaped timber of natural growth" which was "becoming so scarce and expensive."[39] This was not a brand-new idea; in 1718 Peter the Great had told his traveling mechanician A. K. Nartov to try in London to obtain "information on the newly invented improved method of steaming and bending of oak used in the building of ships, and drawings of the furnace used therein."[40]

After obtaining his 1849 patent, Thomas Blanchard continued to work on the problems of "bending larger and larger pieces of wood,"[41] and in 1853 assigned patent rights to the "Ship Timber Bending Company" for the use of his invention in bending ships' timbers and parts of household furniture.[42] This company paid Blanchard $600,000 worth of the company's stock, which suggests they began with a very large capitalization. It also suggests that Blanchard had a strong "interest" in the success of the company. They "purchased a lot of ground on Green Point . . . [and] . . . erected thereon a spacious building with the necessary machinery for bending timber."[43] Greenpoint, part of the area Neziah Bliss developed on Long Island, had become an active ship-building location.

Reading between the lines, one can perceive that Blanchard was kept busy getting the machinery at Greenpoint to work well. When the English Parliamentary Commissioners visited Boston in the spring of 1854, they "called at the residence of Mr. Blanchard . . . with a view of consulting him relative to the best mode of obtaining [gunstocking] machinery" but they "found that he was absent at New York on business." A little later on their tour they went to New York and crossed the river "to see some machinery lately invented by Mr. Blanchard for bending timber for the knees of vessels," but they were disappointed again, for they "found that the machines used had not yet been perfected and were not in working order."[44] Blanchard must have succeeded that summer in getting the machinery to work, for somewhat later visitors to the yard in 1854 reported that "they had two machines now in use, one for ship timbers, or futtocks, and one for bending frames for furniture and ships' knees."[45] They observed that in the larger machine "A piece of white oak 15 feet 8 inches long, and 10 x 9 3/4 inches in section, was bent complete for a ship's futtock, in seven minutes from the time it was taken from the steam bath." In the smaller machine, pieces 7 feet long and 6 1/2 x 5 1/4 inches in section were taken from the bath and formed into right-angled knees in three minutes each. And "one piece of black walnut 6 inches wide, one inch thick, and 6 feet long, intended for chair bottom frames, was formed in one minute from the time it was taken from the bath."[46]

The larger machine observed in 1854 differed in operation from the smaller machine. In the larger machine, after end pressure was applied by a screw to the steamed timber, its "two ends are then drawn around in opposite directions" by "powerful gearing."[47] A lengthwise iron band with ends bent at right angles fit over the outer side of the timber and bent with it while maintaining the end pressure. No picture accompanies its descriptions that year in the *Journal of the Franklin Institute,*[48] but apparently bending was achieved not by a rotating form, as in Blanchard's patent description, but by the folding of a hinged table to which the timber was fastened by iron "dogs." The smaller machine observed was of the type described in Blanchard's patent, in which the two ends of the timber are not bent from the middle, but one end is wrapped around the rotating form.

Within two years, however, Blanchard devised a more powerful version of this machine with the rotating form, for bending thicker timbers, and secured a second woodbending patent for it on October 21, 1856[49] (see figure 8.5, bottom). It constrained the timber not only by an outside band or chain and by "abutments" on the ends, but also by additional molds in which it moved or that moved with it, "submitting it to pressure upon every side and upon the ends during the operation of bending, by which means it is prevented from swelling, bursting or cracking at the point bent."[50] In 1855 a reporter described Blanchard's new heavy-duty machine and remarked "The largest sticks that have yet been bent are but ten inches in diameter; but there appears no reason why sticks of much larger size should not be handled with almost equal facility. The only difficulty to meet would be the increased strength and size of machinery."[51] Blanchard later wrote "I finally succeeded as late as 1854 or 1855 in bending ship knees of the heaviest class, 14 inches square."[52]

All observers expected good results from Blanchard's machinery: "[It] will effect a very great reduction in the cost of ship-timber," it "was likely to produce an important effect on ship-building and cabinet making," and was "certainly an important invention, well suited to the present times."[53] His bending machine won a prize at the Paris Exposition of 1855, recognized as "la machine à courber les bois de marine."[54]

Although the Ship Timber Bending Company had "commenced operations in this new and important undertaking . . . with the most gratifying prospect of success,"[55] it soon "became embarrassed and failed."[56] In June 1855 it licensed its rights for the manufacture of household furniture in the cities of New York and Brooklyn to one Henry Sheldon. Two months later it sold the rest of its rights for only $22,000 to two men who in turn assigned them to the American Timber Bending Company in early September.[57] "Severe and varied" tests of ship timbers bent by Blanchard machines were conducted in 1856 for the United States Navy, at the Novelty Works in New York City, and the results were "highly satisfactory."[58] Nevertheless, the American Timber Bending Company lasted only four years before it went into receivership in February 1860.[59]

Blanchard's bending technology made its way to England through patent management. A London-based company, the "Timber Bending Patents Company (Limited)" bought the patent rights, and invited inspection of "the apparatus at work" in 1857.[60] A Captain A. B. Beecher, R.N. estimated that a Blanchard bending machine costing "little more than £700, competent to bend oak 16 inches square . . . will bend ten [fourteen-foot] pieces of timber in ten hours," tripling their value from £30 to £90. After allowing "expenses etc." of a pound a day each for three men, he calculated that the machine would leave "a clear gain of £57," so that "in fourteen working-days a machine would nearly defray the cost of its purchase." Even if he had overrated its economy by as much as 75 percent, he remarked,

> ample margin is left for immense profits. . . . It cannot be denied that the new process of bending timber will reduce the cost of ships of all sizes twenty-five per cent . . . and greatly increase their strength and durability, by avoiding the necessity for using cross-grained timber.[61]

To what extent did shipbuilders actually adopt Blanchard's machine? Despite such enthusiastic reports on both sides of the Atlantic in the 1850s, Blanchard's backers went bankrupt, as did others in the general business crisis of 1857.[62] In his application in 1863 for extension of his 1849 patent, Blanchard argued that although the company had "proved commercially a failure," from which he had realized only $12,000, the machine on which it was based had nevertheless effected a "revolution in the cost and labor of ship building." Before, suitable pieces of naturally curved timber for ships' knees and futtocks "were obtained with difficulty after searching endless forests." But of late, all yards possessing my machine are sure of having as much curved timber as they want, provided the straight timber can be obtained. It is no exaggeration to say that hundreds of thousands of dollars have thus been saved, and hundreds of vessels added to our commercial fleets; while the strength imparted by the bending process as has long been demonstrated has lessened the average of marine disasters and given grace and lightness to the structure of the largest ships.[63]

From this statement one can infer that the Ship Timber Bending Company, or its successors, had in fact sold bending machines to some American shipyards, and that these had been used to good effect in this era of the clipper ship, even if one discounts heavily for bias in Blanchard's opinion that they had brought about a "revolution in ship building."

Ship-timber bending and patenting thereof did not die with Blanchard or his patent. In 1866 John Willis Griffiths of Brooklyn, New York, former president of the Ship Timber Bending Company, obtained U.S. Patents #51,826 and #51,827 for his ship-timber bending machine and method.[64] Rights to these patents were later bought by the Union Ship Timber Manufacturing Company, whose Steam Bending Works were located in Boston in the late 1860s and 1870s, where Griffiths was superintendent for a time. The U.S. Navy Department bought rights to the Griffiths machine in 1872, and Griffiths obtained another patent for a woodbending machine in 1875.[65] Yet even so, Blanchard's "revolution in ship building" was still tentative in the 1880s, when the U.S. Census Report on the subject was describing it as experiment, rather than accepted practice, at the Boston Navy Yard:

> It is in this yard that some experiments have been made with a machine for bending the oaken frame timbers of ships so as to make them in one piece from keel to gunwale. The machine cost $160,000, and bent a large number of knees and timbers in a satisfactory manner.[66]

With greater hindsight, however, we know that the larger revolution in building ships that eventually overtook the bending of ship timbers in the late nineteenth century was the shift from wood to iron and steel.

## FURNITURE

Following his effort to bend ever-larger timbers, which culminated in his 1856 patent for a heavy-duty machine, Blanchard took out two more woodbending patents in 1858.[67] These patents appear to reflect a recognition that other applications would in fact prove more profitable than the ship timber application. Their timing may also be related to the litigation that ensued between Morris and Blanchard's assignees. They were aimed at specialized uses of fairly light bentwood: one was for shovel handles, and the other for closed figures such as chair bottom hoops or frames for pictures and writing slates. The latter, patented May 4, is very similar to Blanchard's 1849 machine. But where the 1849 patent simply alludes to the possibility that the usually circular rotating mold may be "elliptical or any figure required," this one specifies that the shape of the rotating pattern correspond with the whole form desired for a closed hoop of wood: oval, round-cornered quadrilateral, etc., and makes the molds easily removable (see figure 8.5, top). When a manufacturer of school slates in Philadelphia wanted to use a bentwood frame, he first demurred at Blanchard's price of $2,000 for the patent right, but then agreed to pay Blanchard 5 percent on the sales of the slates for a number of years. The slates proved so popular that "The amount he paid Blanchard exceeded two thousand dollars the first year."[68]

Blanchard's patented "Method of Bending Shovel handles" of 1858 is a much simpler "implement or device" intended for bending "chair legs and similar articles," as well as shovel handles, into a slight S-curve. To do so it did not apply extra end pressure or use a rotating form, but merely clamped the steamed wooden stick between two appropriately shaped top and bottom molds. Abutments at the ends prevented the handle or leg from lengthening, or "distending longitudinally."

As in the case of the blockmaking machines, which Blanchard patented *after* selling the rights to his irregular turning lathe for blockmaking, no separate assignments are recorded for these 1858 improvements.[69] Separately, these two 1858 patents would be useful to manufacturers of school slates or mirror and picture frames, on the one hand, or to shovel manufacturers on the other. But together they would be useful to chairmakers for making bentwood legs and frames for cane-bottom seats. From the language and timing of the patent assignments involved, I infer that these "improvements" were included under the Blanchard woodbending rights that the American Timber Bending Company sold in 1858 to two related chair manufacturers in Massachusetts. They were the Walter Heywood Chair Company of Fitchburg and the Heywood Chair Manufacturing Company of Gardner.

Walter Heywood (1804–1880) and his several brothers had begun making chairs in Gardner over thirty years earlier, but their partnership had split up and reorganized at various times. From 1839 Levi Heywood (1800–1882) was the dominant force in the Gardner enterprise, which in 1851 became the Heywood Chair Manufacturing Company but later grew into the more famous furniture manufacturers, the Heywood-Wakefield Company.[70] From January to May of 1858 Walter Heywood's company in Fitchburg and Levi Heywood's company in Gardner shared rights to Blanchard's woodbending patent for making chairs in Worcester County only, for which they paid $5,000; then they expanded their rights to the whole of New England, just two days before the issue date of Blanchard's second woodbending patent of that year.[71] The American Timber Bending Company reserved "the right to use one machine in the City of Boston, for bending chair legs" but allowed the Heywoods the right to "the construction of cane seat settees [as well as chairs] in their own manufactories only." With Blanchard's machine and its 1858 improvements, the Heywoods of Fitchburg and Gardner were able to make chair legs and seat frames for cane-bottom chairs and settees as well as bowed backs and arms for Windsor-type chairs. For the New England assignment they paid $7,500, bringing the total to $12,500, payable in installments over several months. According to the company's centennial history in 1926, Francis Thonet, of the famous Gebrüder Thonet firm, bentwood chair manufacturers in Vienna, later visited Levi Heywood's factory and paid him a compliment: "I must tell you candidly that you have the best machinery for bending wood that I ever saw."[72] The company history neglects to mention the role that Blanchard's bending machinery had played at the Heywood factory, but credits the compliment to Levi Heywood's woodbending inventions instead.[73]

## SOCIAL CONSTRUCTION OF WOODBENDING TECHNOLOGY

As we have seen, there were few patents granted for bending wood before Blanchard's in 1849. But after his machines went into use in the 1850s, a great many more woodbending patents were granted in the period from the late 1850s to the early 1870s, perhaps indicating a "bandwagon" effect. Among these patents were Blanchard's own woodbending patents of 1856 and 1858, the patent in 1856 to John C. Morris of Cincinnati, and four patents granted to Levi Heywood in the 1860s.[74] Heywood joined Morris in forming the Morris and Heywood Wood-bending Company.[75]

John C. Morris, who had became acquainted with bending machines at Bowman's, a machine shop where he worked in Cincinnati, took out his patent in 1856. Morris intended his machine, like Blanchard's, to have a wide range of applications "for wagon felloes, ship-timber, plow handles, chair stuff, and for all other purposes in which wood is required to be bent."[76] As we have seen, protracted patent infringement litigation ensued in the late 1850s between Morris and his assignees on one side and Blanchard's assignees on the other side. Each side sued the other. In 1858 the court tracked down Illinois plowmaker Leonard Andrus and his erstwhile millwright, David Gans, who had "gone farming" in the meantime, and asked them to describe Gans's unpatented plow-handle machine of 1844. In 1866 they testified again, for the trials were still going on.[77]

Thomas Blanchard withdrew his patent and had it reissued in 1859, with a somewhat clearer description and a new introduction explaining the defects of pre-Blanchard machines for bending timber, in particular that the timber was likely to "rise up and leave the mould" at its weak spots.[78] Blanchard's 1849 patent specification ended with the disclaimer of "any particular form of machinery to carry my new method into operation" and a simple claim to originality for "my method of bending fibrous materials by means of the upsetting movements . . . and relaxing movements combined." But his reissue ends with a stronger warning that "the details of the mechanism may be varied greatly without departing from the principles of my invention." Blanchard's new wording doesn't change the meaning of what he claims, but it changes the emphasis, so that it sounds broader.

John C. Morris withdrew *his* patent and had it reissued in 1862. In it he added a prefatory statement distinguishing "two principal groups or classes" of machines for bending wood, from one end inward to the other or from the middle outward in both directions[79] (see figure 8.9). He then says "my improvements relate to the second class of machines." Morris's original 1856 patent specification does not posit these two classes, but simply claims as original "the clamps . . . to prevent end expansion and the levers . . . working on fixed fulcrums." His reissue, however, not only claims originality for "hooks, . . . pins, or their equivalents to restrain the wood in shape" but also for "a wood bending form to which timbers are made to conform by bending them from the center or inner end of the desired curve, outward." In so doing, Morris very much expanded the meaning of his patent, and staked a broad claim within a "class" of

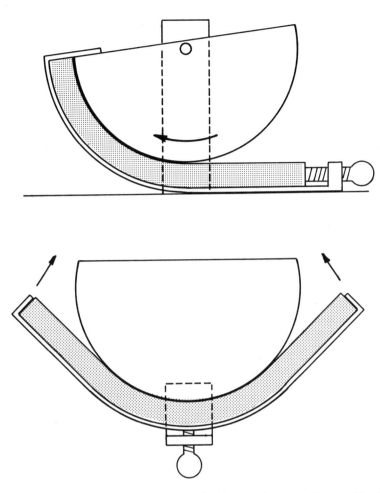

FIGURE 8.9. Two methods of bending wood. Above is shown the Thomas Blanchard method, with rotating form, metal band, and end abutments to contrain the workpiece, and with upsetting screw to apply end pressure to it. As the form rotates clockwise, the wood wraps around it. Below is shown the John C. Morris method, with metal band and end abutments to constrain the workpiece, and the stationary form to which both ends are bent while its middle remains clamped. Morris called Blanchard's method bending "inward" and his own method bending "outward." (Drawing by R. B. Gordon.)

woodbending machines, which he himself had just defined. He also conveniently left unmentioned previous unpatented use of this method, such as the ship-timber bending machine Blanchard had used in 1854, before he succeeded bending heavy timbers with a rotating form.[80]

*231*

At the end of 1862—that is, the year in which his irregular turning patent finally expired—Blanchard unsuccessfully petitioned the House and Senate for a fourteen-year extension of his 1849 woodbending patent.[81] A year later he obtained an ordinary seven-year extension from the Patent Office, by arguing that his bending invention had very much benefited the ship-building industry, but because of the failure of the Ship Timber Bending Company, he had netted only $14,700 total from all uses of his patent. His petition alludes to "my infirmities of old age" and to "a sense of duty to . . . my heirs."[82] It was possibly his last act of patent management; he died four months later, on April 16, 1864. As a piece of property, the woodbending patent survived him until December 1870, in the hands of his assignees and *their* assignees. Blanchard's nephew A. V. Blanchard traveled from Palmer to Cincinnati to sue licensees of the Morris patent; Morris sued A. V. Blanchard's assignees, the Royer Company of Cincinnati.

In the spring of 1866, during the lawsuit of *Morris vs. Royer et al.,* one witness for the defense, George H. Knight, a consulting engineer and patent solicitor, denied the validity of Morris's distinction of two classes of machines for bending, saying "I regard the direction of bending as purely optional, bending in either or both directions being expedients perfectly well known and familiar to the craft" before either Blanchard's or Morris's patent was issued. Knight therefore regarded "the Morris machine as embodying substantially the construction and mode of operation patented to Blanchard, [with] some apparent differences . . . " due to the different applications to articles having different shapes and sizes, such as plow handles, wheel felloes, or ship timbers.

But other witnesses and the judge and jury thought differently from Knight on this point: they were persuaded that the two modes of bending were indeed "substantially different" ways of accomplishing the same end, and therefore separately patentable. The Blanchard faction lost both cases in 1867, as defendants and as plaintiffs. In the latter case, the judge gave a scolding to both sides:

> I have no doubt that Thomas Blanchard, now deceased, was an ingenious mechanic, and a man of much more than ordinary inventive talent. I have no doubt that the machine that he invented, and for which he obtained a patent, is a valuable invention, creditable to him and useful to the public. And I am equally clear that Morris, in his machine, has exhibited inventive talent of a high order, and has produced a useful and practical wood-bending machine. It is to be regretted that these parties did not permit each one to go on in the

enjoyment of his grant under his particular patent, and that it should have been found necessary to resort to litigation to settle their rights.[83]

This opinion, we should note, reflects a very different view from that of the judge in 1849 in *Blanchard Gunstock Turning Factory vs. Eldridge, et al.,* as regards the function of patent law in protecting intellectual property. In that case, Eldridge's reversion to Woolworth's 1819 technology for last turning was not sufficient to protect him from Blanchard's 1820 patent, but in this case Morris not only took refuge in, but also successfully laid claim to, a mode of bending ("outward") that was already in unpatented use before Blanchard's patent as well as his own. In both instances, however, the definition of a significant difference between two machines for achieving the same end—a shaped shoe last or a bent wheel felloe—was socially constructed, not only through the patenting process itself, but also through the ensuing "resort to litigation." The judge's allusion in 1867 to the fact that Blanchard the inventor was already dead hints at an implicit weakening of strength in the property rights of his assignees, relative to those of a currently living inventor.

The Blanchard faction promptly appealed the decision of the Circuit Court to the Supreme Court, and won its reversal two years later, on the grounds of procedural errors in the lower court.[84] By this time the Blanchard patent had only one more year to run, but in 1870 Morris managed to get a seven-year extension of his. The upshot of the whole proceeding was to blur the identification of mechanized woodbending with either Blanchard or Morris. As mentioned above, both types of machine were built beyond 1870 and were still used in wood-wheel works surviving until recently.[85] This contrasts with the case of the irregular turning lathe, in which the social definition of Blanchard's invention eventually subsumed Woolworth's. But both cases of social construction were the outcome of people's perceptions of an evolving technology, as affected by their views of property rights. The duality of the patent as public knowledge and as private property, which Blanchard's story demonstrates, has continued in tension in American society, with effects in both directions, down to the present day.

**9**

# SUMMARY AND
# CONCLUSIONS

As we have seen, Thomas Blanchard's long career as an inventor of machines partook of many important developments in American technological history in the nineteenth century. In various ways people exploited his woodworking inventions, not only in rationalized factory production at armories, but also in manufacturing such diverse other items as shoes and furniture, in building and outfitting river boats and clipper ships, in felling forests and plowing prairies, and in traveling over land.[1]

Blanchard's most famous invention, the irregular turning lathe, made it possible for the first time to shape a highly irregular object by a continuous machine operation. Some previous lathes were capable of cutting irregularities into the surface of a disk or a cylinder, but none were able to cut all around such a highly irregular solid body as a gunstock or a shoe last. Pre-Blanchard lathes were unable to do this because of the limitations intrinsic in cutting by rapid rotary motion of the workpiece against the cutter. Blanchard gave the cutter rapid rotary motion against the workpiece, instead. Blanchard's lathe allowed the workpiece to rotate slowly while a rapidly rotating and slowly traversing cutter cut into it as deeply as permitted by the connected "friction wheel," which was tracing over the shape of a model rotating synchronously with the workpiece. Thus the shape of the model controlled the depth of the cutting and was duplicated in the workpiece.

Blanchard invented his irregular turning lathe in order to make gunstocks, after Asa Waters, Jr., the arms manufacturer in his home town of Millbury, Massachusetts, had drawn him into the armsmaking milieu to improve the action of a gunbarrel-turning lathe. Once Blanchard had proceeded to invent a different kind of lathe for turning gunstocks, he still needed to demonstrate its usefulness for the Springfield Armory and to arrive at a figure for his compensation from the U.S. Ordnance Department, which was to be set at half the amount his machine would save. To do this, Blanchard became an "inside contractor" for gunstocks at Springfield Armory. During his sojourn at the Armory in the 1820s, Blanchard built a sequence of fourteen machines for "half-stocking" muskets. He hired his own work force to operate the machines on this production line, in which "half" of the total work of stocking was performed. Counting

238 ◆ Summary and Conclusions

the remaining handwork, overall labor productivity for stocking guns went up by about one-half during the years his machines were in use. As far as it can be calculated, the saving on labor costs more than paid for the cost of installing and running the machines. After he left, the Armory continued to use his machines, to improve them, and eventually to replace them in the 1840s with newer ones based on his designs. With these second generation machines, productivity went up even more. Blanchard's machines and their "second generation" descendants reduced the hand labor needed to make gunstocks, but certainly did not eliminate it.

Besides the machine for shaping the external contours of a musket stock, Blanchard's production line included machines for drilling holes and cutting the various irregular-shaped cavities or recesses in the wooden stock, to fit some of the metal parts of the musket—the barrel, the lock, the barrel bands, the butt plate, and certain screws. These various "inletting," "recessing," or "bedding" machines resembled the irregular turning lathe in the general idea of guiding a cutter by a tracer to copy an irregular pattern, but they were not lathes. The type of cutter they used was quite different from the cutter of an ordinary lathe. It was also quite different from that of the Blanchard lathe: instead of rotating on a horizontal axis between bearings like a circular saw, the cutter of an inletting machine rotated at the end of a vertical spindle like a drill. The patterns to be traced were also quite different, being recesses of varying shapes and depths instead of solids of varying contours. Still another difference was that the workpiece did not, of course, rotate in these machines; it remained stationary during each inletting operation.

Machines for copying that used this kind of vertical-spindle cutter were also being put to use in England at about the same time, but for copying sculptures and bas-reliefs instead of inletting. In such copying machines, as in Blanchard's inletting machines, the motions of a tracer were copied by the vertical-spindle cutter, but the pattern was in this instance not an irregular cavity, but an irregular surface on a solid. They could not copy an object all the way around in one continuous operation, although they could copy relief on curved surfaces up to about 90 degrees of arc. For a sculpture in the round, some of them could copy successive portions of the object's surface in several operations, with partial rotation of the object, coordinated with partial rotation of the model, in between operations of the cutter.

Blanchard never patented his inletting machines, but received a fee from the U.S. government for their use at the federal armories, as well as for the use of his lathe. The French patent for a sculpture-copying machine that Blanchard obtained in 1855 indicates that those he demonstrated on several public occasions in the 1840s and 1850s were vertical-spindle machines derived from his inletting machine, rather than horizontal-spindle machines like his irregular turning lathe. But (if they were like the 1855 version) they were self-acting, having also a continuous slow rotation of workpiece and model. Blanchard seemed upon a few convenient occasions to regard this machine as part of his irregular turning invention, as when he lobbied in 1847 for extension of his patent by "turning the heads of Congress."

For the American system of manufactures, Blanchard's work at the Springfield Armory in the 1820s had two kinds of consequences: organizational and mechanical. His production line of machines for making gunstocks demonstrated the organizational advantages of having a rationally coordinated sequence of special-purpose machines for producing a standard item in large quantities, and some mechanical features of these woodworking machines were adapted into important metal-working machine tools, such as vertical-spindle milling machines and profilers (see figure 9.1).[2] Since the Armory was an important training ground for mechanics who were mobile, not only among the public and private gun manufactories but also among the other machine shops of New England, these mechanics diffused both of these aspects of Blanchard's work into American manufacturing technology during and after his sojourn in Springfield. The metalworking profiler was (with the milling machine) one of the "American" machine tools that made interchangeable parts for small arms by the midcentury and for sewing machines, typewriters, bicycles, etc., later on. These mostly-metal consumer durables were made in factories where attention was paid to rational arrangement of the production system, for which armory practice, and especially Blanchard's sequentially arranged stocking machines, provided a paradigm.

Thirty years later, after Cyrus Buckland and other Springfield Armory mechanics reworked Blanchard's gunstocking machines into a "second generation" production line, they were the centerpiece of the American machinery (including also the Blanchard-influenced metalworking machine tools) that the British government bought in the mid-1850s in order to set up the Enfield Armory outside London. One important reason it had not impressed its earlier English viewers when it was patented and demonstrated there in the 1820s was that they saw it in isolation, not in the context of the rest of the gunstocking machines that

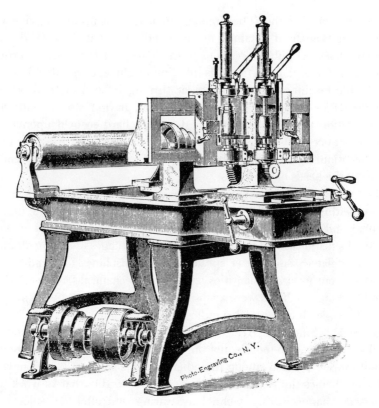

FIGURE 9.1. Two-spindle edging machine, or profiler, c. 1880. This versatile machine tool for edge-milling irregular shapes in metal was a descendant of the Blanchard inletting machine. Movement of a guide pin around a former or pattern (not shown) controlled the shape of cuts on one or two workpieces (not shown). The operator used the two ball handles to move the table holding the workpiece(s) transversely, and the frame holding the vertical-spindle rotary cutters, or "mills," laterally. He used the levers to raise and lower the spindles to a depth that was variable between adjustable stops. He could also use this machine to cut forms and jigs, and to sink dies. (From F. R. Hutton, "Report on Machine-Tools and Woodworking Machinery" *Tenth Census of the United States (1880): Statistics of Power and Machinery Used in Manufactures,* p. 154.)

Blanchard was only then developing at Springfield. He developed these other, unpatented machines for the explicit purpose of taking the best advantage of his lathe's capabilities.

When he left Springfield and adapted his irregular turning lathe to the making of ships' tackle blocks and deadeyes in New York City in the 1830s, Blanchard again developed a sequence of special-purpose machines, within which context his lathe would function to best advantage. Although he obtained patents for ten such blockmaking machines, he apparently assigned the rights to them as a unit in advance, under his lathe patent. As described in the specifications for his ten patents of August, 1836, Blanchard's machines for blockmaking differed from the famous Portsmouth blockmaking machinery in England, both in the way they performed individual tasks, for example, mortising, and in the way the production sequence was arranged. The Portsmouth machinery manufactured solid-shell blocks only, and left to handwork the larger blocks, whose shells were made up of separate pieces, but Blanchard mechanized the production of both kinds of block. The block mill at the Royal Dockyard in Portsmouth was paid for by government funds and was a showpiece for elegant, all-metal machinery that continued in operation for over a century. In contrast, the blockworks that Blanchard's assignees built at Winooski Falls, Vermont, was paid for by private capital and was short-lived, destroyed by fire started by friction in wooden bearings. Both manufactories, however, contained a rationally designed sequence of machines for quantity production of uniform parts that were assembled into a standard product.

After designing production lines for gunstocks and ships' blocks, Blanchard continued to invent more individual machines when he lived in Boston from 1840 to 1864, but designed no more production lines. To take the best advantage of his lathe in other production processes, he did not need to imbed it in a sequence of additional machines as in the armory or the block mill. After they were shaped, gunstocks needed inletting in various spots, and ships' blocks needed boring, scoring, and mortising. External shaping alone, however, sufficed to finish, or nearly finish, other products of the Blanchard lathe, such as ax handles, shoe lasts, and wheel spokes. It is true that thirty years after inventing his lathe, which was capable of turning the irregular contours of plow handles, Blanchard invented a machine capable of bending them, and then "packaged" the two machines by assigning them together to plow handle manufacturers. Compared to the machines he had developed for gunstocking and blockmaking, however, this package was not an extended sequence. Similarly, his lathe and his woodbending machine were both used in making wheels for wagons and carriages, and so were his sanding machine and unpatented tenoning machine, but he did not attempt to integrate them with other appropriate machines into a complete wheel-making production line.

Blanchard's second major woodworking invention was the woodbending machine that he invented and patented in 1849 for plow handles, and for other uses in 1856 and 1858. Blanchard's method never stretched the fibers of wood beyond their natural limits, for his machine applied endwise pressure on the piece of wood and then relaxed it gradually during bending. As with the lathe, one could adapt his bending machine to different products by using different shaped patterns or "formers." Makers of handles for agricultural implements, of furniture, and of carriage and wagon parts applied the Blanchard bender successfully to their various needs for bentwood. The Ship Timber Bending Company, in which Blanchard was himself heavily involved, intended to supply bentwood knees and futtocks to the whole ship-building industry, but it failed financially after just a few years, although Blanchard's machines did succeed in bending timbers of the large sizes needed. Blanchard's three woodbending patents show a concern for different applications of his basic invention, not a concern for production line design.

## APPLICATION DIVERGENCE AND TECHNOLOGICAL CONVERGENCE

Even—or perhaps, especially—outside the context of production lines of his own design, Blanchard's irregular turning and woodbending inventions were individually applied in his lifetime to the production of shoes and hats, of carriages, wagons, and horse-drawn agricultural implements, of hand tools, of furniture, and for a while, of ships. In each of these production processes, which were not necessarily integrated into factories at single locations, but were frequently carried out in scattered specialized units of various sizes, Blanchard's machines played a crucial role, albeit a less conspicuous role than his machines at the Springfield Armory played in the production of muskets and rifles.

Each of Blanchard's inventions had a wide variety of possible relationships to other machines. The user of a Blanchard "spoke lathe," for instance, might be a diversified woodworker who also made ax handles with his Blanchard lathe and sold his output both to wheel makers and to ax makers. Or he might be a wheel maker himself, who used machines, including either a Blanchard or a Morris felloe bender, to make all parts of wheels, and sold the wheels to carriage makers. Or he might be a carriage maker, using Blanchard lathes to make whiffletrees as well as wheel spokes and Blanchard benders to make seat rails as well as wheel felloes.

Blanchard's machines not only fitted easily into any of a range of workshops or factories of different sizes and purposes, they could also be converted fairly easily from making one product to another. In both the bending machine and the lathe, conversion was for many purposes mostly a matter of changing the pattern to be copied. Thus Blanchard patent assignees who were wheel makers in the midwest diversified their product to include handles for agricultural and nonagricultural implements. Woodburn and Scott in St. Louis and Royer, Coleman and Young in Cincinnati, who both had assignments for wheel-making purposes in the 1850s, bought additional assignments in the 1860s to make, respectively, handles for carpenters' and stone-cutters' tools, and handles for plows and cultivators.[3] In a later period, wheel makers Hoopes, Brother, and Darlington in West Chester, Pennsylvania found that during periods of slack demand for wooden wheels (which lengthened as automobiles replaced carriages and metal wheels replaced wooden ones), they could make chair backs and plow handles, baseball bats and wooden skis.[4]

Economic historian Nathan Rosenberg has called this phenomenon "technological convergence," by which "industries which were apparently unrelated from the point of view of the nature and uses of the final product became very closely related on a technological basis."[5] From that perspective, we can think of Blanchard's irregular turning lathe and woodbending machine as agents of technological convergence in nineteenth-century American manufacturing. Viewed from the perspective of the inventor and of the manufacturer who already owns or licenses a machine, "technological convergence" becomes "application divergence." For the inventor it enhances opportunities to earn additional returns on his invention; for the manufacturer it enhances opportunities to earn a return on the machine and the acquired experience of its operators. For both of them it provides some measure of security against the vagaries of demand for any particular product. For the same reasons, technological convergence (or application divergence) also benefited the machine makers as well as the machine inventors and machine users of the nineteenth century, and gave them the flexibility to survive into the twentieth century despite big changes in demand for their products. Builders of woodworking machinery, such as the Defiance Machine Works, established in Ohio in 1850, that began as suppliers to makers of wheels, carriages and wagons, found that they could also sell irregular lathes and woodbending machines to manufacturers of early automobiles and of wooden objects unrelated to carriages. The Defiance catalogue in 1910 offered "complete equipments" of the following kinds of machinery:

. . . automobile wheel and body, hub, spoke, wheel, bending, wagon, carriage, plow handle, broom, rake, fork and brush handle, hammer, hatchet, pick and chisel handle, all kinds of spool and bobbin, barrel bung, oval wood dish, billiard ball and cue, golf stick, shoe lasts, neck-yoke, singletree, shaft, pole and barrel hoop machinery, and a general line of standard and special Wood-Working Machinery, all of which contain many new features of advantage and convenience.[6]

The reader will recognize that this variegated list is an indication of technological convergence and would be much shorter in the absence of irregular turning lathes and woodbending machines. Technological convergence, then, was fostered by the incentives of the patent management system to find divergent applications for any given patented invention.

## PERSPECTIVES ON INTELLECTUAL PROPERTY MANAGEMENT

The career of Thomas Blanchard as an inventor ended during the Civil War. He received his last patent in 1862; married for the third time in 1863, and died in Boston in his seventy-sixth year, in April 1864. Unlike many other famous inventors, he did not die penniless or unrecognized for his inventions. But the recognition and reward that Blanchard enjoyed during his lifetime did not come to him automatically. They came because he engaged not only in inventive activity but also in successful management of his intellectual property, within a social system that rewarded inventive activity by rewarding such management. Among the items that Thomas Blanchard singled out for mention in his will was his set of Patent Office annual reports and his machine models, such as those he had used at various times during his many court trials in protection of his patents. These items were symbolic of the network of relations within which Blanchard had necessarily operated as an American inventor in the first half of the nineteenth century. This network involved him in interaction with other inventors, with Patent Office examiners, with patent agents and patent lawyers, with Supreme Court and other federal judges, with congressmen, and, very importantly, with assignees and licensees.

This social system in which an inventor of Blanchard's time had to operate in order to earn recognition and reward for his inventions had a variety of effects on the inventor himself, on the developing economy and technology of America, and upon the very history of that technology. For the inventor himself, the patent granted by the government for his invention meant that he had legally enforceable exclusive property rights in his invention, which he could sell or license for a fee. For the duration of the patent he had the right to divide this property into different parcels, both by geographic territory and by application, and to sell or license each parcel according to its market value.

Thus the patent not only established an inventor's intellectual property rights, but also facilitated the use of his property by allowing him to divide it up and pass the entrepreneurial risks onto as many other shoulders as he could find through the assignment and licensing system that was part of the patent system. If the inventor was, like Thomas Blanchard (and unlike Azariah Woolworth), good enough at patent management, he didn't need to risk his own money in the shaky developing economy of the early nineteenth-century United States. He didn't need to be an entrepreneur himself, nor did he need to seek a single large entrepreneur to support him, as manufacturer Matthew Boulton had supported inventor James Watt. Small entrepreneurs could take on small individual risks and collectively provide a sufficient reward to the inventor through royalty fees.

In fact, Thomas Blanchard did assume partial entrepreneurship at various times in his career—for instance during his period as inside contractor at Springfield Armory in the 1820s, and when he accepted $600,000 worth of stock instead of cash from the Ship Timber Bending Company in the early 1850s. Blanchard also ran his own machine shop in Boston after 1840 to construct machines on order. However, these episodes of entrepreneurship were not the only way in which he reaped reward from his patents for his inventions. His royalty fees were another way, and particularly in relation to his woodbending machine, a more satisfactory way, considering that the Ship Timber Bending Company foundered not long after its launching.

The patent system functioned to the inventor's benefit not only by creating his property rights and those of his assignees, and by relieving him of the need to be an entrepreneur, but also by acting as a clearinghouse of information. The Patent Office itself was rather tardy in assuming the responsibility for publishing detailed information about patented inventions, but others—such as the Franklin Institute in Philadelphia and the *Scientific American* in New York City—took on this task. The Franklin Institute had to fight with William Thornton, the first Patent Office Superintendent, in order to establish the principle that patent information could be disseminated even during the life of the patents, but succeeded in doing so in 1825, and began publishing abstracts in 1826.[7] Only in 1853 did the *Annual Report* of the Commissioner of Patents begin including pictorial abstracts of the year's patents.

Before this kind of information was published, inventors had to rely on hearsay and visits in person to find out how any invention actually worked. David Wilkinson, for instance, had to travel to several states up and down the East Coast in the mid-1790s to see whether others had already invented his screw-cutting lathe,[8] and Thomas Blanchard had to visit James Harrison's shop in Waterbury, Connecticut in 1819 to see Woolworth's lastmaking machine. Once descriptions and illustrations of patented devices were published, they didn't totally eliminate the need for such journeys, but they immensely eased the task for would-be inventors of keeping themselves informed. This publication of patent information, of course, advertised the invention to a geographically wider pool of potential assignees and licensees with whom the inventor was not already personally acquainted. This advertisement worked to his advantage, counteracting the disadvantage of losing his secrecy.

The advance sale of patent rights to assignees could facilitate the development phase of an invention, in which the inventor was working to embody his design in actual usable objects—in Blanchard's case, machines. Blanchard seems to have done this on several occasions—most clearly when developing his production line of blockmaking machinery in the 1830s. In December 1835 he made one nationwide assignment of his lathe patent for the purpose of making tackle blocks, and never thereafter assigned the ten blockmaking machines that he patented in August 1836. For assignment purposes, everyone concerned seemed to regard those ten patents as improvements on his 1820 invention, even though most of the ten were not adaptations of the Blanchard lathe, but were for quite different types of machine—mortising, inletting, or riveting. Another instance of this procedure was Blanchard's sale in 1853 to the Ship Timber Bending Company of rights to his 1849 woodbending machine, whose patent specification describes how to bend plow handles. This was before he had actually developed machines suitable for bending ship timbers, which he did sometime in 1854. From the inventor's viewpoint, it was clearly an advantage to have a mechanism, such as assignment of prospective improvements, for obtaining advance financial support while developing them.

Thus we can see that the system of patent management within which a nineteenth-century American inventor operated helped the inventor in a number of ways beyond the basic act of granting him a monopoly of rights to his own intellectual property for a specified number of years. But he had to pay a price for these various advantages: the onus of protecting the rights through litigation was on the inventor, unless he had sold them all off. In order to maintain the market value of his property, he had the responsibility of going to court if necessary to prevent its infringement. In such lawsuits the inventor was protecting the property's market value not only for himself but also for his assignees and licensees, who would otherwise be at a disadvantage vis-à-vis their competitors who used the property without paying for it. Assignees also had the right and responsibility to conduct lawsuits, for the sake of other assignees, licensees, and the inventor, as well as for their own sake.

Hence we find Blanchard buying back an assignment from an assignee who was ineffective at suing infringers, and find assignments that spell out the circumstances under which the assigner instead of a dilatory assignee will exercise the right to sue for infringement. We also find previous infringers becoming licensees and cheerful enough witnesses against later infringers. As mentioned in chapter 3, the more useful the invention really was and the more widely applicable, the more infringements were likely to take place, and the more time and money the inventor or his assignees would have to spend on litigation. Even if the litigants regarded it as unpleasant, litigation was not a sign of defects in the patent management system within which they were operating; it was a normal and inevitable feature of the system. It was also through litigation, as well as through the interaction of patent agents and patent examiners during the application process, that the social construction of the invention took place. The network of assignees and licensees that grew up around a patent also constituted a pool of potential innovation and of joint action in restraint of trade or lobbying for favors in the political arena.

These various implications of the patent management system for the inventors also had their counterpart implications for the nation's developing economy and technology. From the point of view of the nation, the system not only served to promote new inventions, which is its basic rationale, but the procedure mentioned above for advance assignment of prospective improvements also seems to have served for support of the development stage of inventions. This can be seen as a private-enterprise alternative to fostering such development by public funds. At the Portsmouth Dockyard in England, the development of blockmaking machinery over several years was paid for by the Royal Navy, which was its own customer. Similarly, at the Springfield Armory in Massachusetts, the Ordnance Department provided shop space, materials, and power for Blanchard's development of his gunstocking machinery, and was the customer for his gunstocks. The development of Blanchard's machinery for blockmaking had no such publicly funded support, but he was able to sell the patent rights to those machines in advance of actually patenting them.

From the point of view of promoting development of the nation's economy and technology, it was of course helpful to have patent information disseminated widely by the private agencies that did so, and later on by the publication of the Patent Office Annual Reports. Even during the period of a patent's restriction on use of that information, such dissemination would promote general technical sophistication among mechanics and inventors. Also from that point of view, the availability of multiple assignments and licenses of a given patented invention in different territories speeded the diffusion of that invention without necessarily waiting for the actual production and shipment of the invented device. In the case of fairly heavy and bulky machinery like Blanchard's, it was probably often much easier in the early decades of those patents for a would-be user at some distance to pay for the designs and to build the machine himself with local materials and labor, than to have Blanchard or one of his assignees build and ship an actual machine. Thus the diffusion of Blanchard's machines could take place through the mail and did not have to wait for the full-fledged development of the woodworking machine industry.

Blanchard's patent history demonstrates several other effects of the patent management system on the nation's economy and technology. One was that by its incentives to the patentee to find multiple applications for his invention, the system encouraged "convergent technology," as discussed earlier. Another was the "one-way ratchet" or "progressive" effect on technology, mentioned in chapter 3, resulting from vigorous enforcement and broad interpretation of patent rights in the courts. This would tend to prevent small-scale use of obsolete equipment, to the benefit of larger companies adopting up-to-date patented equipment. It would therefore tend to promote survival of larger manufacturing firms over smaller ones. Another effect observable in Blanchard's assignment records and in his dealings with his lastmaking licensees is the formation of interest or pressure groups around the protection of the patent rights, such as the lobby they formed for federal legislation against importation from Canada of items made by U.S.-patented machinery. Assignments that include price-maintenance agreements[9] also indicate the patent management system could work to promote formation of interest groups for the control of markets. In a later era such groups were outlawed.

Beyond the effects that the management system for intellectual property rights had both upon the careers of inventors and upon the development of the nation's economy and technology, it had profound effects upon the social construction of invention and therefore on our very perception of what happened in the history of nineteenth-century American technology. Continuously refined and modified definitions of inventions resulted from interaction among persons in patent litigation after patents were granted as well as in patent examination beforehand. In the case of Thomas Blanchard's woodbending patent, social construction occurred during many years of litigation over the question of what were important and unimportant differences between two litigants' machines. This social construction resulted in a record (to the extent a record exists) in which woodbending devices are largely anonymous rather than associated strongly with any one inventor. In the case of Blanchard's irregular turning patent, however, the social construction over many decades of litigation on points of important and unimportant differences between two types of machine resulted in virtually total suppression, in written history, of the "losing" machine. The irregular turning lathe is synonymous with "the Blanchard lathe," while Azariah Woolworth's invention and its later variants for shaping the same irregular wooden objects have disappeared from historical view.

One may argue that Woolworth-type machines were deservedly dropped from *use* on grounds of economic inefficiency in comparison with Blanchard's superior machine. But the history of technology turns into "Whig history" if it follows a canon of economic rationality in what is chosen for remembrance. The Blanchard lathe is preeminent in the history of nineteenth-century American manufacture of irregular wooden objects because the machine was socially constructed through the operation of the system for patent management. Social construction gradually defined away, as "unimportant" or "mechanically equivalent," the differences between the machines of two contenders for recognition and reward. It reinforced the "great man" perception of history by suppressing recognition of the variety of technical means that were in use at one time for achieving a given end.

The system for patent management simultaneously created its own corrective to this situation, however, which today's historians of technology may use if they wish to correct the "great man" and "Whig" views of history. The corrective is the records that were kept not only of patent applications, but also of patent assignments, patent litigation, patent extension, and patent legislation. From these records one can begin to reconstruct the relationships among the participants in the system and learn what they said about the relevant differences and similarities between the long-since disappeared machines that *they* saw with their own eyes when the machines were new in the world—or maybe not so new. The foregoing is an exercise in such reconstruction, showing how our knowledge of certain machines and their makers was shaped irregular and bent to form.

# NOTES

## 1. Contexts

1. *Report of the Committee on the Machinery of the United States of America* (London: Harrison & Sons, 1855), reprinted in Nathan Rosenberg, ed., *The American System of Manufactures* (Edinburgh, 1969), pp. 87–197, esp. p. 171.

2. For the evolution of this expression, see appendix 1 in David A. Hounshell, *From the American System to Mass Production 1800–1932* (Baltimore, 1984), pp. 331–36. For other scholarship on the American system of manufactures, see introduction to Rosenberg, *American System,* pp. 1–86; Merritt Roe Smith, *Harpers Ferry Armory and the New Technology* (Ithaca, 1977); Otto Mayr and Robert C. Post, eds., *Yankee Enterprise* (Washington, D.C., 1981); Donald R. Hoke, *Ingenious Yankees* (New York, 1990).

3. Recent case histories have pointed to various instances, in American and other western societies, of social construction or shaping of particular technologies, such as bicycles, refrigerators, or turbojet engines. See Wiebe Bijker, Thomas P. Hughes, and Trevor J. Pinch, eds., *The Social Construction of Technological Systems* (Cambridge, Mass., 1987); Donald MacKenzie and Judy Wajcman, eds., *The Social Shaping of Technology* (Milton Keynes, 1985).

4. See Peter L. Berger and Thomas Luckmann, *The Social Construction of Reality* (New York, 1966), for a treatise in the sociology of knowledge that outlines a theoretical bridge to the problems of social psychology. The social psychology of perception is central to my view of the mechanism by which any item of technical "reality" was recognized as "new" (an invention) or "old" (a noninvention) within the society's culture.

5. See, for instance, the various essays in Merritt Roe Smith, ed., *Military Enterprise and Technological Change: Perspectives on the American Experience* (Cambridge, Mass., 1985).

6. For the Franklin Institute, see Bruce Sinclair, *Philadelphia's Philosopher Mechanics, A History of the Franklin Institute 1824–1865* (Baltimore, 1974); for

the American Institute, see Brooke Hindle, "The Underside of the Learned Society in New York 1754–1854," in Alexandra Oleson and Sanborn C. Brown, eds., *The Pursuit of Knowledge in the Early American Republic* (Baltimore: Johns Hopkins University Press, 1976).

7. Monte A. Calvert, *The Mechanical Engineer in America, 1830–1910* (Baltimore, 1976).

8. Merritt Roe Smith, *Harpers Ferry Armory,* passim, esp. pp. 244–247, 283–86; Patrick M. Malone, "Little Kinks and Devices at Springfield Armory, 1892–1918," *IA, The Journal of the Society for Industrial Archeology* 14 (1988): 59–76.

9. Merle Curti, "America at the World Fairs, 1851–1893," *American Historical Review* 55 (1950): 833–56; Robert C. Post, "Reflections of American Science and Technology at the New York Crystal Palace Exhibition of 1853," *Journal of American Studies* 17 (1983): 337–356.

10. Some of the studies reported in Bijker et al., cited above, show Venn or other diagrams in the attempt to describe overlaps and hierarchies of social subsystems relevant to the construction of particular technologies. See, for instance, Ruth Schwartz Cowan, "The Consumption Junction: A Proposal for Research Strategies in the Sociology of Technology," and Edward W. Constant II, "The Social Locus of Technological Practice: Community, System, or Organization."

11. In her article in Bijker et al., Ruth Cowan suggests the utility of analyzing such overlapping influences on a particular technology from one standpoint at a time, and illustrates by analyzing cooking and heating technologies from the standpoint of the "consumption junction." Extending her terminology, one could say the standpoint of the present volume is the "invention junction."

12. In a later era, when some businesses and some technological systems became very big and complex, and individual inventors were increasingly superseded by corporate laboratories, the comparative importance to invention of patent management and other relevant social subsystems probably changed in ways that are beyond discussion here. See Leonard S. Reich, *The Making of American Industrial Research: Science and Business at General Electric and Bell, 1876–1926* (New York: Cambridge University Press, 1985); George Wise, *Willis R. Whitney, General Electric and the Origins of U.S. Industrial Research* (New York: Columbia University Press, 1985.) Major studies describing the patent management behavior of inventors later than Blanchard are: Reese Jenkins, *Images and Enterprise: Technology and the American Photographic Industry 1839 to 1925* (Baltimore: Johns Hopkins University Press, 1975); Robert Friedel and Paul

Israel, with Bernard S. Finn, *Edison's Electric Light* (New Brunswick: Rutgers University Press, 1986); Thomas Parke Hughes, *Elmer Sperry, Inventor and Engineer* (Baltimore: Johns Hopkins University Press, 1971). Edward W. Constant II, however, finds patenting played neither a helping nor a hindering role in *The Origins of the Turbojet Revolution* (Baltimore: Johns Hopkins University Press, 1980).

13. Nathan Rosenberg, "Technological Change in the Machine Tool Industry, 1840–1910," *Journal of Economic History* 23 (1963): 414–43, reprinted in Rosenberg, *Perspectives on Technology* (Cambridge, 1976), pp. 9–31, esp. p. 16.

14. George Wallis, *New York Industrial Exhibition. Special Report of Mr. George Wallis* (London, 1854), reprinted in Rosenberg, *American System*, pp. 199–325, 204.

## 2. From "Whittling Boy" to "Man of Progress"

1. In the twentieth-century literature, whittling is an explicit theme in Roger Burlingame, *March of the Iron Men* (New York: Scribner's, 1938) and *Whittling Boy, the Story of Eli Whitney* (New York: Harcourt Brace & Co., 1941).

2. Henry Howe, *Memoirs of the Most Eminent American Mechanics* (New York, 1840), pp.197–210; Asa Holman Waters, (a) "Biographical Sketch of Thomas Blanchard" (Worcester, 1878), 15 pp.; (b) "Thomas Blanchard," in Rev. William A. Benedict and Rev. Hiram A. Tracy, eds., *History of the Town of Sutton Massachusetts, from 1704 to 1876* (Sutton, 1878), pp. 758–69, identical with (a) except for the addition of six paragraphs; (c) Anon. (Asa H. Waters), "Thomas Blanchard, the Inventor," *Harper's New Monthly Magazine* 63 (July, 1881): 254–60. A more recent extended biographical sketch that draws upon Waters is C. Meade Patterson, "Gunstocking Genius," *The Gun Report* 6 (September 1960): 6–10, 21–24, and 6 (October 1960): 15–19, 24–30.

3. Thomas Blanchard was the sixth of eight children (and the fifth of six sons) born to Samuel and Susanna Tenney Blanchard, who were married in Sutton, Massachusetts on March 17, 1775, and who died in their mid-seventies in 1825 and 1826, respectively. John Calvin Crane and Rev. Robert W. Dunbar, eds., *Centennial History of the Town of Millbury, Massachusetts* (Millbury, 1915), p. 411; Howe, p. 197; *Vital Records of Sutton, Massachusetts to the End of the Year 1849* (Worcester, Mass., 1907), pp. 21, 213, 400, 401.

4. Thomas Blanchard's birthplace in Worcester County was within the town of Sutton at the time of his birth in 1788, but at the request of his father the farm was "set" to Oxford in 1793. Years later, Blanchard had difficulty tracking down

a record of his birth, which is not listed in the *Vital Records of Sutton* cited in note 3. D. Hamilton Hurd, *History of Worcester County, Massachusetts* (Philadelphia, 1889), vol. 2, p. 975; George F. Daniels, *History of the Town of Oxford* (Oxford, Mass., 1892), pp. 41, 338; John C. Crane, "Asa Holman Waters," *Proceedings of the Worcester Society of Antiquity for the Year 1887* (Worcester, 1888), vol. 7, pp. 84–96, p. 92.

5. Howe, pp. 197–199.

6. Asa H. Waters (a), p. 5: "Schools were remote and he seldom attended, for he was afflicted with a perverse impediment of speech. . . . " Mrs. Harriet Dana, a neighbor, said "his mother told me he could talk as well as any of her children till he mocked old Mrs. S—— so much he couldn't talk himself." (Daniels, p. 404, n. 1.) For Blanchard's spelling, see his letter to Roswell Lee, February 5, 1819, Springfield Armory Records, Letters Received, quoted in chapter 5 of this volume.

7. Quoted in Daniels, p. 404, n. 1. Apple-paring machines were invented and patented in great numbers in the 19th century.

8. Howe, p. 199.

9. Stephen Blanchard was born October 26, 1775; John Brewer Blanchard was born March 2, 1780. Daniels, p. 403.

10. It was patented May 4, 1813. Before the revision in 1836 of the patent system, U.S. patents had no serial numbers, but are identified only by name and date. On June 1, 1813 Blanchard published an ad for his machine, quoted in Crane and Dunbar, p. 95. In the ad, Blanchard offered a reward for information about any infringers on his patent.

11. Howe, p. 200–201. The patent was granted jointly to Blanchard and one Samuel Rogers of Boston. A tackmaking machine had been patented by Jesse Reed of Hanover, Massachusetts on August 1, 1816, but there was apparently no dispute over the patent of Blanchard and Rogers. If Blanchard had the machine in hand by age twenty-four (18 plus 6) that would be about 1812, yet no source suggests he waited three to four years to patent it, so there is a dating discrepancy here. A more recent source than Howe, but equally undocumented, traces tackmaking machinery to Jesse Reed's father in Kingston, Massachusetts, and says the patents of Rogers, Blanchard, and Reed were all bought by Benjamin and Elihu Hobart of Abington, for $30,000 in 1815. See Orra L. Stone, *History of Massachusetts Industries* (Boston-Chicago, 1930), vol. 2, pp. 1192–95.

12. Crane and Dunbar, p. 97. In New England towns, field drivers were elected for the duty of driving stray cattle and other animals out of fields and notifying owners.

13. *Vital Records of Millbury, Massachusetts to the End of the Year 1849* (Worcester, 1903), pp. 13 and 65 show dates of the Blanchards' publishing intention to marry and their children's births. If practice was similar in Millbury to that in coastal Hingham, premarital conceptions, such as daughter Laura's, occasioned 15 percent to 25 percent of the first-child births at the time, a percentage declining from its peak of 20 percent to 30 percent a quarter-century earlier. See chart 4.1, p. 132 in James A. Henretta, *The Evolution of American Society, 1700–1815* (Lexington, Mass.: D.C. Heath, 1973).

14. Crane and Dunbar, p. 81–82. Millbury was "set off" from Sutton and incorporated in June 1813. A chronology of uses of the millsites on streams in Millbury is in Hurd, pp. 1111–14. Elbridge Kingsley and Frederick Knab, *Picturesque Worcester* (Springfield, Mass., 1895) shows an exterior view of "The Old Blanchard Mill—West Millbury," and an interior photo of the "Workshop of Blanchard, the Inventor," on p. 132.

15. Hurd, p. 1113.

16. Waters (b), p. 760.

17. *A List of Patents Granted by the United States from April 10, 1790 to December 31, 1836* (Washington, D.C.: G.P.O., 1872), p. 196. Merritt Roe Smith, *Harpers Ferry Armory* pp. 117–27, discusses several other barrel-turning machines that appeared between 1816 and 1819 in addition to that of Waters. Waters is also credited with originating the use of powered trip hammers for welding gun barrels.

18. Waters (c), p. 255.

19. A. H. Waters, Sr. and Son, Millbury, Ledger 1815–1820, p. 169, in Waters Family Papers. The opposite page of the ledger shows that Blanchard returned the barrels years later, on April 26, 1823, and was duly credited with the $2.00.

20. Waters (a), p. 7; Waters (b), p. 761. See chapter 4 for the difference between Blanchard's gunstocking and barrel-turning lathes.

21. Howe, p. 202.

22. Smith, *Harpers Ferry Armory,* pp. 125–29.

23. *Boston Advertiser,* Sept. 14, 1819, quoted in Crane and Dunbar, p. 101. On July 28, 1819, Asa Waters charged Blanchard $3.00 for attending his trial two days (Waters ledger, p. 169). He was probably called to testify on the priority of Blanchard's machine. An interference suit occurs between two would-be paten-tees of the same invention within the caveat period of an application for a patent. See chapter 3 for patenting procedures.

24. Howe, p. 209; Stephen Blanchard, deposition in *Thomas Blanchard vs. Chandler Sprague,* U.S. Circuit Court, Massachusetts District, 1839, Record Group 21, National Archives, Boston Branch. See chapters 3 and 7 for discussion of Azariah Woolworth's competing invention of a lastmaking machine.

25. *Vital Records of Millbury* . . . , pp. 13, 131.

26. J. H. Temple, *History of Palmer* (Springfield, Mass., 1889), p. 260.

27. *Vital Records of Millbury* . . . , p. 13, indicate births of Sarah on June 30, 1822, and of Thomas, Jr., on December 3, 1825. A picture of the Blanchard home in Springfield is shown in Charles Wells Chapin, *Sketches of the Old Inhabitants and Other Citizens of Old Springfield* (Springfield, Mass., 1893), p. 51.

28. See Chapter 5 for a discussion of Blanchard's production line for gunstock-ing at Springfield.

29. Crane and Dunbar, p. 104; Chapin, *Old Springfield,* p. 52; Mason A. Green, *Springfield 1636–1886* (Springfield, Mass., 1888), p. 390.

30. Howe, pp. 206–7.

31. Melancthon W. Jacobus, *The Connecticut River Steamboat Story* (Hartford, 1956), pp. 15–17.

32. Chapin, *Old Springfield,* p. 53. Green, *Springfield 1636–1886,* p. 410, says a Brattleboro company gave Blanchard the order for the *Vermont,* but Howe, p. 208, says Blanchard built it at his own expense.

33. Jacobus, p. 19.

34. Jacobus, p. 20.

35. Jacobus quotes an earlier account of this incident by Henry Burnham, in Abby Maria Hemenway, ed., *Brattleboro Windham County Vermont, Early History . . .*, (Brattleboro, 1880), p. 39. Burnham says that it took place in 1827 and identifies Blanchard's boat as the *Barnet*. In Henry Howe's still earlier and much tamer version of 1840, the boat was the *Vermont*, the trip took place in autumn 1828, and no mention is made of falling overboard (Howe, p. 208).

36. Jacobus, p. 21.

37. John L. Sullivan, in a letter to *Mechanics Magazine* 1 (January-June 1833): 220, mentions past operation of Blanchard steamboats on the Connecticut, the Kennebec, and the Allegheny rivers. Sullivan acquired the right to Blanchard's steamboat patent and proposed using two of them in the construction of a "steam camel" for buoying sea vessels up the Hudson to Albany.

38. Thomas Blanchard, "An Estimate of the Cost of Machinery for makeing Gun Carriages for the UStates," February 2, 1830. Letters Received, Office of the Chief of Ordnance, Record Group 156, National Archives. The Ordnance Department apparently misunderstood Blanchard's estimate and noted a total almost twice his estimated costs.

39. March 25, 1831, "Steamboat for the Passage of Rapids."

40. Jacobus, pp. 27, 31; Green, *Springfield 1636–1886,* pp. 469–70.

41. Jacobus, p. 30; Green, *Springfield 1636–1886,* p. 411.

42. Jacobus, p. 28.

43. Charles Wells Chapin, *History of the "Old High School. . ." 1828 to 1840* (Springfield, Mass., 1890), p. 28, shows a table of attendance and proficiency for the high school students (all male) for January 16, 1832 to March 31, 1832, which includes the name of Blanchard's oldest son George.

44. Longworth's *Directory of New York City, 1833–34,* p. 128, gives Thomas Blanchard's occupation as machinist and address as 241 Cherry Street; p. 134 of the 1834–35 directory lists him at *Dry Dock*.

45. Chapin, *Old Springfield,* p. 53.

46. U.S. Patents #3, August 1, 1836; #4, #5, #6, #7, #8, #9, August 10, 1836; #17, #18, and #19, August 31, 1836. The patent system was reorganized in July 1836, at which time patents started receiving serial numbers.

47. This patent of June 19, 1837 (U.S. Patent #230) says he was residing then in New York City, and the purchaser of the assignment that September was a New York City hatmaker, Alonzo Alvord. *Digests of Patent Assignments,* "B" vol. 1, p. 6, Record Group 241, National Archives.

48. The "Schedule of Real Estate" of Thomas Blanchard, deceased, Commonwealth of Massachusetts, Suffolk County Court, July 26, 1864, lists "Land and Buildings in Newark, New Jersey—Value unknown to Appraisers" in addition to Blanchard's residence at 169 Tremont Street and his shop and stable on Dover Street in Boston.

49. Letters dated January 24 and March 12, 1838, from Blanchard to John Robb, Superintendent of Springfield Armory, are written from Springfield, New Jersey. Miscellaneous Letters Received, 1838–1840, Springfield Armory Records, Record Group 156, National Archives.

50. *Thomas Blanchard vs. Chandler Sprague,* U.S. Circuit Court, Massachusetts District, 1839, Record Group 21, National Archives, Boston Branch. The machinist, Timothy McNamara, traveled 414 miles to Boston for the trial; so did Blanchard. He was fifty-one years old; so was Blanchard.

51. Stimpson's Boston Directories for 1840 and 1841 show machinist Thomas Blanchard's house address on Broadway near F Street and E Street, for 1843 on Howard Street, for 1844 on Brighton Street. Those for 1845 to 1849–50 list him as engineer living at 49 Dover Street; Adams's New Directory lists him at 73 Dover Street from 1849–50 to 1855.

52. Thomas Blanchard's gravestone (1568 Spruce Street, Mt. Auburn Cemetery, Cambridge, Massachusetts) says Delia was twenty-six years old when she died in 1867.

53. Simon, six years older than Blanchard, was already "Simon of Boston" when he married a Sutton girl in 1817. *Vital Records of Sutton . . . ,* pp. 21, 214. Simon's son Stillman S. Blanchard was the trustee of Blanchard's will in 1864; he became a boot and shoe manufacturer, and was elected to both houses of the Massachusetts legislature in the 1890s. Blanchard, North Dakota is named for him. *Men of Progress, One Thousand Biographical Sketches . . . of Leaders . . . in . . . Massachusetts* (Boston: New England Magazine, 1896), pp. 200–201.

54. Adams's *Boston City Directory* shows Thomas Blanchard at 169 Tremont Street from 1856 until he died. The architecture of Bulfinch's "Colonnade Row" on Tremont Street, built in 1810, is shown in Walter Muir Whitehill, *Boston, A Topographical History* (Cambridge: Belknap, 1963), p. 68, fig. 38.

55. Blanchard's probate inventory of July 26, 1864 valued his Tremont Street residence at $27,000; his shop and stable on Dover Street at $3,000. His personal estate, including outstanding loans, totaled $67,303.65 plus "Doubtful Notes" outstanding that totaled $956.29.

56. *Professional and Industrial History of Suffolk County Massachusetts,* vol. 3 (Boston, 1894), p. 456. This sketch about Blanchard notes the "singular coincidence" that Blanchard's house at 169 Tremont Street had formerly belonged to Judge Story.

57. Waters (c) (1881), p. 260.

58. Alfred S. Roe, "Thomas Blanchard," in George F. Hoar, "Worcester County Inventors," *New England Magazine,* 35 (n.s.) (1904–05): 359–61, esp. p. 361; Waters (a), p. 11; Waters, (c), p. 257; Exposition Universelle de 1855, *Rapports du Jury Mixte International,* vol. 2 (Paris, 1856), p. 580.

59. Thomas Blanchard, MS application for patent extension, February 28, 1863, in patent extension records, National Archives. The patent #6,951 for "Bending Wood" was dated December 18, 1849.

60. *Exposition Universelle,* vol. 1, pp. 579–80; vol. 2, pp. 273–74.

61. U.S. Patents #15,944, "A Method of Bending Wood," October 21, 1856; #19,541, "A Method of Bending Shovel Handles," March 2, 1858; #20,137, "A Machine for Bending Wood," May 4, 1858.

62. Blanchard, 1863 extension application. The assignment to Quinby on June 12, 1851 (for $50,000) was not recorded at the Patent Office, but a copy appears in *Blanchard vs. Sprague,* U.S. Circuit Court, Boston District, 1859. The assignments to A. V. Blanchard Company were October 1, 1852 (for $10,000) and December 21, 1852 (for $8,000), and are recorded in *Transfers of Patent Rights,* Liber H4, pp. 415 and 417.

63. Henry Howe, p. 209, already credited Blanchard with twenty-four patents, writing before 1840. Several sources mention his inventing an envelope folding machine, of which no patent record survives. Restoration of patents destroyed in the December 1836 Patent Office fire required action by the patentee, who in some cases would not bother to do so if the patent had already expired. The present tally for Blanchard's known pre-1840 patents is only eighteen.

64. Now in the National Portrait Gallery, Washington, D.C.

65. Chapin, *"Old High School"*, p. 45. The loss of his son in 1850 may help explain his 1852 sale to his nephews in Palmer of a major share of his patent rights.

66. Daniel Klubock, Bar Counsel, Board of Bar Overseers of the Supreme Judicial Court, Massachusetts, letter December 6, 1982; Thomas Blanchard's Will, January 12, 1864; records of *Boston Safe Deposit and Trust Company vs. Thomas Blanchard, Jr., & others,* Suffolk County, March 15, 1907—June 18, 1907; Thomas Blanchard's gravestone indicates Alfred Maddock died November 19, 1862, at the age of twenty-four years, and that Delia died April 26, 1867.

67. A. S. Roe, p. 361.

## 3. Social Construction of Invention Through Patent Management

1. In addition to money and fame, Fritz Machlup has identified three other motivations for invention: fun, service to mankind, and Veblen's "instinct of workmanship." See "The Supply of Inventors and Inventions," in Richard R. Nelson, ed., *The Rate and Direction of Inventive Activity: Economic and Social Factors* (Princeton, 1962), p. 144. In the present discussion, money and fame are what the social system can provide directly as rewards for invention; the other motivations are possibly also social in origin, but are not at issue here.

2. For the slow emergence of reward for invention out of royal grants of privilege, see Maximilian Frumkin, "Early History of Patents for Invention," *Transactions of the Newcomen Society* 26 (1947–49): 47–56.

3. Roger Hahn, *The Anatomy of a Scientific Institution: The Paris Academy of Sciences, 1666–1803* (Berkeley: University of California Press, 1971), pp. 66–70.

4. The beginning of patents for invention in England is usually dated to the Statute of Monopolies in 1624. Two excellent studies of the English patent management system before its reform in 1852 are Christine MacLeod, *Inventing the Industrial Revolution: The English Patent System 1660–1800* (Cambridge, 1988), and Harold I. Dutton, *The Patent System and Inventive Activity During the Industrial Revolution 1750–1852* (Manchester, 1984). For a brief account of "the origin and growth of the patent system in Britain," see Allan Gomme, "Patents of Invention," (London, 1952).

5. For useful brief accounts of these changes, see Morgan Sherwood, "The Origins and Development of the American Patent System," *American Scientist* 71

(Sept.-Oct. 1983): 501–506; H. A. Meier, "Thomas Jefferson and a Democratic Technology," in Carroll W. Pursell, Jr., ed., *Technology in America* (Cambridge, Mass., 1981), p. 29; and Nathan Reingold, "U.S. Patent Office Records as Sources for the History of Invention and Technological Property," *Technology and Culture* 1 (1960): 156–67. For more detail, see P. J. Federico, ed., "Outline of the History of the United States Patent Office," *Journal of the Patent Office Society* 17 (July 1936).

6. Robert C. Post, *Physics, Patents, and Politics: A Biography of Charles Grafton Page* (New York, 1976), p. 51.

7. Post, *Physics,* p. 51; also Munn & Co., *The United States Patent Law* (New York, 1871), p. 17.

8. The requirement of models ended in 1880. See Kendall J. Dood, "Patent Models and the Patent Law 1790–1880," *Journal of the Patent Office Society* 65 (April and May 1983): 187–216, 234–74; and Dood, "Why Models?" in *American Enterprise: Nineteenth Century Patent Models* (New York, 1984). For the vicissitudes of making and housing models, see William and Marlys Ray, *The Art of Invention: Patent Models and Their Makers* (Princeton, 1974).

9. By 1870 Munn & Co. was boasting that they had handled nearly 20 thousand patents in over 20 years of experience. Munn & Co. . . . *Patent Law,* p. 17. On Munn & Co. see Michael Borut, "The *Scientific American* in Nineteenth Century America" (Ph.D. dissertation, New York University, 1977), pp. 89–151. By 1860 there were nearly three dozen patent agencies in Washington D.C. See Post, *Physics,* p. 160.

10. Reingold, p. 160 likens the patent application process to an editorial conference between a writer and editor before publication.

11. Post, *Physics,* p. 50–51.

12. Robert C. Post, "'Liberalizers' vs. 'Scientific Men' in the Antebellum Patent Office," *Technology and Culture* 17 (1976): 24–54.

13. Section 18, 5 Stat. 117, Act of July 4, 1836, quoted in Reingold, p. 163.

14. On reissues, see Kendall Dood, "Pursuing the Essence of Inventions: Reissuing Patents in the 19th Century," forthcoming in *Technology & Culture.*

15. Ridsdale Ellis, *Patent Assignments* (New York, 1955), chap. 5.

16. Jeannette Mirsky and Allan Nevins, *The World of Eli Whitney* (New York, 1952), chaps. 8 and 9 discuss this choice and the tribulations of partners Miller and Whitney in attempting to follow it.

17. Joseph and Frances Gies, *The Ingenious Yankees* (New York, 1976), p. 120.

18. These comparisons are observable in the "patented" patent application files and in patent litigation records, both held in various locations by the National Archives.

19. John C. Crane, "Asa Holman Waters," in *Proceedings of the Worcester Society of Antiquity* 7 (1888): 85. Blanchard wrote to Roswell Lee June 9, 1819 to tell him of Kenney's interference suit, to be decided by three commissioners, "and you are appointed by the Secretary of State as the principle one" (original spelling). Springfield Armory Records, Record Group 156, National Archives. On July 28, 1819, Asa Waters debited Thomas Blanchard $3.00 for "two days attending court." I infer this was Kenney's interference suit and that Waters probably testified as a witness. A. H. Waters, Sr., and Son, Millbury, Ledger 1815–1820, p. 169, in Waters Family Papers.

20. Henry Howe, *Eminent American Mechanics,* p. 209; William Hovey, affidavit April 4, 1849, Samuel Cox affidavit March 11, 1849, both in *Blanchard vs. Eldridge et al.,* U.S. Circuit Court, Eastern District Pennsylvania, March 8, 1849, Record Group 21, National Archives, Philadelphia Branch.

21. The 1819 and 1820 versions of Blanchard's patent specification were both restored following the December 1836 fire at the Patent office and were copied into *Restored Patents,* vol. 4, 1817–22, pp. 297–302 and pp. 349–63, respectively. The thirty or so volumes of *Restored Patents* are in Records of the Patent Office, Record Group 241, National Archives Cartographic Section, Alexandria, Virginia.

22. Azariah Woolworth, deposition of January 16, 1849, in *Blanchard Gunstock Turning Factory v. Isaac Eldridge et al.* Woolworth was a native of Longmeadow near Springfield, Massachusetts, according to Joseph Anderson, *The Town and City of Waterbury* (New Haven, 1896), vol. 2, p. 454.

23. Descriptions of Woolworth's machines #1 and #2 are found in: Azariah Woolworth's deposition, January 16–17, 1849, in *Blanchard Gunstock Turning Factory vs. Isaac Eldridge et al.,* 1848, U.S. Circuit Court, Eastern District, Pennsylvania, Record Group 21, National Archives, Philadelphia Branch; opinions of Timothy McNamara, Stephen Blanchard, William Hovey, and Daniel

Treadwell, in Simon Greenleaf, Master's Report in *Thomas Blanchard vs. Chandler Sprague,* 1838, U.S. Circuit Court, Massachusetts District, Record Group 21, National Archives, Boston Branch.

24. Stephen Blanchard, affidavit in *Thomas Blanchard v. Chandler Sprague,* U. S. Circuit Court, Massachusetts 1838, Record Group 21, National Archives, Boston Branch.

25. The affidavit of Phineas Dow, August 10, 1848 in *Blanchard Gunstock Turning Factory vs. Isaac Eldridge et al.* includes a copy of Woolworth's patent specification. Record Group 21, National Archives, Philadelphia Branch.

26. On the compromise, see Samuel Cox affidavit in *Blanchard Gunstock Turning Factory vs. Isaac Eldridge et al.* For Isaac Eldridge's version, see his letter to the *Scientific American* 4 (October 21, 1848): 38.

27. The records for assignments of rights to Blanchard's various patents are scattered through the volumes of *Transfers of Patent Rights,* Libers A to Z in each of series 0 to 9, dating from ca. 1836 to 1870. These are held by the National Archives at the Federal Records Center, Suitland, Maryland. They are digested in *Digests of Patent Assignments,* "B" volumes 1 to 4, Record Group 241, National Archives. These digests, which also constitute the index to the complete assignments, are themselves indexed by the patentee's name in separate volumes, also in Record Group 241, National Archives. For a list of Blanchard's irregular turning and woodbending assignment territories, and instructions on locating nineteenth-century assignment records, see Carolyn C. Cooper, "Thomas Blanchard's Woodworking Machines: Tracking 19th-century Technological Diffusion," *IA, The Journal of the Society for Industrial Archeology* 13 (1987): 41–54.

28. James Hendley affidavit July 11, 1848, in *Thomas Blanchard vs. John Haynes,* U.S. Circuit Court, New Hampshire District, 1848; Chandler Sprague, deposition in *Thomas Blanchard vs. Chandler Sprague et al.,* U.S. Circuit Court, Massachusetts District, 1859; both in Record Group 21, National Archives, Boston Branch.

29. Collins Stevens, depositions in *Blanchard v. Sprague,* 1838, U.S. Circuit Court, Massachusetts District, and on September 16, 1856 in *Thomas Blanchard v. Warren Wadleigh and Isaac Lane,* U.S. Circuit Court, New Hampshire District, 1857, both in Record Group 21, National Archives, Boston Branch.

30. Until the Civil War ruined the southern market for carriages, James M. Quinby prospered on the whole, in spite of overextension while mayor of Newark in 1852. In 1856 he was employing about 150 hands. His former employer,

Amos K. Carter, whose business Quinby had bought out, was reputedly honest but seemed to be constantly in debt. He was reported in 1849 to be "making money at his business but spends it in lawsuits vs. parties for infringing a patent right of which he is owner." On return from a business tour in Europe he disappeared in the shipwreck of the *S.S. Pacific* in early 1856, leaving his family destitute. New Jersey, vol. 20, pp. 35, 84, 87, in R. G. Dun and Co. Collection, Baker Library, Harvard University Graduate School of Business Administration; Edwin T. Freedley, *Leading Pursuits and Leading Men. A Treatise on the Principal Trades and Manufactures of the United States* (Philadelphia, 1856), p. 110.

31. See Thomas Blanchard, "The Memorial of Thomas Blanchard Inventor, praying further protection for his patent rights," January 8, 1850, referred to the Committee of Patents April 24, 1850, HR 31A-G 13.2, Record Group 233, National Archives. This petition requests enactment of a law applicable to more than just shoe lasts. It was to "prevent the importation into this country . . . of articles manufactured in that country [Canada] by means of machinery or inventions patented in the United States, and made in those Provinces in evasion of the Patent Laws of the United States."

32. *Blanchard vs. Sprague*, 1859.

33. Report of the Committee on the Judiciary, House of Representatives number 273, 31st Cong. 1st sess., April 24, 1850, Record Group 233, National Archives. I am grateful to Steven Lubar for sending me this quotation.

34. Pro and con petitions in Records of the Committee on Patents, 31st Cong., HR 31A-G13.2, Record Group 233, National Archives.

35. Thomas Blanchard, "Petition to the Senate and House of Representatives," Dec. 28, 1833, presented to the House Jan. 6, 1834, pp. 4, 5. A copy made June 13, 1838 is in file of *Blanchard vs. Sprague*, 1838.

36. *Blanchard vs. Sprague*, 1838; *Federal Cases, comprising Cases Argued and Determined in the Circuit and District Courts of the United States* (St. Paul: West, 1894), vol. 3, p. 645–46.

37. In August 1855, Blanchard obtained French patent #14,290 for a sculpture-copying machine that had a small vertical-spindle rotary cutter instead of the large horizontal-spindle cutter of his lathe. *Descriptions des Machines et Procédés pour Lesquels des Brevets d'Invention ont été pris sous le Régime de la Loi du 5 Juillet, 1844,* 2nd ser., vol. 51 (1855), p. 186. See chapter 7 for discussion of this machine.

38. Anon. (Asa H. Waters) (c) "Thomas Blanchard the Inventor," *p.* 258.

39. *Scientific American* 3 (April 22, 1848): 245.

40. *Scientific American* 3 (May 12, 1848): 270.

41. "Outrage upon Inventors' Rights," *Scientific American* 3 (July 22, 1848): 349.

42. See correspondence in patent application files for U. S. Patent No. 6253 granted April 3, 1849 to Elbridge Webber and Charles Hartshorn, Record Group 241, National Archives, Suitland, Maryland.

43. D. Hamilton Hurd, ed., *Worcester County,* vol. 2, p. 976.

44. *Thomas Blanchard vs. John Haynes,* U.S. Circuit Court New Hampshire District, 1848; *Federal Cases* 3: 628–29.

45. *Thomas Blanchard vs. Eli Whitney,* U.S. Circuit Court Connecticut District, Sept. 1855; *Federal Cases* 3: 651.

46. See, for instance, Timothy Clark, U.S. Patent No. 4932, Jan 19, 1847; Smith Beers, U.S. Patent No. 7806, Dec. 3, 1850; Philo Beers, U.S. Patent No. 7937, Feb. 18, 1851. Blanchard's protest (with original emphasis) is in the application file for Philo Beers's patent, Record Group 241, National Archives, Suitland, Maryland.

47. Woolworth had made models of his machine for previous Blanchard suits in the 1830s, but had fallen into obscurity as well as bad times. He was rediscovered in Hartford in summer 1848 and mentioned in the *Scientific American* 3 (August 5, 1848): 365 as an unnamed "inventor . . . who claims to have invented the Last Machine some years before Mr. Blanchard." Summoned to Philadelphia, he was housed, clothed and nursed by the defendants in the trial when he fell "sick and deranged." Azariah Woolworth, deposition January 16–17, 1849, *Blanchard Gunstock Turning Factory vs. Isaac Eldridge et al.,* U.S. Circuit Court, Pennsylvania Eastern District, October session 1848.

48. Isaac Eldridge affidavit, February 21, 1849 in *Blanchard vs. Eldridge,* in Equity, U. S. Circuit Court Eastern District, Pennsylvania, October Session 1848, Record Group 21, National Archives, Philadelphia Branch.

49. W. W. Hubbell, master's report February 27, 1849 in *Blanchard Gunstock Turning Factory vs. Eldridge et al.,* 1849.

50. Judge Kane's opinion appears in *Scientific American* 4 (May 19, 1849): 27, and in *Federal Cases* 3: 622–623.

51. Ibid.

52. Isaac Eldridge affidavit, October 5, 1849, *Blanchard vs. Eldridge,* 1848.

53. John F. Frazer, John C. Cresson, and Charles B. Trego, "Report of the Commissioners," December 1, 1849 in *Blanchard vs. Eldridge* 1848. For credentials of the commissioners, see Bruce Sinclair, *Philadelphia's Philosopher Mechanics,* pp. 254–58 and *passim.*

54. Ibid.

55. *Equity Docket Books* 3 (1848–1858), U.S. Circuit Court for the Eastern District Pennsylvania, October Session 1848, p. 25, Record Group 21, National Archives, Philadelphia.

56. Justice Grier's opinion in *Blanchard vs. Biddle Reeves, Isaac Eldridge, et al.* U. S. Circuit Court, Eastern District Pennsylvania, September Term 1850, is reported in *Federal Cases* 3: 639, 640.

57. Grier's opinion in *Blanchard vs. Biddle Reeves et al.,* cited in note 56.

## 4. Lathes Before Blanchard and How His Was Different

1. In this discussion, an "irregular" shape is one whose right-angle cross-sections across its axis of rotation are not circular.

2. In the portrait lathe, last among the pre-Blanchard lathes discussed below, there are two parallel axes of rotation, and they are oriented from front to back, i.e. transversely on the machine.

3. Rev. Robert Willis, "Machines and Tools for Working in Metal, Wood, and Other Materials," *Lectures on the Results of the Great Exhibition of 1851* (London: David Bogue, 1852), p. 305.

4. Adolf Rieth and Karl Langenbacher, *Die Entwicklung der Drehbank* (Stuttgart, 1954), p. 3.

5. The terms "cylinder" and "cylindrical" refer throughout this discussion to a cylinder of revolution, i.e., a right circular cylinder. A disk is a cylinder with a

large ratio of diameter to length, but I shall use "cylinder" for those that are long with a relatively small diameter, which are turned between centers, to distinguish them from disks.

6. A possibly turned bowl was found in a Mycenaean grave of 1200 B.C. L.T.C. Rolt, *Tools for the Job: A Short History of Machine Tools* (London, 1965) p. 17, but an Etruscan bowl from the eighth century B.C. is the oldest certainly turned survival. Robert S. Woodbury, *History of the Lathe to 1850* (Boston, 1961), pp. 25, 32, cites the earliest material and pictorial evidence of turning between centers from the first and third centuries B.C., i.e., later than the evidence for dishwork.

7. In an intentionally interrupted cutting, of course, the cutter may have rounded the corners but not cut deeper than the original—perhaps flat—sides of a workpiece.

8. See figure 6.2 for pole lathe among blockmakers' tools. Also, Joshua Rose, *Modern Machine-Shop Practice* (New York: Scribner's, 1888), vol. 1, p. 129. Woodbury shows medieval pole lathes, pp. 41–43; Rolt shows one in use relatively recently for turning bowls, p. 31.

9. Rolt, p. 22, dates this to the mid-14th century; Woodbury (1961), p. 44–46, discusses the 15th and 16th century drawings that may show lathes driven by crank and flywheel

10. See figure 6.2, which shows blockmakers' tools, for a great wheel lathe.

11 Abraham Rees, ed., *Cyclopaedia: Or, a New Universal Dictionary of Arts and Sciences* (London, 1819), s.v. "rose engine." David Pye, *The Nature and Art of Workmanship* (Cambridge, 1968), p. 24, distinguishes "workmanship of risk," in which "the result of every operation during production is determined by the workman as he works and its outcome depends wholly or largely on his care, judgement and dexterity," from "workmanship of certainty," in which "the result of every operation during production has been predetermined and is outside the control of the operative once production starts."

12. For a brief survey of machine tool control that brings its history into the present, see K. R. Gilbert, "The Control of Machine Tools—A Historical Survey," *Transactions of the Newcomen Society* (1971–72) 45: 119–127 and plates 22–27.

13. Edwin Battison distinguishes between a "mechanical" or hand-cranked slide rest and a "self-acting" or machine-cranked slide rest in his introduction to

the English translation of A. S. Britkin and S. S. Vidonov, *A.K. Nartov: an Outstanding Machine Builder of the 18th Century* (Jerusalem, 1964), p. i.

14. For compound slide rests, see figures 4.5, 4.6, 4.8, 4.9.

15. Rolt, p. 24, Woodbury p. 47, Edwin A. Battison, "Screw-Thread Cutting by the Master-Screw Method Since 1480", *Contributions from the Museum of History and Technology* (Washington, D. C., 1964), p. 107–8. The machine, recently reinterpreted as equipment for cutting breechplugs for matchlock guns, may have been intended only to inscribe the spiral path to be deepened by hand filing. It was preceded by a similar machine illustrated in a 1471 manuscript by Martin Mercz, "Kunst aus Büchsen zu schiessen," on the art of firing guns. Vernard Foley and Susan Canganelli, "The Origin of the Slide Rest," parts 1 and 2, *Tools and Technology, The newsletter of the American Precision Museum* (1984): 1–7, 17–22.

16. See, for instance, Rudolf Kellermann and Wilhelm Treue, *Die Kulturgeschichte der Schraube* (Munich, F. 1962).

17. Rolt, pp. 36 and 63; Woodbury, pp. 67 and 82–86.

18. Joseph Moxon, *Mechanick Exercises; or the Doctrine of Handy-Works applied to the Art of Turning,* 1680, cited by Willis, p. 305. The 1703 edition of Moxon has been reprinted by the Early American Industries Association. Its section on turning, pp. 185–236, is illustrated with plates showing many of the features discussed here, including "oval" and "swash" turning, pp. 225–27 and 231–32.

19. By far the most complete and thoroughly annotated bibliography on this subject is Sydney George Abell, John Leggat, and Warren Greene Ogden, Jr., comps., *A Bibliography of the Art of Turning and Lathe and Machine Tool History* . . . 3rd ed. (North Andover, Mass., 1987).

20. Rees, *Cyclopaedia,* s.v. "rose engine."

21. Woodbury, pp. 53–54, ascribes the principle of the traversing spindle to Leonardo da Vinci's screw-cutting lathe of about 1500 in his *Codice Atlantico.*

22. More precisely, the spindle's motion is along an arc of a circle whose center is on an axis below the bench

23. Supposed to have been invented by a turner named Guillot, according to

Maurice Daumas, *A History of Technology and Invention,* vol. 2 (New York, 1979), p. 271.

24. For details of master screws and keys, see Denis Diderot and Jean le Rond D'Alembert, *Encyclopédie, Recueil des Planches* (Paris, 1772), vol. 10, plates 13,16.

25. For pictures of these decorative effects, see Kener E. Bond, Jr. "Rose Engine and Ornamental Lathes," *Metalsmith,* Fall, 1981: 23–27.

26. Rees, *Cyclopaedia,* s.v. "rose engine."

27. Ibid. For details of rosette patterns of both types, see Diderot and D'Alembert, vol. 10, plates 22–25.

28. Rees, *Cyclopaedia,* s.v. "Turning" explains it and ascribes its invention to mathematician Abraham Sharp (1652–1742). A.K. Nartov's oval turning lathe of 1722 has an eccentric chuck, shown in Britkin and Vidonov p. 49. Woodbury says he can find no evidence to support some writers' ascription of the ellipse chuck mechanism to Leonardo da Vinci, n. 28, p. 60.

29. Rees, *Cyclopaedia,* s.v. "rose engine." For examples of ornamental turning in the eighteenth century, see Diderot and D'Alembert, vol. 10, plate 62.

30. Britkin and Vidonov, also V. V. Danilevskii, *Nartov and his Theatrum Machinarum* (Jerusalem, 1966).

31. Britkin and Vidonov, p. 70; Danilevskii, p. 203. The column was designed but never erected.

32. Britkin and Vidonov, pp. 66–67; Danilevskii, p. 153.

33. A. E. Musson and Eric Robinson, *Science and Technology in the Industrial Revolution* (Manchester, 1969). p. 221.

34. Hulot *père,* who died in 1781, had also made lathes and written about them. Hulot *fils* made two for George III around 1766. L.E. Bergeron, *Manuel du Tourneur* (Paris, 1816) vol. I, p. x. Warren G. Ogden Jr. has kindly supplied information and bibliographical references about the two Hulots.

35. Bergeron, vol. 2, pp. 424–437, *Atlas,* plate 52. In 1849 this section and plate were translated and reprinted in Boston as a pamphlet, *The Image Lathe.*

This reprint was probably prompted by the patent suit of Thomas Blanchard against John Kimball, which was under way at that time.

36. Franklin Peale, deposition October 14, 1850, in *Thomas Blanchard vs. John Kimball,* U.S. Circuit Court, Massachusetts District, May term 1851. Record Group 21, National Archives, Boston Branch.

37. The volumes of plates for the *Encyclopédie* are very large and must have been expensive even in their own day; it seems unlikely that they would be readily available to Blanchard even on his trips outside Millbury before 1819.

38. As Woolworth's machine showed, the action of the separate powered cutter could, less advantageously, have been reciprocating instead of rotational. It was necessary that the cutter be independently powered, not that it be rotary.

39. The 1820 version of the patent specification refers throughout to this hanging frame as a "lathe" in the same sense as the lay or batten in a loom. See figures 3.2 and 5.2 for last- and stock-turning lathes, respectively.

40. Instead of relying on its weight alone, the 1819 version of the patent specification has a spring pressing the frame toward the wheels to keep them in contact with the workpiece and model.

41. Thomas Blanchard, patent specification for "a machine for turning Gun Stocks . . ." September 6, 1819, Records of the Patent and Trademark Office, *Restored Patents* vol. 4 (1817–1822), pp. 297–302. National Archives, Cartographic Section, Alexandria, Virginia. The other two "principles" concerned the parallelism of the model and work with the tracing and cutting wheels and the combination and application of all parts and movement of the machine "to produce the desired effect," p. 297.

42. Henry Howe, *Eminent American Mechanics,* p. 209. Howe mentions no names, but I surmise this is an allusion to Blanchard's conflict with the "Woolworth" faction.

43. Thomas Blanchard, patent specification for "an Engine for turning or cutting irregular forms . . ." January 20, 1820, Records of the Patent and Trademark Office, *Restored Patents* vol. 4, 1817–1822, pp. 349–63, pp. 353, 359.

44. Blanchard, 1820 specification, p. 362.

45. The machine he saw operating in Waterbury had a powered reciprocating cutter, but he was probably told about the burr cutter to be added to it.

46. In, for instance Robert Hooke's gear cutter in the 17th century, Robert S. Woodbury, *History of the Gearcutting Machine* (Cambridge: MIT Press), p. 47; *History of the Milling Machine* (Cambridge: MIT Press), p. 23. These are both reprinted in *Studies in the History of Machine Tools* (Cambridge: MIT Press, 1972).

47. Blanchard, 1819 specification, p. 297.

48. Blanchard, 1820 specification, p. 359.

49. Blanchard, 1820 specification, p. 353. This statement does not appear in the 1819 specification.

50. Blanchard, 1820 specification, p. 363.


## 5. The Gunstocking Production Line at Springfield Armory

1. Roswell Lee to Thomas Blanchard, January 20, 1819, Springfield Armory Records, Record Group 156, National Archives, hereinafter referred to as "SAR."

2. Thomas Blanchard to Roswell Lee, February 5, 1819, SAR. (Blanchard's spelling.)

3. The parts called "the mounting" of a musket in Ordnance Department nomenclature of that era were: bands, guard plate, tang pin, trigger, side plates, side pins, heel plate, screws for heel plate and guard, and bandsprings. *Regulations for the Inspection of Small Arms, 1823,* (Washington D.C., 1823) p. 12–13, in Eli Whitney Papers, Yale University Archives. "Pins" screwed into threaded metal; "screws" screwed into wood.

4. See, for example, Jacob Abbott, "The Armory at Springfield," *Harper's New Monthly Magazine* 5 (July 1852): 145–161. At Springfield Armory Abbott saw the stocking machines that are here termed "second generation."

5. David A. Hounshell, *From the American System to Mass Production 1800–1932* (Baltimore, 1984), pp. 35, 38.

6. SAR, monthly payrolls, 1819, Record Group 156, entry 1379, National Archives.

7. SAR, monthly work returns for stockers, 1819, Record Group 156, entry 1371, National Archives. Felicia J. Deyrup, *Arms Makers of the Connecticut*

*Valley* (Northampton, Mass., 1948), appendix D, table 4, p. 245. From "production workers" Deyrup excludes clerical, supervisory, and maintenance workers.

8. Attendance and output ranged widely among the Springfield Armory stockers: in January 1819, thirty-six stockers stocked 1185 muskets, averaging 32.9 each, but the individual output ranged from 3 to 48. That December, thirty-three stocked 944 guns, averaging 28.6 each, with a range of 10 to 36. SAR, stockers' work returns, 1819, Record Group 156 entry 1371, National Archives.

9. Major James Dalliba, "Armory at Springfield," *American State Papers,* Class 5: *Military Affairs,* vol. 2, Report 246, 1819, p. 538.

10. SAR, Thomas Blanchard to Roswell Lee, June 9, 1819.

11. SAR, monthly work return for stockers, June 1820, Record Group 156, entry 1371, National Archives. Of the 1146 muskets stocked that month, 389 were "Stockd with Turnd Stocks." Twenty-one of the twenty-eight stockers used them, but only five used them exclusively; fifteen of the others used both "turned" and "rough" stocks; four used only "rough" stocks; one was paid by the day instead of the piece, so his output is not known. Local tradition at the Armory dated the lathe's arrival as 1822, hence the label to that effect on the extant machine. Since Blanchard wrote in 1833 that all his machines burned up in 1825 and had to be rebuilt, the label's claim that the surviving machine is the "original" is dubious.

12. Superintendent Roswell Lee to Chief of Ordnance George Bomford, August 22, 1822. Lee said 12,500 stocks had been turned on an account opened April 5, 1820, but didn't say where the machine was located. SAR, letters sent, Record Group 156, National Archives.

13. Thomas Blanchard to Roswell Lee, February 21, 1821, SAR. (Blanchard's spelling.) The bracketed word is unclear in original; it may be "part" or "plate."

14. Blanchard to Lee, February 21, 1821, SAR, letters received, Record Group 156, National Archives.

15. Ibid.

16. Blanchard to Lee, April 13, 1821, SAR, letters received, Record Group 156, National Archives.

17. For inside contracting in civilian factories, see John Buttrick, "The Inside Contract System," *Journal of Economic History* 12 (Summer 1952): 205–21.

18. Roswell Lee to Colonel George Bomford, Chief of the Ordnance Department, June 19, 1822, SAR.

19. Lee to Bomford, June 19, 1822, SAR.

20. Ibid.

21. According to Lee, Blanchard was "ambitious to make all he can, hires men & boys at very low wages, that know little or nothing of the business, & is often changing hands." Roswell Lee to George Bomford, July 16, 1825, SAR, quoted in Merritt Roe Smith, *Harpers Ferry Armory,* p. 136.

22. Thomas Blanchard, "Petition to the Honorable the Senate and House of Representatives in Congress Assembled," December 28, 1833, copy dated June 13, 1838 in *Thomas Blanchard vs. Chandler Sprague,* U.S. Circuit Court, Massachusetts District, May term 1838. Record Group 21, National Archives, Boston Branch.

23. Blanchard "worked at machinery" July through November at $2.00 a day, before resuming his role as half-stocking contractor in December. Springfield Armory monthly payroll records for 1825, Record Group 156, National Archives. In his patent extension petition of 1833 he remembered this period as "six months."

24. Monthly work returns for stockers and lower water shop and payrolls for 1825–30, SAR, Record Group 156, National Archives. Blanchard resumed receiving payment for half-stocking muskets in December 1825 through June 1826, was off the payroll July through September, resumed half-stocking October-July 1827, and was off again from August to April 1828. Then for a year, May 1828 through April 1829, he was paid as a pieceworker to use some of his own machines to fit on locks, bands, and butt plates. From May through September 1829 the payroll records his new royalty payments of 9 cents per musket; in October and thereafter his name disappears from the payroll. Meanwhile, the work returns for the lower water shop begin showing other individuals performing stocking machine operations in 1828; a full complement of six such workers is shown from January 1829 onward.

25. Contract Between Thomas Blanchard and George Bomford, February 7, 1828, SAR; Thomas Blanchard, "Petition to the Honorable the Senate and House of Representatives in Congress Assembled," December 28, 1833, copy dated June 13, 1838 in *Thomas Blanchard vs. Chandler Sprague,* U.S. Circuit Court, Massachusetts District, May term 1838.

26. Chief of Ordnance George Bomford to Secretary of War James Barbour, November 13, 1827, SAR. Five years after Blanchard obtained renewal of his patent in 1834 he agreed with the Ordnance Department on January 29, 1839 to accept payment of "one-half the clear . . . savings . . . to the U.S. from the use of my improvements during the full period of 14 years." After this was ascertained and he received a final balance of $6653.44, on July 18, 1839 he relinquished all his patent rights to the United States for the use of "said patented machines at any and all public Armories or Arsenals." *Transfers of Patent Rights,* Liber D, p. 151, National Archives, Suitland, Maryland.

27. Blanchard-Bomford contract, February 7, 1828. Records of the Office of the Chief of Ordnance, Record Group 156, National Archives. (Numbers supplied.) Bomford used the term "breech plate" for Lee's term "heel plate." Virtually the same wording of the list, in the same order, is reproduced in Claud E. Fuller, *Springfield Muzzle-Loading Shoulder Arms* (New York, 1930), p. 19, which attributes it to Bomford's letter to Barbour, November 13, 1827. Charles H. Fitch gives the list of machines without attribution in his "Report on the Manufactures of Interchangeable Mechanism," *Tenth Census of the United States (1880)* vol. 2: *Report on the Manufactures of the United States,* (Washington, D.C., 1883), p. 630.

28. Fitch, ". . . Interchangeable Mechanism," p. 630.

29. For a history of the Ordnance Department's role in establishing interchangeability, see Merritt Roe Smith, "Military Entrepreneurship," in Otto Mayr and Robert C. Post, eds., *Yankee Enterprise,* pp. 63–102.

30. For brief sketches of Buckland and Warner, see Charles Wells Chapin, *Sketches of the Old Inhabitants and Other Citizens of Old Springfield,* pp. 86–89 and 390–93. Also, Charles H. Fitch, "The Rise of a Mechanical Ideal," *Magazine of American History* 11 (1884): 516–27.

31. Nathan Rosenberg, ed., *The American System of Manufactures,* reprints their reports. The "New York Industrial Exhibition Special Report of Mr. George Wallis" and "of Mr. Joseph Whitworth" were printed in London in 1854; the latter is hereinafter cited as "Whitworth." It makes up pp. 329–89 of Rosenberg's book. "The Report of the Committee on the Machinery of the United States of America" appeared in 1855. This committee consisted of Lt. Col. Robert Burn and Lt. Thomas Warlow, both of the Royal Artillery, and Mr. John Anderson, Ordnance Inspector of Machinery. Their report is hereinafter cited as "Anderson." It comprises pp. 89–197 of the book. John Anderson describes fifteen gunstocking machines, pp. 137–42; Joseph Whitworth names sixteen, p. 364–65, and

lists their operating times. Each was reporting his observations at Springfield Armory.

32. For the orders for machines, see Anderson, pp. 180–91.

33. "The Royal Small-Arm Manufactory, Enfield" parts 1–6, *The Engineer* 7 (March 25–June 25, 1859): 204–5, 258–59, 294–95, 348–49, 384–85, and 422–23, hereinafter cited as *"Engineer."*

34. *Engineer,* April 15, 1859, p. 258.

35. Fitch, ". . . Interchangeable Mechanism" (1883), p. 632.

36. Anderson, p. 137.

37. Whitworth, p. 364.

38. Anderson reported on fifteen machines, Whitworth on sixteen.

39. Blanchard to Lee, February 5, 1819, SAR.

40. Anderson, p. 181. The fees were $50 for each machine.

41. For an interesting discussion of skills and their social construction, see Charles More, *Skill and the English Working Class, 1870–1914* (London, 1980).

42. Blanchard, petition "To the Honorable the Senate and House of Representatives in Congress assembled," December 28, 1833, copy in records of *Blanchard vs. Sprague,* May term 1838, U.S. Circuit Court Massachusetts District, Record Group 21, National Archives, Boston Branch.

43. Whitworth, p. 364; Anderson, p. 138.

44. Blanchard to Lee, June 9, 1819, SAR, Record Group 156, National Archives.

45. Blanchard, patent extension petition, December 28, 1833.

46. except of course for the rough-turning lathe (#3) and [#2], which was the identical machine at both times.

47. Blanchard to Lee, February 5, 1819, SAR.

48. Anderson, pp. 117, 141, 191.

49. Stockers' and lower water shop work returns, May 1835, SAR. The piece rates for machine work on the stock totaled $0.1941.

50. Springfield Armory Inventory of Machinery, December 1834. Springfield Armory Museum Library.

51. One for "spotting to thickness" cost $552.00, one for "second or fine turning stock" was $730, and one for "giving the profile of the stock, cutting in sideplate, band springs and rod springs" was $915.00.

52. Inventory of Machinery at Springfield Armory, September 30, 1842. Springfield Armory Museum Library.

53. Piece rates are shown in the January payrolls for the cited years, SAR, Record Group 156, entry 1379, National Archives, and in Anderson, p. 146. For more detail, see Carolyn C. Cooper, "'A Whole Battalion of Stockers': Thomas Blanchard's Production Line and Hand Labor at Springfield Armory," *IA The Journal of the Society for Industrial Archeology* 14 (1988): 50–52.

54. Whitworth, p. 365.

55. Anderson, p. 142. "Boring for the ramrod" is not to be confused with cutting a groove for the ramrod, which was performed by machine. Fitch (p. 634) says "the open part of the [ramrod] cut is bedded by a mill" but that the attempt to mechanize drilling for the closed ramrod hole was not successful until 1860, i.e., after Anderson, Whitworth, and the *Engineer* reporter had written their observations. This was confirmed by Thomas Greenwood in 1862, who listed as machine operations both cutting the groove for the ramrod and boring the hole for the ramrod in continuation of the groove. Thomas Greenwood, "On Machinery for the Manufacture of Gunstocks," *Proceedings of the Institution of Mechanical Engineers* (1862), p. 330.

56. Including, in Fitch's list, "boring ramrod-groove" (the closed part) in addition to "bedding for ramrod-groove." Fitch, p. 629.

57. Fitch, p. 630.

58. Ibid.

59. Ibid.

60. John C. Crane, "Asa Holman Waters," p. 87.

61. Springfield Armory's antebellum peak of production was in 1851, when it turned out 23,000 muskets, rifles, and carbines. Deyrup, *Arms Makers* . . . appendix B, table 2, p. 233. Harpers Ferry's peak year for whole new longarms was 1847, when it produced 15,054 muskets and rifles. M.R. Smith, *Harpers Ferry Armory* . . . , table 1. In the pre-1840 period, that of Blanchard's "first generation" production line, the top output was obtained by Springfield in 1829–31, when production was 16,500 muskets annually.

62. Springfield Armory payrolls, July 1853, January 1864, Record Group 156, entry 1379, National Archives.

63. Deyrup, table 2, p. 233 shows Springfield Armory output of 17,000 muskets, rifles, and carbines in 1853; 276,200 in 1864. (Production had jumped from 13,803 in 1861 to 102,410 in 1862.) Dividing 17,000 by 15 and 276,200 by 180 gives the number of guns stocked per gunstocker in 1853 and 1864; dividing by an assumed 300 days of work per year gives the estimated number of guns stocked per worker in a day in those years, i.e., 3.78 in 1853 and 5.11 in 1864.

64. Of the 15 men performing stocking operations in July 1853, 8 were "shaping and completing" stocks at a piece rate indicative of handwork; one was "assembling muskets," which was also handwork. Of the 180 performing stocking operations in January 1864, 109 were "completing stocks," at a piece rate indicative of handwork. Springfield Armory payrolls, July 1853, January 1864, Record Group 156, entry 1379, National Archives.

65. Musket production at Harpers Ferry and Springfield Armory 1828–33 totaled 155,195. Deyrup, *Arms Makers* . . . table 2, p. 233; M. R. Smith, *Harpers Ferry Armory* . . . , table 1. Deyrup, p. 98, says Springfield Armory paid Blanchard "about $1,000" in 1828 and 1829, but this is much less than the $2,880 he should have received for Springfield's 32,000 muskets produced in those two years. Smith, p. 137, n. 50, says Harpers Ferry Superintendent Stubblefield continually defaulted on royalty payments to Blanchard between 1819 and 1829.

66. A copy of this contract, in Blanchard's handwriting, between Springfield Armory Superintendent John Robb and Thomas Blanchard, and a petition of January 7, 1839 by Blanchard to Congress to make an appropriation for paying him, are in the records of the Committee on Claims of the 26th Cong. HR 26A-G2.1, National Archives.

67. Blanchard's final settlement of July 18, 1839 with the U.S. for his irregular turning lathe is recorded in *Transfers of Patent Rights,* Liber D, p. 151, National Archives, Suitland, Maryland. The record doesn't say what the total "clear savings" were calculated to be, nor how much he had already received.

68. Eugene Ferguson, "History and Historiography," in Mayrand Post, *Yankee Enterprise,* p. 3; M. R. Smith, *Harpers Ferry Armory,* pp. 323–26; Robert A. Howard, "Interchangeable Parts Reexamined: The Private Sector of the American Arms Industry on the Eve of the Civil War," *Technology and Culture* 19 (1978): 649.

69. Edward Lucas to John Robb, April 5, 1839, SAR Miscellaneous Letters 1838–1849, Record Group 156, National Archives.

70. Blanchard built two stocking machines at Harpers Ferry—for turning the stocks and bedding the barrel—in 1819, and nine more in early 1828, at a price of $1,600, according to M. R. Smith, *Harpers Ferry Armory,* p. 137. Estimating the cost of the earlier two at $250 (their valuation at Springfield in 1834), we can say that the stocking machines at Harpers Ferry cost about $1,850, and the set at Springfield cost about $1,425 (as valued in 1834).

71. 209,820 muskets x 28 cents = $58,749; $15,000 for waterpower + $1850 for machines = $16,850; $41,899 savings / 209,820 muskets = $.19969 average saving per musket. This calculation of course makes the assumption that the labor savings of 28 cents per musket set in immediately in 1820, which, as the evidence presented above indicates, is not true. Lucas pointed out that rifle production at Harpers Ferry did not involve Blanchard machinery, so only muskets come into this calculation.

72. At Springfield Armory, expenditures for lands (including water privileges), buildings, mill-dams, flumes, and other permanent improvements from 1795 through 1821 totaled $114,887.64, while repairs of buildings, mill-dams, etc., totaled $19,736.05 in the same period, for a grand total of $134,623.69. By 1839, the grand total for these items of land, capital equipment and repairs to same was $346,211.34, of which $10,057.94 was for land. These figures suggest that the guess of $150,000 for mill-dams, flumes, waterwheels, etc. (exclusive of buildings) might be on the low side, but not totally unrealistic. George Bomford, "Statement of the expenditures of the United States' Armory at Springfield, Massachusetts . . . from its establishment to the close of the year 1821," November 30, 1822, in *American State Papers,* Class 5, *Military Affairs* vol. 2, p. 478; Abstract A, "Total Expenditure of Money at National Armory, Springfield, Massachusetts From its Establishment to June 30, 1878," Record Group 156, National Archives.

73. To use the figures for Springfield Armory that are comparable to those Lucas used for Harpers Ferry, start with the pre-1820 labor piece rate of $1.12 per stock, and subtract the $0.895 labor cost per stock in 1839; then multiply the difference, $0.225, by the 283,400 muskets produced at Springfield 1820–39, to obtain the labor savings total of $63,765. Subtract from this the assumed capital cost of $16,425 for the waterpower ($15,000) and the machines ($1,425), to find $47,340 as the savings due to Blanchard's machines at Springfield Armory 1820–39, or $0.167 per musket. Adding this to the $41,899 saved at Harpers Ferry, we find $89,239 for both armories. Divided by the 493,220 muskets produced both places from 1820 through 1839, this yields a per-musket savings of 18 cents.

74. Lucas volunteered the opinion that "the saving effected by Blanchard's Machines, may or may not be greater than it would be by other Machinery, that might be put into operation for the purpose of saving manual labour in the stocking of guns" and that it was "less than it has heretofore been estimated." He did not explain how he calculated his answer to the question "What is the actual saving (if any) on a Musket from the use of Mr. Blanchard's Machinery? Answer. Eight & 87/100 cents." Lucas to Robb, July 18, 1839, SAR.

75. Even if we repeat the calculation for Springfield ascribing to Blanchard's machines a cost of $36,046 to include 10 percent of the total of *all* of the 1795–1839 expenditures for land, buildings, mill-dams etc., and repairs to them, which seems excessive, and subtract that from the labor savings of $63,765, we still derive a savings of $27,719 at Springfield due to Blanchard's machines. If we only double that to guess minimally at the combined armories' savings ($55,438) and then subtract a maximally assumed royalty of $32,042 for Blanchard, we arrive at a rock-bottom net savings of $23,396. An alternative calculation might be simply to accept Edward Lucas's estimation that Blanchard's machines saved $0.0887 per musket, apply it to the 1820–39 production at both armories, and emerge with the figure of $43,748.61 for the overall savings. After subtracting Blanchard's half for 1820–33 ($0.04435 x 356,020 = $15,789.49), the government would, on this calculation, have saved only $27,959.12. Even in these two "anti-Blanchard" scenarios, the government has saved some money, not lost it, by supporting Blanchard's "R&D" and continuing to use his machines for a decade thereafter.

76. Anderson, p. 138.

77. *London Journal of Arts and Sciences* 5 (1822): 238–245, plus plate 12, which shows the lathe set up to make right and left lasts for shoes; *Repertory of Arts,* 6 (n.s.) (July-December, 1836): 392.

78. "Report from the Select Committee on Small Arms," *Parliamentary Papers* (1854), vol. 18, Q.7273 and Q.7274, quoted in Nathan Rosenberg, "America's Rise to Woodworking Leadership," in Brooke Hindle, ed., *America's Wooden Age: Aspects of its Early Technology,* (Tarrytown, N.Y., 1975), p. 201, n. 42. Reprinted in Rosenberg, *Perspectives on Technology* (Cambridge, 1976).

79. This is the general theme of H. J. Habakkuk, *American and British Technology in the 19th Century* (Cambridge, 1962).

80. Russell Fries, "British Response to the American System," *Technology and Culture* 16 (July 1975): 377–403.

81. P. V. Hagner, Brevet Major and First Lieutenant of Ordnance, U.S. Army, Report October 25, 1849 to Chief of Ordnance, reprinted in Stephen V. Benet, *A Collection of Annual Reports and Other Important Papers Relating to the Ordnance Department,* vol. 2, (Washington, D.C., 1878), p. 312.

82. Rosenberg, "America's Rise . . . ," pp. 46–48, 201, n. 42.

83. Cooper, " 'A Whole Battalion of Stockers' " gives examples of the puffery.

84. This is of course an anachronistic distinction for the purpose of analysis; industrial engineering had not yet been named in the 1820s.

85. For distinctions among mass and flow production and related concepts, see F. S. Demyanyuk, *The Technological Principles of Flow Line and Automated Production,* (London, 1963), vol. 1, pp. 1–29.

86. This is the theme, for instance, of A. H. Holman's 1881 article about Blanchard, and of modern historians of the American system.

*Appendix A*. Blanchard's Production Line for Half-Stocking Muskets

1. *Engineer,* p. 258; Anderson, p. 138. Unfortunately, no picture is available of the slabbing machine.

2. Anderson, p. 138.

3. In 1854 Whitworth timed the slabbing machine at 3 1/2 to 4 minutes; the rough-turning lathe at 4 to 4 1/2 minutes.

4. Thomas Blanchard to Eli Whitney, Jr., December 22, 1842, in file of

*Thomas Blanchard vs. Eli Whitney,* U.S. Circuit Court, Connecticut District, September term, 1855, National Archives, Boston Branch.

5. Eli Whitney, Jr., ordered one from Blanchard in December 1842 for $600, including the right to run it until the patent would expire in 1848. Letters by Eli Whitney, Jr., to Thomas Blanchard, December 20, 1842; to Thomas Warner, December 29, 1842. Eli Whitney Papers, Yale University Archives.

6. Anderson, p. 139. "Boring" does not normally connote "milling," "cutting," or "forming the bed for," but these must be what is meant by the phrase "boring for the barrel," (machine #4 in 1828), since a semicircular groove cannot be bored.

7. Ibid.; Whitworth, pp. 364–65; *Engineer,* p. 258.

8. Whitworth, p. 365. To avoid confusion with operations at the "breech" end of the barrel, I use the term "butt plate" instead of the 1828 term "breech plate."

9. Anderson, p. 140.

10. Thomas Greenwood, "On Machinery for the Manufacture of Gunstocks," p. 333.

11. See K. R. Gilbert, "The Ames Recessing Machine: A Survivor of the Original Enfield Rifle Machinery," *Technology and Culture* 4 (Spring 1963): 207–211; and the Science Museum's catalog, *The Machine Tool Collection* (London: H.M.S.O., 1966), p. 94 and plate 32. Merritt Roe Smith, "The American Precision Museum," *Technology and Culture* 15 (July 1974): esp. 422, 430–31. Smith also gives a brief history of the Robbins and Lawrence Company, whose building now houses the museum.

12. Blanchard to Lee (February 19, 1821), SAR.

13. Fitch, "Report . . . ," p. 630.

14. Ibid.

15. *Engineer,* p. 294.

16. Anderson, p. 142.

## 6. The Blockmaking Production Line at Winooski Falls

1. Before July 4, 1836 U.S. patents were not numbered but identified only by name of patentee and date of issue. From that date the reformed Patent Office began numbering patents in chronological order; hence the low numbers of Blanchard's blockmaking patents, which were issued on August 1, 10, and 31, 1836.

2. Bertrand Gille, "Machines," in Charles Singer, E. J. Holmyard, A. R. Hall, and Trevor I. Williams, eds., *A History of Technology* (Oxford, 1956), 2: 630.

3. "A Particular Account of the Origin and Progress of Mr. Taylor's Machines for Making Blocks, Shivers, and Pins," *Hampshire Repository* (London, 1801), 2: 87.

4. K. R. Gilbert, *The Portsmouth Blockmaking Machinery* (London, 1965); Carolyn C. Cooper, "The Portsmouth System of Manufacture," *Technology and Culture* 25 (April 1984):182–225; Cooper, "The Production Line at Portsmouth Block Mill," *Industrial Archaeology Review* 6 (Winter 1981–82): 28–44.

5. *Edinburgh Encyclopaedia,* s.v. "block machinery."

6. *Encyclopaedia Britannica,* 7th ed., s.v. "block machinery."

7. For instance, in the Rees *Cyclopaedia,* published in 1819, the Portsmouth block mill's operation was not described in its entry on blockmaking, but constituted the totality of its article on "Machinery."

8. David Brewster, ed., *Second American Edition of the New Edinburgh Encyclopaedia . . ., vol. 6 (New York: Whiting and Watson, 1813). The article "Block Machinery" appears on pp. 581–93.*

9. *Darwin H. Stapleton, ed., The Engineering Drawings of Benjamin Henry Latrobe* (New Haven, 1980), p. 239.

10. M. D. Leggett, *Subject Matter Index of Patents Issued from the United States Patent Office from 1790 to 1873* (Washington, D.C., 1874), p. 840. This patent of April 1, 1802 was apparently not restored to the record after the Patent Office fire of 1836, for it is not listed in the alphabetical index for the relevant volume of *Restored Patents,* Record Group 241, National Archives, Alexandria, Virginia.

11. Stapleton, p.53. I am indebted to Darwin Stapleton for drawing my attention to Latrobe's observations.

12. Thomas Blanchard, patent specification of January 20, 1820, *Restored Patents* 4: 362, 363.

13. Blanchard, patent specification of September 6, 1819, *Restored Patents* 4: 297.

14. William Woodworth soon thereafter invented a planing machine with a rotary cutter. Thomas Blanchard later recalled his acquaintance with Woodworth and their conversations about rotary cutters in a deposition of March 29, 1847 in *William Van Hook vs. Reid Throckmorton et al.,* U.S. Circuit Court, Southern District of New York (National Archives microfilm publication M884, roll 23).

15. *History of Columbia County, New York* . . . (Philadelphia, 1878), p. 258. The block mill's approximate location is marked today by Block Factory Road.

16. *Documents Relative to the Manufactures in the United States, Collected and Transmitted to the House of Representatives* [22d Cong., 1st sess.] . . . *by the Secretary of the Treasury* (The "McLane Report"), vol. 1 (Washington, D.C.: Duff Green, 1833) footnote, p. 454.

17. George White, M.D., deposition May 12, 1849 in *Jacob P. Wilson vs. Daniel Barnum,* (equity) U.S. Circuit Court Eastern District Pennsylvania, April Session 1849, Record Group 21, National Archives, Philadelphia Branch.

18. *Digests of Patent Assignments,* "B" volume 1, p. 1. *Longworth's New York City Directory, 1834–35* lists Thomas Blanchard's address as "Dry Dock"; *Longworth's . . . Directory 1835–36,* p. 101 lists that address for Neziah Bliss. The New York Dry Dock Company had been incorporated in 1824. Robert G. Albion, *The Rise of New York Port, 1815–1860* (New York, 1939), p. 299.

19. *Restored Patents* vol. 30: 253, 281, 285, 289, 301, for Patents #5, #6, #3, #4, and #19, respectively, all dated August 11, 1835. The affidavit for Patent #17, p. 225, is dated "August 11, 1836," but is signed by the same witnesses as the other five, so it may actually date from 1835 also.

20. Duplicate copies of Blanchard's blockmaking patents were received by the Patent Office September 11, 1837, and recorded anew "in conformity to the act of Congress passed 3d March 1837." Patent files, National Archives, Suitland, Maryland. Blanchard's assignment to Bliss was digested on the first page of the

first volume of [restored] *Assignment Digests* for the letter "B," National Archives. The corresponding first restored Liber of the *Transfers of Patent Rights* containing the full record of the earliest restored assignments appears to be missing.

21. John Homer Bliss, *Genealogy of the Bliss Family in America . . . 1550 to 1880* (Boston, 1881); Henry R. Stiles, *History of the City of Brooklyn*, (Brooklyn, 1869) vol. 2, text and footnote pp. 410–12. I am grateful to Albert Maass for this reference and other information concerning Neziah Bliss. Carroll W. Pursell, Jr., *Early Stationary Steam Engines in America* (Washington D.C., 1969), pp. 24 and 98, discusses the Novelty Iron Works and Neziah Bliss, (misnamed "Hezekiah Bliss.")

22. Memorandum of agreement between Eliphalet Nott and Neziah Bliss, July 18, 1834, in *Documents of the Senate of the State of New York, 76th Session, 1853*, vol. 2 (Albany, 1853), Document #68, p. 13.

23. In *Washburn vs. Gould*, U.S. Circuit Court, Massachusetts District, c. 1844, James E. Serrell testified having seen, at an unspecified time in the past, Blanchard's machine at a block factory on the corner of Dry Dock and Tenth Street. The Novelty Iron Works was at Dry Dock and Twelfth Streets, shown in *Harper's Magazine* 2 (May 1851): 723, reproduced in Pursell, *Early Stationary Steam Engines*, p. 99.

24. "Winooski Patent Block Manufacturing Company," *Burlington Free Press* (April 1, 1836), p. 3. Bliss is not listed among the block and pump manufacturers of New York City in *New York As it Is*, 1837 edition, but the Winooski Patent Block Manufacturing Company is so listed, p. 22, with an address on Fletcher Street, not near Dry Dock.

25. Unless otherwise indicated, quotes in the remainder of this chapter are from the patent specification under discussion in each section.

26. David Steel, *The Elements and Practice of Rigging and Seamanship* (London, 1794), "Blockmaking," p. 158.

27. Ibid., p. 155.

28. *Edinburgh Encyclopaedia*, s.v. "block machinery," p. 584.

29. *Encyclopaedia Britannica* s.v. "block machinery," R. S. Peale Reprint (1892), vol. 3, p. 833. The 1878 version of the 9th edition omits this comment.

30. "Winooski . . . ," *Burlington Free Press* (April 1, 1836), p. 3.

31. Frank G. Woollard, *Principles of Mass and Flow Production* (London, 1954).

32. Richard Beamish, *Memoir of the Life of Sir Marc Isambard Brunel* (London: Longmans, 1862), p. 98.

33. U.S. Patent #19, *Restored Patents* 30: 301.

34. "An act, to incorporate the Winooski Block Manufacturing Company," *Laws of Vermont, 1835* (Montpelier: E. P. Walton & Son, 1835), pp. 107–108.

35. "Winooski . . .," *Burlington Free Press* (April 1, 1836), p. 3.

36. David Lowenthal, *George Perkins Marsh: Versatile Vermonter* (New York, 1958), p. 41.

37. *National Cyclopaedia of American Biography* (New York: 1893) vol. 3, p. 462. Peter Stuyvesant's land north-east of the Novelty Works, was among those tracts that Bliss and Nott at least contemplated buying, in addition to Stuyvesant Cove, which they bought from Nicholas Stuyvesant. *Documents of the Senate of the State of New York, 76th Session, 1853,* vol. 2 (Albany, 1853), Document 68, p. 11.

38. The Catlin MSS are in the Wilbur Collection at Bailey-Howe Library, University of Vermont. One of Guy's early exploits is described by H. N. Muller, "Floating a Lumber Raft to Quebec City, 1805: The Journal of Guy Catlin of Burlington," *Vermont History* 39 (Winter 1971): 116–24.

39. "Winooski . . . ," *Burlington Free Press* (April 1, 1836), p. 3.

40. "Winooski . . . ," *Burlington Free Press* (April 1, 1836), p. 3 and "Destructive Fire," *Burlington Free Press* (December 28, 1838).

41. The twelve pump and block makers of Boston mentioned in the McLane Report of 1833, vol. 1, p. 454, had a combined total value of $24,000 in "real estate, buildings and fixtures" and $7,200 in "tools, machinery and apparatus other than fixtures."

42. "Winooski . . . ," *Burlington Free Press* (April 1, 1836), p. 3.

43. *New York As It Is, In 1837* appends a separately paginated *Classified Mercantile Directory, for the Cities of New-York and Brooklyn.* Its p. 22 lists the

Winooski Patent Block Manufacturing Company as one of five pump and block manufacturers.

44. "Winooski . . . ," *Burlington Free Press* (April 1, 1836), p. 3.

45. Cooper, "The Portsmouth System . . . ," p. 195.

46. "Destructive Fire," *Burlington Free Press* (December 28,1838). As mentioned above, their predecessor, the Livingston Patent Block Company, had already accomplished this in Boston, according to the McLane report of 1833.

47. Ibid. Gudgeons, the ends of shafts turning in bearings, could overheat if they ran too fast. The newspaper posed an editorial query: "Does not the use of wood for bearings, greatly increase the hazard in this respect?"

48. "Destructive Fire," *Burlington Free Press* (December 28, 1838).

49. Zadock Thompson, *History of Vermont, Natural, Civil, and Statistical, in Three Parts . . . ,* (Burlington, 1842), part 3, p. 57.

50. Blanchard's assignment to Quinby of July 9, 1852 solely for "cutting or turning any irregular . . . forms . . . used in and by the Navy or other Marine Service of the United States," recorded in *Transfers of Patent Rights,* Liber R2, p. 430, refers to a much broader unrecorded assignment of June 12, 1851 that included oars, tackle-blocks, and the other quoted objects of manufacture. Quinby was to pay Blanchard $50,000 for it. Record Group 241, National Archives.

*Appendix B.* Blanchard's Production Line for Pulley-Blocks and Deadeyes

1. Unless otherwise indicated, quotes in this appendix are from the patent specification under discussion in each section.

2. Cooper, "Portsmouth System," pp. 191 and 205 show the Taylor-Dunsterville and the Portsmouth mortising machines, respectively. Here, the latter is shown in the top row in figure 6.5.

3. U.S. Patent #5, August 10, 1836, an ". . . improvement in the machine for mortising and boring the solid wooden shells of ships tackle Blocks." *Restored Patents,* vol. 30, pp. 253–59.

4. "Methods of and Machinery and Apparatus for Working Metal, Wood, and

Other Materials," Great Britain Patent #1951, April 23, 1793 (London: Eyre & Spottiswoode, 1854), p. 30.

5. At Portsmouth a single "boring machine" (top row, figure 6.5) bored both the pin hole and the holes for starting the mortises; the mortising machine then lengthened the mortises.

6. U.S. Patent #4, August 10, 1836, for "Improvements for Stock Shaving or rounding the edges or joints and ends of Ships Tackle Blocks." *Restored Patents,* vol. 30, pp. 289–94.

7. Rees, *Cyclopaedia,* s.v. "Machinery," and plate 6, or Gilbert, p. 14 and pp. 22–25. In our figure 6.5, the shaping engine is in the top row.

8. U.S. Patent #8, August 10, 1836, for a "machine for cutting the scores around Ships Tackle Blocks and dead eyes." *Restored Patents,* vol. 30, pp. 261–63.

9. U.S. Patent #19, August 31, 1836, "machinery . . . applicable to forming or shaping the sides of blocks, the shells of which are made in pieces and commonly known as plank or made blocks." *Restored Patents,* vol. 30, pp. 301–305.

10. U.S. Patent #6, August 10, 1836, "certain new and useful improvements in the machinery for . . . making the end pieces of plank or made blocks." *Restored Patents,* vol. 30, pp. 281–283.

11. U.S. Patent #9, August 10, 1836, for "new and useful improvements in the methods of riveting Plank or made Blocks." *Restored Patents,* vol. 30, pp. 277–79.

12. U.S. Patent #17, August 31, 1836, for ". . . cutting out the Sheave and Pins of Ships Tackle Blocks and Pulleys from the rough log and boring the sheaves. . . ." *Restored Patents,* vol. 30, pp. 225–28.

13. Pins of blocks used in powder holds aboard Navy ships were wooden instead of iron, to lessen the danger of a spark exploding the powder.

14. U.S. Patent #3, August 1, 1836, " . . . the machine for turning and finishing wooden sheaves and pins for ships Tackle Blocks and pullies." *Restored Patents,* vol. 30, pp. 285–88.

15. See Cooper, "Portsmouth System," p. 203 for illustration comparing the sheave-cutting machines in M. I. Brunel's blockmaking patent and at Portsmouth. Brunel's was more traditional.

16. U.S. Patent #18, August 31, 1836, for "improvements in the methods of cutting in or countersinking metal or other Bushes in the sheaves for Ships tackle Blocks." *Restored Patents,* vol. 30, pp. 241–44.

17. For the Portsmouth coaking machine, see Rees, *Cyclopaedia,* s.v. "Machinery"; K. R. Gilbert, *The Portsmouth Blockmaking Machinery,* p. 31; and Gilbert, *The Machine Tool Collection,* (London, 1966), p. 93.

18. Charles H. Fitch, "Report on the Manufactures of Interchangeable Mechanism," p. 630.

19. If, however, Blanchard's 1820s solution was actually the same adjustment that he later used for inletting bushings in 1836, then the copying feature of the second-generation inletting machine may have been a post-Blanchard solution to the problem. This seems less likely.

20. David Steel, *The Elements and Practice of Rigging and Seamanship,* p. 158.

21. U.S. Patent #7, August 10, 1836, for ". . . improvement in the machine for Boring holes and cutting the Laniard screws in dead eyes, used on board shipping." *Restored Patents,* vol. 30, pp. 297–300. "Screws" should read "scores."

## 7. Diffusion and Application Divergence of the Blanchard Lathe

1. Application divergence viewed from a different perspective is technological convergence, which Nathan Rosenberg has discussed in "Technological Change in the Machine Tool Industry, 1840–1910."

2. Azariah Woolworth, deposition January 16, 1849, in *Thomas Blanchard vs. Isaac B. Eldridge et al.* (in equity), U.S. Circuit Court, Pennsylvania Eastern District, October session, 1848. Record Group 21, National Archives, Philadelphia Branch.

3. Blanche Hazard, *The Organization of the Boot and Shoe Industry in Massachusetts Before 1875)* (Cambridge, Mass., 1921), esp. p. 97.

4. For a history of the Lyman Blake-Gordon McKay stitcher and the development of shoe machinery thereafter, see M. A. Green, "How Shoes are Made By

Machine," in Waldemar Kaempffert, ed., *A Popular History of American Invention* (New York, 1924), vol. 2, pp. 404–34. For an extended discussion of the transformation of shoe manufacturing as a process of "learning by selling," see Ross Thomson, *The Path to Mechanized Shoe Production in the United States* (Chapel Hill, 1989).

5. For shoemaking techniques and equipment before mechanization, see D. A. Saguto, "The 'Mysterie' of a Cordwainer," *Chronicle of the Early American Industries Association* 34 (March, 1981): 1–7; David N. Johnson, *Sketches of Lynn* (Lynn, Mass., 1880), pp. 31–38 and pp. 332–37.

6. For convenience, the following discussion refers only to shoe lasts, but applies to boot trees also.

7. Leonard Smith, deposition quoted in Simon Greenleaf, master's report in *Thomas Blanchard vs. Chandler Sprague,* U.S. Circuit Court, Massachusetts District, 1838, p. 23. Record Group 21, National Archives, Boston Branch.

8. Torrey Bates, *The Shoe Industry of Weymouth* (Weymouth, Mass., 1933), p. 21.

9. Hazard characterizes Phase 2 of the putting-out system, 1810–37, as a period of specialization in processes and rise of the central shop, which she says "developed rapidly after 1820." In the central shop the pieces of leather were cut before being put out for binding and the uppers were inspected before they and rough-cut soles were put out for bottoming (pp. 42, 44).

10. Unfortunately, boot-and-shoe output figures are not readily available before "the Barber Statistics" for Massachusetts in 1837, reproduced in Hazard, appendix 18, pp. 207–10. In Essex County in 1837 the town of Lynn alone produced over 2 1/2 million pairs of boots and shoes and Haverhill and Marblehead produced more than a million pairs each, but this was already twenty years after Woolworth's invention.

11. Samuel Cox, depositions December 6, 1837 in *Blanchard vs. Sprague,* 1838; and October 7, 1848 in *Blanchard vs. Eldridge,* 1848.

12. *Transfers of Patent Rights,* Liber F, p. 92.

13. Henry Orne had guided the writing of Woolworth's patent application, according to Woolworth's testimony in *Blanchard vs. Eldridge,* 1848.

14. Charles White, deposition in *Blanchard vs. Sprague,* 1838.

15. Samuel Cox testimony quoted in Simon Greenleaf, master's report January 25, 1838, p. 10, in *Blanchard vs. Sprague,* 1838.

16. James Hendley, affidavit July 11, 1848 in *Blanchard vs. Haynes,* U.S. Circuit Court, New Hampshire District, 1848, Record Group 21, National Archives, Boston Branch. Hendley obtained his assignment in July 1834; Blanchard bought it back from him in 1847.

17. Samuel Cox, in *Blanchard vs. Sprague,* 1838. Cox said that after trying and rejecting the Blanchard lathe he was forced to resume machine production in the 1820s when Charles White had begun lowering last prices.

18. Greenleaf, master's report in *Blanchard vs. Sprague,* 1838, pp. 22–23. Greenleaf converted shillings and pence to dollars and cents in deriving the bill to Sprague for damages. A pair of lasts cost 63 cents, or 3 shillings 9 pence.

19. Collins Stevens and William Ellison, depositions in *Blanchard vs. Haynes,* 1848.

20. Nathaniel Faxon, testimony quoted in Simon Greenleaf's master's report, *Blanchard vs. Sprague,* 1838, pp. 40–43, said he sold $2,000 worth. At 63 cents a pair, this would be 3174 pairs. Faxon's business seems large enough to justify guessing he was a "manufacturer" in the putting-out system of shoemaking.

21. *Professional and Industrial History of Suffolk County* (Boston, 1894) vol. 3, p. 459. The boot and shoe figures tally exactly with those in "The Barber Statistics," Hazard, p. 209.

22. Collins Stevens, deposition in *Blanchard vs. Sprague,* 1838.

23. In calculating Sprague's bill for damages, Greenleaf derived a daily net of $4.09 after allowing him 12 1/2 percent for discount and 10 percent for "commissions on sales."

24. Agreement between Blanchard and Sprague, U.S. Circuit Court, Massachusetts District, May term, 1839. Charles White's annual fee, mentioned above, was $100, so Sprague's fee of $50 doesn't seem punitive.

25. H. Y. Ghilson, cited by George S. Hillard, master in chancery, in *Thomas Blanchard vs. Obadiah Morse et al.,* in equity, May term 1849, U. S. Circuit

Court, Massachusetts District, Record Group 21, National Archives, Boston Branch.

26. "Affidavits of Last Manufacturers" to Committee on Patents, 31st Cong., HR 31A-G13.2, Record Group 233, National Archives.

27. Sprague in *Thomas Blanchard vs. Chandler Sprague, et al.,* U.S. Circuit Court, Massachusetts District, 1859. Record Group 21, National Archives, Boston Branch.

28. This is the average of the prices on the list, not necessarily of the prices of lasts produced, of which there were probably more in one category than in others.

29. Thomas Blanchard in *Blanchard vs. Sprague,* 1859.

30. Four times Sprague's output of 7757 for January 1 to April 1, 1858 equals an estimated output of 31,028 for 1858.

31. Hazard, p. 91, n. 3. Chandler Sprague was the only lastmaker listed in North Bridgewater, indeed in all of Plymouth County, in George Adams, *New England Business Directory, 1856,* p. 188. Lastmaking prosperity depended heavily, of course, on the prosperity of the shoe industry at large, and the intervening year of 1857 was a very bad year for business in general. So Sprague's output may well have fallen from 40,000 to 31,028 between 1855 and 1858. But if the census was correct as to his income, it would suggest he concentrated his output in the high-priced categories of lasts.

32. *Blanchard vs. Chandler Sprague,* 1859. See Case #1,516 in *Federal Cases* 3: 640–45.

33. Collins Stevens, affidavit September 16, 1856, in *Thomas Blanchard vs. Warren Wadleigh and Isaac Lane,* U.S. Circuit Court, New Hampshire District, 1857, Record Group 21, National Archives, Boston Branch.

34. Ibid.

35. Ibid.

36. See, for example, Daniel Treadwell, deposition June 25, 1838; and Thomas Ashcroft, quoted in Simon Greenleaf, pp. 6–7, both in *Blanchard vs. Sprague,* 1838.

37. Stevens, deposition in *Blanchard vs. Sprague,* 1838.

38. Seth Boyden, deposition January 18, 1848, in *Blanchard vs. Eldridge,* 1848. Since this deposition by Boyden is the only reference to hatblock lathes in the patent litigation and assignment records I have examined, and other information is so skimpy, I have omitted discussion of this application of the Blanchard lathe. Boyden's testimony proves, however, that Blanchard's lathe was used for this purpose well before the first patent specifically for hatblock turning—U.S. Patent #26,691—was issued to J. H. Masker, also of Newark, New Jersey, on January 3, 1860.

39. Samuel Cox, deposition October 20, 1848 in *Blanchard Gunstock Turning Factory vs. Joseph Browne,* U.S. Circuit Court, Pennsylvania Eastern District, April Session 1846, Record Group 21, National Archives, Philadelphia Branch.

40. See, for example, Harold R. Quimby, *Pacemakers of Progress* (Chicago, 1946), p. 281; Bates, 1933, quotes Johnson, 1880, to say that "Even as 'late as 1880, most women's shoes were made on absolutely straight lasts,' " p. 21.

41. Frederick J. Allen, *The Shoe Industry* (Boston, 1916), p. 75.

42. R. F. Farey, "Measurements and Lasts," in Ernest Bordoli, ed., *The Boot and Shoe Maker,* vol. 2, (London, 1936), p. 218.

43. Hazard, pp. 91, 217, 234.

44. *Transfers of Patent Rights,* Liber F, p. 109, to Gibbs and Boies (September 5, 1840) for tool handles; Liber S, p. 146, to Samuel Reed (September 9, 1840) for wheel spokes. "One Machine now in operation" by one Mansfield of Braintree, Massachusetts was excepted from Reed's assignment eight months later for all New England, Liber S, p. 165 (May 5, 1841). U.S. Patent Office records, Federal Record Center, Suitland, Maryland.

45. Thomas Blanchard, U.S. Pat. #3008, March 21, 1843, variously titled "Improvement in the Machine for Turning Irregular Forms . . . being a back and under rest" (specification), or "Spoke Lathe" (drawing).

46. *Scientific American* 3 (Sept. 9, 1848): 401.

47. I am grateful to John Bowditch of the Henry Ford Museum for sending me pictures of this machine.

48. Abner Lane, deposition of July 21, 1856 in *Thomas Blanchard vs. Warren Wadleigh and Isaac N. Lane,* 1857. Saw teeth are "set" or bent a little to each side alternately, so as to cut a "kerf" or path a little wider than the thickness of the saw blade, to keep the blade from binding as it cuts deeper.

49. Yet another mid-nineteenth century variant of the Blanchard lathe that does without a back and under rest for cutting ax handles or wheel spokes was recorded in 1980 by the Historic American Engineering Record at Ben Thresher's mill in Barnet Center, Vermont. Its "swinging yoke" carries the slowly rotating workpiece and model past the cutter and tracer, and see-saws as the tracer follows the contours of the model. I am grateful to Richard K. Anderson, the HAER delineator of this machine, for giving me a copy of his drawings (sheet 11 of 11, HAER VT-10).

50. When making ax handles on one recent occasion, it cut a spiral flat-bottomed kerf that is wider than 1/4 inch—perhaps 3/8 to 1/2 inch wide, edged by a narrow deeper cut. The crooked-knife cutters removed the material between the successive loops of the spiral saw kerf. On that test occasion, the saw teeth and crooked-knife cutters were not properly adjusted in depth; hence the narrow deeper cut left by the saw teeth. I am grateful to Merritt Roe Smith for showing me these ax handles and describing the operation of the machine, which he witnessed.

51. Abner Lane, 1856, in *Blanchard vs. Wadleigh and Lane,* 1857.

52. Abraham Wheaton, testimony in *Blanchard Gunstock Turning Factory vs. Evert Shipman, Hart J.G. Norton, and Elias A. Yale,* U.S. Circuit Court, Connecticut District, 1851, Record Group 21, National Archives, Boston Branch.

53. James B. Miller, deposition in *Blanchard Gunstock Turning Factory vs. James B. Miller,* U.S. Circuit Court, Eastern District Pennsylvania, 1848, Record Group 21, National Archives, Philadelphia Branch.

54. Even if Miller were to run his lathe 300 days a year, he would only have to pay Blanchard $150 at his rate of production, so his was a smaller operation than that of Gibbs and Boies. The assignment to Gibbs and Boies was made twice for the same territory: *Transfers of Patent Rights,* Liber F, p. 109, September 5, 1840, and Liber I1, p. 304, October 20, 1842. In the later assignment Blanchard is acting as "President of [the Blanchard Gunstock Turning Factory] Corp."

55. *Spelman Gibbs & Jarvis Boies vs. Thomas Blanchard,* U.S. Circuit Court, Connecticut District, May 1847, Record Group 21, National Archives, Boston

Branch. The complaint doesn't say what Blanchard's price was for renewal of the assignment.

56. Jarvis Boies depositions July 14, 1853, in *Thomas Blanchard vs. Thomas J. S. Rogers* and in *Thomas Blanchard vs. Charles and Augustus Bond,* U.S. Circuit Court, New Hampshire District, Record Group 21, National Archives, Boston Branch.

57. Referred to in assignment of Leland's rights to his heirs, H.J., D.C., and John S. Leland, *Transfers* . . . , Liber L4, p. 339, June 27, 1857.

58. *Transfers* . . . , Liber A6, p. 18, January 23, 1855. By this time James M. Quinby had replaced Carter as part-owner of the right with Leland and Boies.

59. *Transfers* . . . , Liber A6, p. 20, June 29, 1860. Peter H. Smith, "The Industrial Archeology of the Wood Wheel Industry in America" (Ph.D. dissertation, George Washington University, 1971), discusses Jacob Woodburn's participation in development of the Sarven Hub for carriage wheels, p. 124.

60. Thomas Blanchard, application for an extension of the patent of December 18, 1849, for "An Improved Method of Bending Timber and other Fibrous Substances," February 28, 1863, Record Group 241, National Archives.

61. *Transfers* . . . , Liber H4, p. 415, October 1, 1852; Blanchard, patent extension application, 1863.

62. Edwin T. Freedley, ed., *Leading Pursuits and Leading Men, A Treatise on the Principal Trades and Manufactures of the United States* (Philadelphia, 1856), p. 41.

63. James Coleman, William Mitchell, depositions July 2, 1866 in *James Morris vs. Theodore Royer, Samuel T. J. Coleman, and John Young,* U.S. Circuit Court, Southern Ohio District, 1867, Record Group 21, National Archives, Chicago Branch; Charles Cist, *Sketches and Statistics of Cincinnati in 1859* (Cincinnati, 1859), p. 245.

64. *Transfers* . . . , Liber Q7, p. 219, January 4, 1864. Both Samuel T. J. Coleman, 36, and James Coleman, 71, testified in 1866 for the defense in *James Morris vs. Royer, et al.,* 1867.

65. Thomas Blanchard, U.S. Patent #10,497, "Machine for Polishing Plow Handles and Other Articles," February 7, 1854.

66. See, for instance, F. R. Hutton, "Report on Machine Tools and Wood-Working Machinery" (Washington, D.C., 1885), pp. 286–90. In 1830 Blanchard proposed to build a machine of this sort to help make gun carriages at Allegheny Arsenal. Major R. L. Baker to George Bomford, February 5, 1830, Letters received, Office of the Chief of Ordnance, Record Group 156, National Archives.

67. Major R. L. Baker to Col. George Bomford, February 5, 1830, with enclosure by Thomas Blanchard, "An Estimate of the Cost of Machinery for makeing Gun Carriages for the UStates." Letters Received, Office of the Chief of Ordnance, Record Group 156, National Archives. An additional note by another hand indicates a misunderstanding of the estimate and adds up the machine costs to a total of $8,655 instead of less than $5,000. I am indebted to Merritt Roe Smith for drawing my attention to this document.

68. *Transfers . . .* , Liber S, p. 163, September 9, 1840.

69. Peter J. Leary, *Newark, New Jersey Illustrated* (Newark, 1893), p. 200.

70. *Transfers . . .* , Liber S, p. 165, May 5, 1841.

71. Leary, p. 200.

72. S. G. Reed, letter to the editor of *The Hub* 18 (Nov. 1876): 316. Reed wrote that he "commenced making wheels with machinery in 1831."

73. *Transfers . . .* , Liber U1, p. 6, December 18, 1848 and p. 8, December 20, 1848.

74. George Adams, *New England Business Directory* (Boston, 1856), p. 262.

75. I. D. Ware, *The Carriage Builders' Reference Book* (Philadelphia, 1877), p. 270.

76. Leary, p. 200. The partners were brothers E. and O. A. Whittemore and Phineas Jones. Reed in 1876 wrote to *The Hub* that he and E. Whittemore established the wheel factory at Elizabethport, after which "Phineas Jones took my share," p. 316.

77. The first such assignment recorded was in 1844, to Peter Legg of Kingston, New York, for turning spokes and other carriage parts in Kingston and adjoining counties, plus counties along both banks of the Hudson River from

Troy to Sing Sing, and for selling them in western New York, Ohio, and Michigan. *Transfers...*, Liber N2, p. 385, November 13, 1844.

78. Reed, 1876, p. 316.

79. *Transfers . . .* , Liber K2, p. 345, July 20, 1849, and p. 349, June 21, 1851.

80. Cist, p. 330–31.

81. Cist, p. 302.

82. *Transfers . . .* , Liber V4, p. 264, June 16, 1857.

83. *Transfers . . .* , Liber T4, p. 339, September 9, 1857.

84. *Scientific American* (January 14, 1882), p. 19.

85. *Transfers . . .* , Liber R2, p. 89, January 1, 1850; *Transfers . . .* , Liber I3, p. 111, July 21, 1854. The assignees were Samuel Gaty, John McCune, Gerard B. Allen, and James Collins.

86. J. Thomas Scharf, *History of St. Louis City and County* (St. Louis, c. 1883), vol. 2, p. 1259.

87. *Transfers . . .* , Liber R2, p. 93, May 15, 1852.

88. *Transfers . . .* , Liber E4, p. 86, October 17, 1855.

89. David Wooster, deposition Sept. 20, 1847 in *Blanchard Gunstock Turning Factory vs. David Wooster and Lewis Smith,* U.S. Circuit Court, Connecticut District, 1849, Record Group 21, National Archives, Boston Branch. I have found no definition for a "sett of spokes," but a set of spokes for a carriage with four 12–spoke wheels would be 48 spokes. Other common sizes of wheels had 14 spokes or 10; some carriages had smaller front wheels and larger rear wheels.

90. Philo Beers, affidavit June 1, 1848, in *Thomas Blanchard vs. Philo Beers,* U.S. Circuit Court, Connecticut District, September term, 1850, Record Group 21, National Archives, Boston Branch.

91. *Blanchard Gunstock Turning Factory vs. David Hull,* U.S. Circuit Court, Connecticut District, June, 1851, Record Group 21, National Archives, Boston Branch.

92. James M. Quinby, affidavit August 13, 1851 in *James M. Quinby vs. Ezra Seeley & Joseph Wheeler,* U.S. Circuit Court, Connecticut District, September term, 1851, Record Group 21, National Archives, Boston Branch. Carter had reassigned this license of October 25, 1848 to Quinby on November 20, 1848.

93. Henry Stow, affidavit September 8, 1853, in *Thomas Blanchard vs. Albert Goodyear and Henry Ives* and *Thomas Blanchard vs. Philo Beers and Albert Good-year,* in Equity, U.S. Circuit Court, Connecticut District, September term, 1852, Record Group 21, National Archives, Boston Branch.

94. Jesse Duncan, affidavit September 8, 1853 in *Blanchard vs. Goodyear and Ives* and . . . *vs. Beers and Goodyear.*

95. Timothy Clark, U.S. Patent #4932, January 19, 1847; Smith Beers, U.S. Patent #7806, December 3, 1850; Philo Beers, U.S. Patent #7937, February 18, 1851.

96. In his patent specification, Smith Beers made explicit the similarity of his machine to "a machine invented in 1818 and known as the Waterbury last making machine," Smith Beers, "Specification of Letters Patent No. 7806," December 3, 1850, lines 21–24.

97. Henry Stow, deposition May 1851 in *Blanchard Gunstock Turning Factory vs. Timothy Clark,* U.S. Circuit Court, Connecticut District, April session, 1851, Record Group 21, National Archives, Boston Branch.

98. Timothy Clark, deposition in *Blanchard Gunstock Turning Factory vs. John G. Quigley and Moses H. Hunter,* U.S. Circuit Court, Connecticut District, September 1847, Record Group 21, National Archives, Boston Branch.

99. This remark suggests that the pay to workmen making wheels was on a piece rate rather than strictly time basis.

100. Jesse Duncan, affidavit September 8, 1853 in *Blanchard vs. Goodyear & Ives* and . . . *vs. Beers & Goodyear.*

101. *Digests of Transfers of Patent Rights,* "B" volume 1, p. 195, July 31, 1852, and p. 217, October 14, 1853. The brevity of this assignment record does not mean Philo's machine had little effect on wheel production, for the New Haven Wheel Company was large and nationally important. But it does mean that not many different wheel makers used it, unless by unrecorded license.

102. Stow, 1853, in *Blanchard vs. Goodyear & Ives* and . . . *vs. Beers and Goodyear.*

103. Trevor Manufacturing Co., *Handle Machinery* catalog (Lockport, New York, September 1899), National Museum of American History.

104. At that time Henry Stow, a licensee of Blanchard's in New Haven, Connecticut, had testified that with a Blanchard lathe "some [hands] will turn 600 a day as easily as others will 400. We turn from 4[00] to 600 a day." Stow, 1853, in *Blanchard vs. Goodyear and Ives* and . . . *vs. Beers and Goodyear.*

105. For a more extended discussion of sculpture and relief copying machines in nineteenth-century England and America, see chapter 8 of Carolyn C. Cooper, "The Roles of Thomas Blanchard's Woodworking Inventions in Nineteenth-Century American Manufacturing Technology," Ph.D. dissertation, Yale University 1985.

106. quoted in James P. Muirhead, *The Life of James Watt* (New York, 1859), p. 358.

107. E. A. Cowper, "On the Inventions of James Watt and his Models Preserved at Handsworth and South Kensington," *Proceedings of the Institute of Mechanical Engineers* (1883): 599–631, esp. p. 618. The machines and tools from Watt's garret workshop have been preserved and are on display in a replica garret at the Science Museum in London.

108. Sculptor Benjamin Cheverton did not patent his sculpture-copying machine. Joseph Gibbs, a timber merchant in Kent, obtained Great Britain Patent #5,871 for his carving machine; Thomas Jordan, a "mathematical divider" in Pimlico, obtained British patents #10,377 and #10,523 for his 1844 and 1845 machines, respectively.

109. Hezekiah Augur's machine of 1846 was granted U.S. Patent #4,906; his 1849 patent was #6,058. Isaac Singer, who later developed the sewing machine, obtained U.S. Patent #6,310 for his wood-carving machine in 1849.

110. *Scientific American* 2 (August 28, 1847): 390.

111. Thomas Blanchard, specification for "an Engine for turning or cutting irregular forms . . ." January 20, 1820, *Restored Patents,* vol. 4, p. 362, National Archives Cartographic Section, Alexandria, Virginia.

112. George F. Goodman, deposition November 23, 1847, in *Blanchard Gun-stock Turning Factory vs. Joseph Brown,* U. S. Circuit Court, Pennsylvania Eastern District, 1848. Microfilm 969, roll 5, National Archives, Philadelphia Branch.

113. *Scientific American* 4 (March 17, 1849): 205.

114. This was one of 2300 first class medals that were given at the exhibition, ranking after 112 grand medals of honor and 252 medals of honor, but before 3900 second class medals and 4000 honorable mentions. *Rapport sur L'Exposition Universelle de 1855* (Paris, 1857), p. 406.

115. The term in French, as in English, refers to a pointed cutting tool for use in engraving.

116. *Exposition Universelle de 1855, Rapports du Jury Mixte International* (Paris, 1856), vol. 2, pp. 579–80.

117. Ibid., p. 580; *Scientific American* 10 (August 11, 1855): 382.

118. French patent #14,290, *Descriptions des machines et Procédés pour Lesquel des Brevets d'Invention ont été pris sous le Régime de la loi du 5 Juillet, 1844,* 2d ser., 51 (1855): 186 and plate 42.

119. *Scientific American* 2 (August 28, 1847): 390.

120. *Scientific American* vol. 3 #52 (Sept. 16, 1848), p. 411.

121. G. Bernard Hughes, "Mechanical Carving Machines," *Country Life* 116 (Sept. 23, 1954):980–81. Named for the marble of the island of Paros, Parian ware was actually unglazed pottery made of feldspar and china clay.

122. Michele Helene Bogart, "Attitudes Toward Sculpture Reproductions in America 1850–1880," Ph.D. dissertation, University of Chicago, 1979, p. 89. I am indebted to Janet A. Headley for drawing my attention to this work, and for conversations about sculpture copying generally.

## 8. Bending Wood

1. For example, by Aryans in India 2000–1000 B.C., Egyptians fifteenth century B.C., and Celts in Central Europe 500 B.C., according to V. Gordon Childe, "Rotary Motion," in Charles Singer, et al., eds., *A History of Technology,* vol. 1 (Oxford, 1954), p. 212.

2. For pictures of workers wrestling steamed wood into forms for bentwood chairs in the nineteenth century and in the 1970s, see John Dunnigan, "Michael Thonet: One hundred and fifty years of bentwood furniture," *Fine Woodworking* (January/February 1980): 44.

3. Samuel Bentham, specification for Great Britain Patent #1951, of 1793, for "Methods of, and Machinery and Apparatus for, Working Wood, Metal, and other Materials" (London: Eyre & Spottiswoode, 1854), p. 17 (original spelling).

4. Ibid.

5. *American Journal of Improvements in the Useful Arts, and Mirror of the Patent Office in the United States,* vol. 1 (Washington D. C., 1828), pp. 103, 105.

6. Reynolds, U.S. Patent of July 17, 1835; Mulford, U.S. Patent of January 16, 1835. These are the oldest patents brought into evidence in litigation that took place in the 1850s and 1860s between the woodbending patents of Thomas Blanchard and John C. Morris. Because they precede the reorganization of the Patent Office in July 1836, they have no patent numbers.

7. H. M. DuBois, "Bent Timber for Rims," *The Hub* 20 (November 1, 1878): 388.

8. David Gans, deposition January 17, 1866 in *Alonzo V. Blanchard, John D. Blanchard, and Franklin Blanchard vs. Antoine Puttman, Conrad Weaver, and John Bittinger,* U.S. Circuit Court, Southern District of Ohio, March 1867, Record Group 21, National Archives, Chicago Branch.

9. U.S. Patent #6934, December 11, 1849. Hames are part of a horse collar.

10. U.S. Pat. #6951, December 18, 1849.

11. Thomas Blanchard, "Application for an extension of the patent of December 18, 1849 for an improved method of bending timber and other fibrous substances," February 28, 1863, Record Group 241, National Archives. David Gans, however, said he spoiled only about one plow handle in ten in his unpatented machine in Illinois. It was—probably coincidentally—very similar to Blanchard's somewhat later machine.

12. Blanchard extension application, 1863.

13. "When a piece is worked in such a way that its length is shortened and either or both its thickness and width increased, the piece is said to be upset and

the operation is known as "upsetting." Raymond Howard Monroe, ed., *Modern Shop Practice* (Chicago, 1919), vol. 4, p. 239.

14. Thomas Blanchard, Specification for Patent #6951, for "a Method of Bending Timber and other Fibrous Substances," December 18, 1849.

15. Blanchard extension application, 1863.

16. *Transfers of Patent Rights,* Liber H4, p. 415 (October 1, 1852), Record Group 241, National Archives; Blanchard extension application, 1863.

17. William F. Mitchell, testimony July 2, 1866 in *John C. Morris vs. Theodore Royer, Samuel T. J. Coleman, and John Young,* U.S. Circuit Court, Southern District of Ohio, March 1867, Record Group 21, National Archives, Chicago Branch. Spoilage of work was highly variable, depending on timber quality. A. J. Conant, a worker at Royer's, testified March 22, 1866 to a rate of only "one in a thousand . . . with those we are bending there now."

18. Gans, deposition January 17, 1866, in *Blanchard . . . vs. Puttman et al.*

19. Childe, p. 212; Peter Haddon Smith, "Industrial Archeology of the Wood Wheel Industry in America," pp. 11–12.

20. P. H. Smith, p. 13, 14; J. Geraint Jenkins, *Traditional Country Craftsmen* (London, 1978), pp. 115–20. For English wheel-making technology of the mid-nineteenth century, see "A Day at a Coach Factory," *Penny Magazine* 10 (December 25, 1841): 501–8. Also see George Sturt, *The Wheelwright's Shop* (Cambridge, 1976) (reprint of 1923 edition), for the practice of making wagon wheels in rural southern England in the 1880s-90s. In farming districts of England straking survived into the twentieth century in preference to "shrinking on" tires made of a single hoop of iron.

21. Anon. (Asa Holman Waters), "Thomas Blanchard, the Inventor," *Harper's New Monthly Magazine* 63 (June-November 1881): 258. This seems unlikely. Blanchard's patent of 1858 is for bending full hoops, but smaller and lighter than carriage wheels.

22. Hiram Jenks, deposition in *Morris vs. Royer et al.,* 1867.

23. Howard M. DuBois, "Bent Timber for Rims," p. 388.

24. Blanchard, 1849 patent specification.

25. P. H. Smith, ". . . Wood Wheel Industry," photos between pp. 31 and 32; DuBois, p. 388.

26. Transfers . . . , Liber T2, p. 158, August 19, 1852. Record Group 241, National Archives.

27. Peter J. Leary, Newark, N. J., Illustrated (Newark, 1893), p. 192.

28. Blanchard extension application, 1863; Transfers . . . , Liber H4, p. 41, December 21, 1852.

29. Royer, Simonton and Company were Theodore Royer, Joseph Simonton, and John Young. Transfers . . . , Liber P3, p. 462, January 26, 1853. The territory assigned included the counties of Pennsylvania west of the Alleghenies, Ohio, Indiana, Kentucky, Illinois, Missouri, Wisconsin, Iowa, Tennessee, Michigan, Virginia, Mississippi, and Louisiana. Royer paid A. V. Blanchard Company $3,000 in six semiannual payments of $500 each.

30. Transfers . . . , Liber K2, p. 349, June 21, 1851. John Young was the assignee, for Ohio, Indiana, Kentucky, Tennessee, Arkansas, and the western counties of Virginia and Pennsylvania.

31. Charles Cist, Sketches and Statistics of Cincinnati in 1859, p. 330–31.

32. U. S. Patent #14,405, for an "Improved Method of bending wood," March 11, 1856.

33. DuBois, p. 389, 388.

34. The Hub 20 (March 1, 1879): 588; I.D. Ware, Carriage-Builders' Reference Book (Philadelphia, 1876), p. 27.

35. P. H. Smith, " . . . Wood Wheel Industry " p. 31 says the Blanchard-type machine at Hoopes, Brother, and Darlington appears to have been made there, not purchased from a commercial machine manufacturer.

36. Edward P. Duggan, "Machines, Markets, and Labor: The Carriage and Wagon Industry in Late-Nineteenth-Century Cincinnati," Business History Review, 52 (Autumn, 1977): 308–25.

37. Futtocks are curved pieces of which the ribs or frames of the ship are built up; knees are right-angled braces at the sides of the ship for supporting the decks.

38. Robert Greenhalgh Albion, *The Rise of New York Port (1815–1860)* (New York and London, 1939), p. 295.

39. William H. Shock, "Notes on Blanchard's Patent Timber Bending Machine," *Journal of the Franklin Institute,* 58 (July-December 1854): 338–39.

40. V. V. Danilevskii, *Nartov and his Theatrum Machinarum* (Jerusalem and Washington D.C., 1966), p. 48.

41. Blanchard extension application, 1863.

42. *Transfers . . . ,* Liber H3, p. 187, August 18, 1853.

43. Shock, p. 338. See Albion, chapter 14, "The East River Yards," especially p. 297, for a discussion of the shipbuilding milieu of the New York port.

44. Nathan Rosenberg, *The American System of Manufactures,* pp. 100, 106.

45. J. Vaughan Merrick, report, *Journal of the Franklin Institute* 58 (July-December 1854): 286–87.

46. Shock, p. 338–39.

47. Merrick, p. 286.

48. Merrick, Shock.

49. Thomas Blanchard, U.S. Patent # 15,944, for a "new and Improved Method of Bending Timber," October 21, 1856.

50. Blanchard, patent specification, 1856.

51. David Wells, ed., "Bending Ship-Timber," in *Annual of Scientific Discovery . . . for 1855 . . .* (Boston and London, 1855), p. 38.

52. Blanchard, extension application, 1863.

53. Wells, p. 39; Merrick, p. 287; Shock, p. 339.

54. *Rapports du Jury Mixte . . .* vol. 1, pp. 273–4, vol. 2, p. 580.

55. Shock, p. 338.

56. Blanchard, extension application, 1863.

57. *Transfers* . . . , Liber F4, p. 5, August 25, 1855 and Liber G4, p. 37, September 5, 1855. The ten-day holders of rights—clearly not users of the machinery, but financial intermediaries—were named George H. Ellery and Francis B. Cole. Both assignments included not only rights to any renewal or extension but also to "any Improvements which the said Thomas Blanchard might hereafter make in the art of Bending Timber & machinery for the same."

58. "Timber-Bending Machinery," *The Artizan* 15 (February 1, 1857): 27–28.

59. *Transfers* . . . , Liber A6, p. 83, February 2, 1860.

60. *The Artizan,* p. 28.

61. "The New Process of Timber-Bending," *The Nautical Magazine and Naval Chronicle* 26 ( January 1857): 21–22. See also "New Mode of Bending Timber," in the same journal, vol. 25 (October 1856), pp. 557–559.

62. Richard C. McKay sketches a picture of boom times in building clipper ships for the rush to California, followed by a slackening in 1855, then recovery, then serious depression in 1857, in which "New York's East Side shipyards . . . were silent. On every hand great American shipping houses were failing." Richard C. McKay, *South Street: A Maritime History of New York* (New York, 1934), pp. 393, 402–403.

63. Blanchard, extension application, 1863.

64. John Willis Griffiths (1809–1882) designed pioneering clipper ships from the mid-1840s, lectured on shipbuilding science at the American Institute, and wrote a *Treatise on Marine and Naval Architecture* (1849). See Richard C. McKay, pp. 175, 257. His patents of 1866 were both dated January 2. One was for a machine resembling Blanchard's that featured a "bed-plate . . . capable of revolution"; the other was for preparing beveled ship timber "by sawing . . . slabs or boards from the sides . . . but not entirely severing the same . . . ," *Patent Office Report,* 1866, pp. 300–301.

65. I am indebted to Charles Haines for drawing my attention to Griffiths and his woodbending machines. For further information, see Haines's forthcoming dissertation, University of Delaware. The Griffiths patents of 1866 were assigned in 1871, 1872, and 1877, as recorded in *Transfers of Patents,* Liber Z7, p. 348, Liber M15, pp. 184, 185, and Liber I22, p. 184. His patent #171,376, dated

December 21, 1875, was assigned to five persons surnamed Griffiths in late 1875, who reassigned him life tenure in early 1876. These assignments are recorded in *Transfers . . . ,* Liber Z19, p. 232 and Liber H20, p. 37.

66. Henry Hall, *Report on the Ship-Building Industry of the United States, Tenth Census of the United States (1880),* vol. 8 (Washington D.C., 1884), p. 236.

67. U.S. Patents #19,480, "Method of Bending Shovel-Handles," March 2, 1858; and #20,137, "Machine for Bending Wood," May 4, 1858.

68. Anon. (A. H. Waters), "Thomas Blanchard the Inventor," *Harper's* 1881, p. 258. This transaction does not appear in the assignment records. Blanchard assigned the right for frame-making to his nephews in Palmer in 1852, so perhaps this anecdote refers to a time between 1849 and 1852, or perhaps Blanchard retained his patent right to the 1856 bending machine and licensed it to the Philadelphia frame-maker.

69. Nor were there any assignments for Blanchard's 1856 patent unless it be regarded as an "improvement" foreseen in his assignment of 1853 to the Ship Timber Bending Company.

70. *A Completed Century 1826–1926: The Story of Heywood Wakefield Company* (Boston, 1926).

71. *Transfers . . . ,* Liber D5, p. 117, January 12, 1858 and Liber D5, p. 120, May 2, 1858. This assignment allowed the Heywoods to use "improvements upon said patented Machinery . . . under any letters patent which may be hereafter granted to or held by" the American Timber Bending Company.

72. *A Completed Century . . . ,* p. 3. This undated visit was possibly upon the occasion of the 1876 Centennial Exhibition in Philadelphia, where the Thonets displayed their furniture.

73. Levi Heywood, of inventive bent, was reputed to have reinvented the band-saw in 1835, only to learn it wasn't feasible with the quality of sawblades available at that time. Rev. William Dodge Herrick, *History of Gardner* (Gardner, 1878), p. 303.

74. Heywood's patents were: U.S. Pats. #27,447 of March 13, 1860; #72,292 and #72,293 of December 17, 1867; and #80,627 of August 4, 1868.

75. Herrick, p. 305, does not give a date for this company, but the context suggests that it postdated Morris-Blanchard litigation.

76. U.S. Patent #14,405, for an "Improved Method of bending wood," March 11, 1856.

77. Depositions of David Gans and Leonard Andrus, January 17, 1866, in *Blanchard et al. vs. Puttman et al.,* U.S. Circuit Court, Ohio Southern District, March 1867, Record Group 21, National Archives, Chicago Branch.

78. U.S. patent reissue #853, November 15, 1859, quoted in "Opinion and Charge" by Judge J. Leavitt, in *Morris vs. Royer et al.* and *Blanchard et al. vs. Puttman et al.,* 1867, p. 12.

79. U.S. patent reissue #1312, May 27, 1862, quoted by Leavitt in his opinion and charge, p. 10.

80. As mentioned above, Merrick, p. 286, described the heavy duty machine as bending the two ends by drawing them around "in opposite directions" by "powerful gearing."

81. Papers of Senate patent committee, 37th Cong., Record Group 46, National Archives.

82. Thomas Blanchard, extension application, 1863.

83. Leavitt opinion and charge, p. 22.

84. Judgment #206, Supreme Court of the United States, December term, 1868, dated November 29, 1869. National Archives, Record Group 267, Supreme Court appellate case file 5086.

85. The machinery and operations of Hoopes, Brother, and Darlington of West Chester, Pennsylvania were documented by a Smithsonian team in 1969. See Peter Haddon Smith, ". . . Wood Wheel Industry."

## 9. Summary and Conclusions

1. This list alludes only to Blanchard's woodworking inventions. He also invented a horizontal circular shear (1813), tack machine (1817), speed regulator for carriages (1825), steamboat for passage of rapids (1831), mode of making hat batting (1837), mill for reducing substances (1858), a cigarette (1858), and a scoop shovel (1862). Some of these were also useful in the contexts mentioned.

2. See F. R. Hutton, "Report on Machine Tools and Wood-Working Machinery," in *Tenth Census of the United States: Statistics of Power and Machinery Used*

*in Manufactures* (Washington, D.C.: Government Printing Office, 1885), p. 154; and Lt. Col. James G. Benton, *The Fabrication of Small Arms for the United States Service,* Ordnance Memoranda, vol. 22, (Washington, D.C., Government Printing Office, 1878), plate 22.

3. Assignment of H. M. Preston to Woodburn and Scott, June 29, 1860, *Transfers of Patent Rights,* Liber A6, p. 20; assignment of A. V. Blanchard and Company to Royer, Coleman and Company, January 4, 1864, *Transfers . . . ,* Liber Q7, p. 219. Record Group 241, National Archives. The assignees needed additional permission for their new application of the Blanchard lathes and benders, even to use the machines they already had.

4. Peter Haddon Smith, "The Industrial Archeology of the Wood Wheel Industry in America," p. 201. Baseball bats are among the items that do not require a Blanchard lathe for turning, but could be made on one.

5. Nathan Rosenberg (1963), "Technological Change in the Machine Tool Industry," reprinted in *Perspectives on Technology* (Cambridge, 1976), pp. 9–31.

6. Defiance Catalogue #200, p. 13, quoted in P. H. Smith, ". . . Wood Wheel Industry," p. 53.

7. Bruce Sinclair, *Philadelphia's Philosopher Mechanics,* pp. 42–45.

8. David Wilkinson, "Reminiscences," (1846) in Gary Kulik, Roger Parks and Theodore Z. Penn., eds., *The New England Mill Village 1790–1860* (Cambridge, Mass., 1982), p. 88.

9. For example, the assignment by Royer, Simonton and Company to Thomas Wing and William A. Richardson, *Transfers . . . ,* Liber T4, p. 339.

# BIBLIOGRAPHY

## Manuscripts

Eli Whitney Papers. Yale University Archives, New Haven, Connecticut.

Records of the Office of Chief of Ordnance. Record Group 156. National Archives, Washington, D.C.

Records of the Springfield Armory. Record Group 156. National Archives, Washington, D.C.

Waters Family Papers. American Antiquarian Society Library, Worcester, Massachusetts.

## Patent Records

Patent application files. Record Group 241. National Archives, Washington, D.C.

Patent assignments. *Digests of Patent Assignments,* "B" Volumes 1–4. Record Group 241. National Archives, Washington, D.C. *Transfers of Patent Rights,* Libers A-Z, series 0–9, c. 1836–1870. Record Group 241. National Archives, Washington, D.C.

Patent extension files. Record Group 241. National Archives, Washington, D.C.

Patent legislation files. Record Groups 233 (House of Representatives) and 64 (Senate). National Archives, Washington, D.C.

Patent specifications. *Restored U.S. Patents,* Record Group 241. National Archives, Washington D.C. Post-1836 U.S. patents: Record Group 241, National Archives, Washington D.C. and U.S. Office of Patents and Trademarks, Washington, D.C. Pre-1852 Great Britain patents: Science Museum Library, London, England.

## Litigation Records

U.S. Circuit Courts for Maine, Massachusetts, Connecticut, and New Hampshire Districts. Record Group 21. National Archives, Waltham, Massachusetts.

U.S. Circuit Court for Southern New York District. Record Group 21. National Archives, Bayonne, New Jersey.

U.S. Circuit Court for Eastern Pennsylvania District. Record Group 21. National Archives, Philadelphia, Pennsylvania.

U.S. Circuit Court for Ohio District. Record Group 21. National Archives, Chicago, Illinois.

U.S. Supreme Court. Record Group 267. National Archives, Washington D. C.


Books and Articles

Abbott, Jacob. "The Armory at Springfield." *Harper's New Monthly Magazine* 5 (July 1852): 145–161.

Abell, Sydney George, John Leggat, and Warren Greene Ogden, Jr., comps. *A Bibliography of The Art of Turning and Lathe and Machine Tool History. . . .* North Andover, Mass.: Museum of Ornamental Turning Ltd., 1987.

*A Completed Century 1826–1926: The Story of Heywood Wakefield Company.* Boston: 1926.

Adams, George. *New England Business Directory.* Boston: 1856.

"A Day at a Coach Factory." *Penny Magazine* 10 (December 25, 1841): 501–8.

Albion, Robert G. *The Rise of New York Port, 1815–1860.* New York and London: Scribners, 1939.

Allen, Frederick J. *The Shoe Industry.* Boston: Vocation Bureau of Boston, 1916.

*American Journal of Improvements in the Useful Arts, and Mirror of the Patent Office in the United States* vol. 1. Washington D.C.: 1828.

*American State Papers.* Class 5: *Military Affairs.* vol. 2. Report 246.

Anderson, John, Robert Burn, and Thomas Warlow. *Report of the Committee on the Machinery of the United States of America.* London: Harrison & Sons, 1855. Reprinted in Nathan Rosenberg, ed., *The American System of Manufactures,* pp. 87–197. Edinburgh: Edinburgh University Press, 1969.

Anderson, John. "On the Application of the Copying or Transfer Principle in the Production of Wooden Articles." *Proceedings of the Institution of Mechanical Engineers* (1858), pp. 237–48.

*The Artizan* 15 (February 1, 1857): 27–28 and plate 93.

Bates, Torrey. *The Shoe Industry of Weymouth.* Weymouth, Mass.: Weymouth Historical Society Publication #6, 1933.

Battison, Edwin A. "Screw-Thread Cutting by the Master-Screw Method Since 1480." *Contributions from the Museum of History and Technology.* United States National Museum Bulletin 240, paper 37, pp. 105–120. Smithsonian Institution, Washington, D.C., 1964.

Beardsley, Rev. William A. "Hezekiah Augur: Woodcarver, Sculptor and Inventor." *Papers of the New Haven Colony Historical Society* 10 (1951): 258–285.

Benedict, Rev. William A. and Rev. Hiram A.Tracy, eds. *History of the Town of Sutton, Massachusetts, from 1704 to 1876.* Sutton, Mass.: Sanford, 1878.

Benton, Lt. Col. James G. *The Fabrication of Small Arms for the United States Service.* Ordnance Memoranda, vol. 22. Washington, D.C.: Government Printing Office, 1878.

Berger, Peter L. and Thomas Luckmann. *The Social Construction of Reality*. New York: Doubleday, 1966.

Bergeron, L. E. *Manuel du Tourneur*. 2d ed. rev. P. Hamelin Bergeron. Paris: 1816. 2 vols., plus atlas of plates.

—— *The Image Lathe*. Boston: Andrews and Prentiss, 1849. 12 pp. (Translation of vol. 2, pp. 424–437, with planche 52, of above.)

Bijker, Wiebe, Thomas P. Hughes, and Trevor J. Pinch, eds. *The Social Construction of Technological Systems*. Cambridge, Mass.: MIT Press, 1987.

Bliss, John Homer. *Genealogy of the Bliss Family in America . . . 1550 to 1880*. Boston: the author, 1881.

Bogart, Michele Helene. "Attitudes Toward Sculpture Reproductions in America 1850–1880." Ph.D. dissertation, University of Chicago, 1979.

Bond, Kener E., Jr. "Rose Engines and Ornamental Lathes." *Metalsmith* 2 (Fall 1981): 23–27.

Borut, Michael. "The *Scientific American* in Nineteenth Century America." Ph.D. dissertation, New York University, 1977.

Brandon, Ruth. *A Capitalist Romance: Singer and the Sewing Machine*. Philadelphia: Lippincott, 1977.

Britkin, A. S. and S. S. Vidonov. *A. K. Nartov: An Outstanding Machine Builder of the 18th Century*. Translated from the Russian. Jerusalem: Israel Program for Scientific Translations. Washington, D.C.: Smithsonian Institution and National Science Foundation, 1964.

*Burlington Free Press*. April 1, 1836; December 28, 1838.

Burnham, Henry. In Abby Maria Hemenway, ed. *Brattleboro Windham County Vermont, Early History. . . .* Brattleboro: D. Leonard, 1880.

Buttrick, John. "The Inside Contract System." *Journal of Economic History* 12 (Summer 1952): 205–21.

Calvert, Monte A. *The Mechanical Engineer in America, 1830–1910*. Baltimore: Johns Hopkins University Press, 1967.

Chapin, Charles Wells. *History of "The Old High School" . . . 1828 to 1840*. Springfield, Mass.: 1890.

—— *Sketches of the Old Inhabitants and Other Citizens of Old Springfield*. Springfield, Mass.: Press of Springfield, 1893.

Childe, V. Gordon. "Rotary Motion." In Charles Singer, E. J. Holmyard, and A. R. Hall, eds., *A History of Technology*, vol. 1, pp. 187–215. Oxford: Oxford University Press, 1954.

Cist, Charles. *Sketches and Statistics of Cincinnati in 1859*. Cincinnati: 1859.

Clark, D. K. *The Exhibited Machinery of 1862*. London: Day & Son, 1864.

Constant, Edward W. II, "The Social Locus of Technological Practice: Community, System, or Organization." In Wiebe Bijker, Thomas P. Hughes, and Trevor J. Pinch, eds., *The Social Construction of Technological Systems*. Cambridge, Mass.: The MIT Press, 1987.

Cooper, Carolyn C. "The Portsmouth System of Manufacture." *Technology and Culture* 25 (April 1984): 182–225.

—— "The Production Line at Portsmouth Block Mill." *Industrial Archaeology Review* 6 (Winter 1981–82): 28–44.

—— "The Roles of Thomas Blanchard's Woodworking Inventions in Nineteenth-Century American Manufacturing Technology." Ph.D. dissertation, Yale University, 1985.

—— "Thomas Blanchard's Woodworking Machines: Tracking 19th- Century Technological Diffusion." *IA, The Journal of the Society for Industrial Archeology* 13 (1987): 41–54.

—— " 'A Whole Battalion of Stockers': Thomas Blanchard's Production Line and Hand Labor at Springfield Armory," *IA, The Journal of the Society for Industrial Archeology* 14 (1988): 37–57.

Cowan, Ruth Schwartz, "The Consumption Junction: A Proposal for Research Strategies in the Sociology of Technology." In Wiebe Bijker, Thomas P. Hughes, and Trevor J. Pinch, eds., *The Social Construction of Technological Systems*. Cambridge, Mass.: The MIT Press, 1987.

Cowper, E. A. "On the Inventions of James Watt and his Models Preserved at Handsworth and South Kensington." *Proceedings of the Institute of Mechanical Engineers* (1883), pp. 599–631.

Crane, John C. "Asa Holman Waters." *Proceedings of the Worcester Society of Antiquity for the Year 1887,* vol. 7, pp. 84–96. Worcester, Mass.: Worcester Society of Antiquity, 1888.

Crane, John Calvin, and Rev. Robert W. Dunbar, eds. *Centennial History of the Town of Millbury, Massachusetts*. Millbury: 1915.

Daniels, George F. *History of the Town of Oxford*. Oxford, Mass.: 1892.

Danilevskii, V. V. *Nartov and his Theatrum Machinarum*. Translated from the Russian. Jerusalem: Israel Program for Scientific Translations. Washington, D.C.: Smithsonian Institution and National Science Foundation, 1966.

Daumas, Maurice. *A History of Technology and Invention: Progress Through the Ages,* vol. 2, *The First Stages of Mechanization*. Translated from the French by Eileen B. Hennessy. New York: Crown, 1970.

Demyanyuk, F. S. *The Technological Principles of Flow Line and Automated Production*. London: Pergamon, 1963.

*Descriptions des Machines et Procédés pour Lesquels des Brevets d'Invention ont été pris sous le Régime de la Loi du 5 Juillet, 1844*. 2d ser. vol. 51 (1855). p. 186.

Deyrup, Felicia J. *Arms Makers of the Connecticut Valley*. Northampton, Mass.: Smith College, 1948.

Dickinson, Henry W. *The Garret Workshop of James Watt*. Board of Education/Science Museum Technical Pamphlet #1. London: H.M.S.O., 1929.

Diderot, Denis, and Jean le Ronde D'Alembert. *Encyclopédie. Recueil des Planches* vol. 10. Paris, 1772.

Dood, Kendall J. "Patent Models and the Patent Law 1790–1880." *Journal of the Patent Office Society* 65 (April and May, 1983): 187–216, 234–74.
—— "Why Models?" In *American Enterprise: Nineteenth Century Patent Models.* New York: Cooper-Hewitt Museum, 1984.
DuBois, Howard M. "Bent Timber for Rims." *The Hub* 20 (November 1, 1878): 388–89.
Duggan, Edward P. "Machines, Markets, and Labor: The Carriage and Wagon Industry in Late-Nineteenth-Century Cincinnati." *Business History Review* 51 (Autumn 1977): 308–25.
Dunnigan, John. "Michael Thonet: One hundred and fifty years of bentwood furniture." *Fine Woodworking* (January/February 1980): 38–45.
Dutton, Harold I. *The Patent System and Inventive Activity During the Industrial Revolution 1750–1852.* Manchester: Manchester University Press, 1984.
Earl, Polly Anne. "Craftsmen and Machines: The Nineteenth Century Furniture Industry." In Ian M. G. Quimby and Polly Anne Earl, eds., *Technological Innovation and the Decorative Arts,* pp. 307–29. Charlottesville: University Press of Virginia, 1974.
*Edinburgh Encyclopaedia.* New York: Whiting and Watson, 1813. s.v. "block machinery."
Ellis, Ridsdale. *Patent Assignments* 3d ed. New York: Baker, Voorhis, 1955.
*Encyclopaedia Britannica.* 4th-9th eds. s.v. "block machinery."
*The Engineer.* "The Royal Small-Arm Manufactory, Enfield." *The Engineer* 7 (March 25–June 25, 1859): 204–5, 258–59, 294–95, 348–49, 384–85, 422–23.
*Exposition Universelle de 1855, Rapports du Jury Mixte International.* Paris: Imprimerie Imperiale, 1856. 2 vols.
Farey, R. F. "Measurements and Lasts." In Ernest Bordoli, ed., *The Boot and Shoe Maker,* vol. 2. London: Gresham, 1936.
*The Federal Cases, Comprising Cases Argued and Determined in the Circuit and District Courts of the United States [from 1789 to 1880]. . . .* St. Paul, Minn.: West, 1894.
Federico, P. J., ed. "Outline of the History of the United States Patent Office." *Journal of the Patent Office Society* 17 (July 1936) (Centennial Number).
Fitch, Charles H. "Report on the Manufactures of Interchangeable Mechanism." In *Tenth Census of the United States (1880),* vol. 2, *Report on the Manufactures of the United States,* pp. 611–704. Washington, D.C.: Government Printing Office, 1883.
—— "The Rise of a Mechanical Ideal." *Magazine of American History* 11 (June 1884): 516–27.
Foley, Vernard, and Susan Canganelli. "The Origin of the Slide Rest." *Tools and Technology, The Newsletter of the American Precision Museum* 6 (1984): 1–7, 17–22.

Ford, William F. *The Industrial Interests of Newark, N.J.* New York: Van Arsdale, 1874.

Freedley, Edwin T. *Leading Pursuits and Leading Men. A Treatise on the Principal Trades and Manufactures of the United States.* Philadelphia: Edward Young, 1856.

Fries, Russell. "British Response to the American System." *Technology and Culture* 16 (July 1975): 377–403.

Frumkin, Maximilian. "Early History of Patents for Invention," *Transactions of the Newcomen Society* 26 (1947–49): 47–56.

Fuller, Claud E. *Springfield Muzzle-Loading Shoulder Arms.* New York: Bannerman, 1930.

Gerdts, William H. *American Neo-Classic Sculpture: The Marble Resurrection.* New York: Viking, 1973.

Gies, Joseph and Frances. *The Ingenious Yankees.* New York: Crowell, 1976.

Gilbert, K. R. "Machine Tools." In Charles Singer *et al.*, eds., *A History of Technology,* vol. 4, pp. 417–441. London: Oxford University Press, 1958.

—— "The Ames Recessing Machine: A Survivor of the Original Enfield Rifle Machinery." *Technology and Culture* 4 (Spring 1963): 207–211.

—— *The Portsmouth Blockmaking Machinery.* London: H.M.S.O., 1965.

—— *The Machine Tool Collection.* Science Museum Catalogue. London: H.M.S.O., 1966.

—— "The Control of Machine Tools—A Historical Survey." *Transactions of the Newcomen Society* (1971–72), 45: 119–127 and plates 22–27.

Gille, Bertrand. "Machines." In Charles Singer, *et al.*, eds., *A History of Technology,* vol. 2, p. 630. Oxford: Oxford University Press, 1956.

Goddard, Dwight. *Eminent Engineers.* New York: Hill, 1905.

Golden, Michael Joseph. *A Laboratory Course in Wood-Turning.* New York: American Book, 1897.

Gomme, Allan. "Patents of Invention." London: British Council, 1952.

Goodman, W. L. *A History of Woodworking Tools.* London: Bell, 1964.

Green, Mason A. *Springfield 1636–1886.* Springfield, Mass.: C. A. Nichols, 1888.

Green, M.A. "How Shoes are Made By Machine." In Waldemar Kaempffert, ed., *A Popular History of American Invention,* vol. 2, pp. 404–34. New York: Scribner's, 1924.

Greenwood, Thomas. "On Machinery for the Manufacture of Gunstocks." *Proceedings of the Institution of Mechanical Engineers* (1862), pp. 328–40.

Habakkuk, H. J. *American and British Technology in the Nineteenth Century.* Cambridge: Cambridge University Press, 1962.

Hagner, P. V. Report, October 25, 1849 to Chief of Ordnance. Reprinted in Stephen V. Benet, ed., *A Collection of Annual Reports and Other Important Papers Relating to the Ordnance Department,* vol. 2. Washington, D.C.: Government Printing Office, 1878.

Hall, Henry. *Report on the Ship-Building Industry of the United States. Tenth Census of the United States, (1880),* vol. 2. Washington, D.C.: Government Printing Office, 1884.

Hallock, James Lindsey. "Woodworking Machinery in Nineteenth Century America." Master's thesis, University of Delaware, 1978.

Hazard, Blanche. *The Organization of the Boot and Shoe Industry in Massachusetts Before 1875.* Cambridge, Mass.: Harvard University Press, 1921.

Herrick, Rev. William Dodge. *History of Gardner.* Gardner, Mass.: 1878.

Hindle, Brooke, ed. *America's Wooden Age: Aspects of its Early Technology.* Tarrytown, N.Y.: Sleepy Hollow Restorations, 1975.

——, ed. *Material Culture of the Wooden Age.* Tarrytown, N.Y.: Sleepy Hollow Restorations, 1981.

Hislop, Codman. *Eliphalet Nott.* Middletown, Conn.: Wesleyan University Press, 1971.

*History of Columbia County, New York.* Philadelphia: Everts & Ensign, 1878.

Hoar, George F. "Worcester County Inventors." *New England Magazine* n.s. 35 (1904–5): 350–61.

Hoke, Donald R. *Ingenious Yankees.* New York: Columbia University Press, 1990.

Hounshell, David A. *From the American System to Mass Production 1800–1932.* Baltimore: Johns Hopkins University Press, 1984.

Howard, Robert A. "Interchangeable Parts Reexamined: The Private Sector of the American Arms Industry on the Eve of the Civil War." *Technology and Culture* 19 (1978): 633–649.

Howe, Henry. *Memoirs of the Most Eminent American Mechanics. . . .* New York: W. F. Peckham, 1840.

Hughes, G. Bernard. "Mechanical Carving Machines." *Country Life* 116 (September 23, 1954): 980–81.

Hurd, D. Hamilton. *History of Worcester County, Massachusetts.* Philadelphia: 1889. 2 vols.

Hutton, F. R. "Report on Machine Tools and Wood-Working Machinery." In *Tenth Census of the United States (1880): Statistics of Power and Machinery Used in Manufactures.* Washington, D. C.: U. S. Government Printing Office, 1885.

Jacobus, Melancthon W. *The Connecticut River Steamboat Story.* Hartford: Connecticut Historical Society, 1956.

Jenkins, J. Geraint. *Traditional Country Craftsmen.* London: Routledge & Kegan Paul, 1978.

Johnson, David N. *Sketches of Lynn.* Lynn, Mass.: Nichols, 1880.

"Jordan's Patent Machinery for Wood Carving." *The Illustrated Exhibitor and Magazine of Art* (London, 1852) 1: 44.

Kellermann, Rudolf, and Wilhelm Treue. *Die Kulturgeschichte der Schraube.* Munich: F. Burckmann, 1962.

Kingsley, Elbridge, and Frederick Knab. *Picturesque Worcester*. Springfield, Mass.: W. F. Adams, 1895.

Leary, Peter J. *Newark, N. J., Illustrated*. Newark: Board of Trade, 1893.

Leggett, Morton D., comp. *Subject Matter Index of Patents for Inventions, 1790– 1873*. Washington D.C.: U.S. Government Printing Office, 1874. 3 vols.

*London Journal of Arts and Sciences* 5 (1822): 238–245.

Lowenthal, David. *George Perkins Marsh: Versatile Vermonter*. New York: Columbia University Press, 1958.

Machlup, Fritz. "The Supply of Inventors and Inventions." In Richard R. Nelson, ed., *The Rate and Direction of Inventive Activity: Economic and Social Factors*, pp. 143–69. Princeton: National Bureau of Economic Research, Princeton University Press, 1962.

"Machinery for Carving." *Journal of the Franklin Institute* 39 (January-June 1845): 413–14.

MacKenzie, Donald and Judy Wajcman, eds. *The Social Shaping of Technology*. Milton Keynes: Open University Press, 1985.

MacLeod, Christine. *Inventing the Industrial Revolution: The English Patent System 1660–1800*. Cambridge: Cambridge University Press, 1988.

McKay, Richard C. *South Street: A Maritime History of New York*. New York: Putnam, 1934.

McLane, Louis, comp., *Documents Relative to the Manufactures in the United States, Collected and Transmitted to the House of Representatives . . . by the Secretary of the Treasury*, vol. 1. Washington, D.C.: Duff Green, 1833.

Malone, Patrick M. "Little Kinks and Devices at Springfield Armory, 1892– 1918." *IA, The Journal of the Society for Industrial Archeology* 14 #1: 59– 76.

Mayr, Otto and Robert C. Post, eds. *Yankee Enterprise*. Washington, D.C.: Smithsonian Institution Press, 1981.

*Mechanics Magazine* (London) 26 (1836–37): 155.

Meier, H. A. "Thomas Jefferson and a Democratic Technology." In Carroll W. Pursell, Jr., ed., *Technology in America*. Cambridge, Mass.: MIT Press, 1981.

Mercer, Henry C. *Ancient Carpenters' Tools*. Doylestown, Pa.: Bucks County Historical Society, 1929.

Merrick, J. Vaughan. Report. *Journal of the Franklin Institute* 58 (July-December 1854): 286–87.

Mirsky, Jeannette and Allan Nevins. *The World of Eli Whitney*. New York: Macmillan, 1952.

Monroe, Raymond Howard, ed. *Modern Shop Practice*. Chicago: 1919.

More, Charles. *Skill and the English Working Class, 1870–1914*. London: Croom Helm, 1980.

Moxon, Joseph. *Mechanick Exercises; or the Doctrine of Handy-Works applied to the Art of Turning.* London: 1703. Reprinted by Early American Industries Association. Morristown, N.J.: Astragal Press, 1989.

Muirhead, James P. *The Life of James Watt.* New York: D. Appleton, 1859.

Muller, H. N. "Floating a Lumber Raft to Quebec City, 1805: The Journal of Guy Catlin of Burlington." *Vermont History* 39 (Winter 1971): 116–24.

Munn & Co. *The United States Patent Law.* New York: Munn, 1871.

Musson, A. E., and Eric Robinson. *Science and Technology in the Industrial Revolution.* Manchester: Manchester University Press, 1969. .

*The Nautical Magazine and Naval Chronicle* 25 (October 1856): 557– 559; 26 (January 1857): 21–22.

*New York As It Is, 1835. New York As It Is, 1837.* New York: J. Disturnell, 1835, 1837.

Nelson, Richard R., ed. *The Rate and Direction of Inventive Activity: Economic and Social Factors.* Princeton: National Bureau of Economic Research, Princeton University Press, 1962.

Patterson, C. Meade. "Gunstocking Genius." *The Gun Report* 6 (September 1960): 6–10, 21–24; 6 (October 1960): 15–19, 24–30.

Pierpont, Rev. J. "Whittling—A Yankee Portrait." *The United States Magazine* 4 (March, 1857): 217.

Post, Robert C. "'Liberalizers' vs. 'Scientific Men' in the Antebellum Patent Office." *Technology and Culture* 17 (1976): 24–54.

—— *Physics, Patents, and Politics: A Biography of Charles Grafton Page.* New York: Science History Publications, 1976.

—— "Reflections of American Science and Technology at the New York Crystal Palace Exhibition of 1853." *Journal of American Studies* 17 (1983): 337–356.

*Professional and Industrial History of Suffolk County Massachusetts.* Boston: Boston History Company, 1894. 3 vols.

Pursell, Carroll W., Jr., ed. *Technology in America.* Cambridge, Mass.: MIT Press, 1981.

—— *Early Stationary Steam Engines in America.* Washington D.C.: Smithsonian Institution Press, 1969.

Pye, David. *The Nature and Art of Workmanship.* Cambridge: Cambridge University Press, 1968.

Quimby, Harold R. *Pacemakers of Progress.* Chicago: Hide & Leather, 1946.

*Rapport sur L'Exposition Universelle de 1855.* Paris: Imprimerie Imperiale, 1857.

Ray, William and Marlys. *The Art of Invention: Patent Models and Their Makers.* Princeton: Pyne Press, 1974.

Reed, S. G. Letter to the editor. *The Hub* 18 (November 1876): 316.

Rees, Abraham, ed. *Cyclopaedia: Or, a New Universal Dictionary of Arts and Sciences.* London: Longman, Hurst, Rees, Orme, and Brown, 1819. s.v. "blocks," "lathe," "machinery," "rose engine."

*Regulations for the Inspection of Small Arms, 1823.* Washington D.C.: Ordnance Department, 1823.

Reingold, Nathan. "U.S. Patent Office Records as Sources for the History of Invention and Technological Property." *Technology and Culture* 1 (1960): 156–67.

*Repertory of Arts* (n.s.) 6 (July-December, 1836): 392.

Richards, John. *Treatise on the Construction and Operation of Wood-Working Machines.* London: E. & F. Spon, 1872.

Rieth, Adolf, and Karl Langenbacher. *Die Entwicklung der Drehbank.* Stuttgart: Kohlhammer, 1954.

Roe, Alfred S. "Thomas Blanchard." In George F. Hoar, "Worcester County Inventors." *New England Magazine* (n.s.) 35 (1904–05): 359–61.

Roe, Joseph W. *English and American Tool Builders.* New Haven: Yale University Press, 1916.

Rolt, L. T. C. *Tools for the Job: A Short History of Machine Tools.* London: Batsford, 1965.

Rosenberg, Nathan, ed. *The American System of Manufactures.* Edinburgh: Edinburgh University Press, 1969.

—— "America's Rise to Woodworking Leadership." In Brooke Hindle, ed., *America's Wooden Age,* pp. 37–55. Tarrytown, N.Y.: Sleepy Hollow Restorations, 1975.

—— "Technological Change in the Machine Tool Industry, 1840–1910." *Journal of Economic History* 23 (1963): 414–43.

—— *Perspectives on Technology.* Cambridge: Cambridge University Press, 1976.

Saguto, D. A. "The 'Mysterie' of a Cordwainer." *Chronicle of the Early American Industries Association* 34 (March 1981): 1–7.

Salaman, R. A. *Dictionary of Tools Used in the Woodworking and Allied Trades.* London: Allen & Unwin, 1975.

Scharf, J. Thomas. *History of St. Louis City and County.* St. Louis: n.d., c. 1883. 2 vols.

*Scientific American* 2 (August 28, 1847): 390; 3 (April 22, 1848): 245; 3 (May 12, 1848): 270; 3 (July 22, 1848): 349; 3 (September 9, 1848): 401; 3 (September 16, 1848: 411; 4 (March 17, 1849): 205; 4 (May 19, 1849): 27; 10 (August 11, 1855): 382; n.s. 46 (January 14, 1882): 19.

Sherwood, Morgan. "The Origins and Development of the American Patent System." *American Scientist* 71 (September-October 1983): 501–506.

Shock, William H. "Notes on Blanchard's Patent Timber Bending Machine." *Journal of the Franklin Institute,* 58 (July-December 1854): 338–39.

Sinclair, Bruce. *Philadelphia's Philosopher Mechanics, A History of the Franklin Institute 1824–1865.* Baltimore: Johns Hopkins University Press, 1974.

Smith, Merritt Roe. "The American Precision Museum." *Technology and Culture* 15 (1974): 413–37.

—— *Harpers Ferry Armory and the New Technology.* Ithaca: Cornell University Press, 1977.

—— "Military Entrepreneurship." In Otto Mayr and Robert C. Post, eds., *Yankee Enterprise,* pp. 63–102. Washington, D. C.: Smithsonian Institution Press, 1981.

—— "Army Ordnance and the 'American System' of Manufacturing, 1815–1861." In Merritt R. Smith, *Military Enterprise and Technological Change: Perspectives on the American Experience.* Cambridge, Mass.: MIT Press, 1985.

Smith, Peter Haddon. "The Industrial Archeology of the Wood Wheel Industry in America." Ph.D. dissertation, George Washington University, 1971.

Stapleton, Darwin, ed. *The Engineering Drawings of Benjamin Henry Latrobe.* New Haven: Yale University Press, 1980.

Steel, David. *The Elements and Practice of Rigging and Seamanship.* London: 1794.

Stiles, Henry R. *History of the City of Brooklyn.* vol. 2. Brooklyn, N.Y.: By Subscription, 1869.

Stone, Orra L. *History of Massachusetts Industries.* vol. 2. Boston-Chicago: S. J. Clarke, 1930.

Sturt, George. *The Wheelwright's Shop.* Cambridge: Cambridge Univerity Press, 1976. Reprint of 1923 edition.

Temple, Josiah Howard. *History of Palmer.* Springfield, Mass.: Town of Palmer, 1889.

Thompson, Zadock. *History of Vermont, Natural, Civil and Statistical, in Three Parts. . . .* Burlington, Vt.: Chauncy Goodrich, 1842.

Thomson, Ross. *The Path to Mechanized Shoe Production in the United States.* Chapel Hill: University of North Carolina Press, 1989.

Trevor Manufacturing Company. *Handle Machinery* catalog. Lockport, New York: September, 1899.

Usher, Abbott Payson. *A History of Mechanical Inventions,* rev. ed. Cambridge, Mass.: Harvard University Press, 1954.

*Vital Records of Millbury, Massachusetts to the end of the Year 1849.* Worcester, Mass.: Franklin P. Rice, 1903.

*Vital Records of Sutton, Massachusetts to the End of the Year 1849.* Worcester, Mass.: Franklin P. Rice, 1907.

Wallis, George. *New York Industrial Exhibition. Special Report of Mr. George Wallis.* London: Harrison, 1854. Reprinted in Nathan Rosenberg, ed., *The American System of Manufactures,* pp. 199–325. Edinburgh: Edinburgh University Press, 1969.

Ware, I. D. *The Carriage Builders' Reference Book.* Philadelphia: Carriage Monthly, 1877.

Waters, Asa Holman. (a) *Biographical Sketch of Thomas Blanchard.* Worcester, Mass.: Lucius P. Goddard, 1878. 15 pp.

Waters, Asa Holman. (b) "Thomas Blanchard." In Rev. William A. Benedict and Rev. Hiram A. Tracy, *History of the Town of Sutton, Massachusetts, from 1704 to 1876,* pp. 758–69. Sutton, Mass.: Sanford, 1878.

—— (c) (Anon.) "Thomas Blanchard, the Inventor." *Harper's New Monthly Magazine* 63 (July 1881): 254–60.

Whitworth, Joseph. *New York Industrial Exhibition. Special Report of Mr. Joseph Whitworth.* London: Harrison and Son, 1854). Reprinted in Nathan Rosenberg, ed., *The American System of Manufactures,* pp. 329–89. Edinburgh: Edinburgh University Press, 1969.

Wilkinson, David. "Reminiscences." (1846) In Kulik, Gary, Roger Parks, and Theodore Z. Penn, eds., *The New England Mill Village 1790–1860.* Cambridge, Mass.: MIT Press, 1982.

Willis, Rev. Robert. "Machines and Tools for Working in Metal, Wood, and Other Materials." In *Lectures on the Results of the Great Exhibition of 1851.* London: David Bogue, 1852.

Woodbury, Robert S. *History of the Lathe to 1850.* Boston, Mass.: Nimrod Press, 1961. Reprinted in *Studies in the History of Machine Tools.* Cambridge, Mass.: MIT Press, 1972.

Woollard, Frank G. *Principles of Mass and Flow Production.* London: Iliffe, 1954.

# INDEX

| | DATE DUE | | |
|---|---|---|---|
| | | | |
| | | | |
| | | | |
| | | | |
| | | | |
| | | | |
| | | | |
| | | | |
| | | | |
| | | | |